A CHRISTIAN
THEOLOGY OF
MARRIAGE
AND FAMILY

A CHRISTIAN THEOLOGY OF MARRIAGE AND FAMILY

Julie Hanlon Rubio

PAULIST PRESS
New York • Mahwah, N.J.

Chapter 10 is a revised version of "Does Family Conflict with Community?" *Theological Studies* 58 (December 1997); a revised version of chapter 5 was published as "The Dual Vocation of Christian Parents," *Theological Studies* 63 (December 2002).

Cover design by Valerie Petro
Book design by ediType

Library of Congress Cataloging-in-Publication Data

Rubio, Julie Hanlon.
 A Christian theology of marriage and family / Julie Hanlon Rubio.
  p. cm.
 Includes bibliographical references and index.
 ISBN 0-8091-4118-3
 1. Marriage – Religious aspects – Catholic Church. 2. Family – Religious aspects – Catholic Church. 3. Catholic Church – Doctrines. I. Title.
 BX2250 .R825 2003
 261.8′3585 – dc21

                                                                    2002156307

Published by Paulist Press
997 Macarthur Boulevard
Mahwah, New Jersey 07430

www.paulistpress.com

Printed and bound in the
United States of America

To Stephen, Thomas, and Dominic Rubio

Contents

PART TWO
APPLICATIONS

Acknowledgments

When I was a graduate student at Harvard Divinity School in the spring of 1991, my advisor, Francis Schüssler Fiorenza, gave me the proofs of an essay on marriage that eventually appeared in his two-volume *Systematic Theology*. He thought that since I was young, romantic, and recently engaged, I would not find his community model of marriage to be very inspiring. However, that essay put into words much of what I had already been thinking and inspired me to continue reflecting. Around the same time, Austin Fleming, my pastor at St. Ann's in Boston, gave me his book of prayers for engaged couples and a book by Paul Covino on the new liturgical guidelines for weddings, both of which spoke to the need for communal participation in the wedding ceremony and the marriage itself. These books and Professor Fiorenza's essay were central to my own wedding planning, and eventually they became crucial in my scholarship as well. Dr. John P. Crossly at the University of Southern California guided me through my dissertation, "A Social Ethic of the Family," which was my first real attempt to argue that Christian marriage and family life are essentially social.

This book grew out of my own experience as a young wife and mother and my continued quest to bridge the gap between social justice and family issues. I wrote it in small chunks of time over a period of many years while my children attended preschool, and later elementary school. A strong network of friends and neighbors, including the women of the Tuxedo Park Babysitting Co-op, helped me piece together the child care I needed to finish the book.

My research assistants at St. Louis University, Juliet Mousseau, Brian Matz, and Christine Baudin, provided invaluable assistance at many stages in the project, and my department chair, J. J. Mueller, S.J., provided the research release time I needed to finish the book. Editors Christopher Bellito and John Eagleson helped me clarify my academic prose. My colleague Mark Chmiel gave me moral support and, in his writing on his late wife (Mev Puleo), a real-life model of the theology I wanted to bring out in this book. I have learned so much from conversations with other parents, my colleagues: Florence Caffrey Bourg, Thomas Kelly, David Fillingim, Kenneth Parker, and Michael McClymond; my sisters-in-law: Mary Machado, Maggie Craig, Molly Rubio, Maria Rubio, and Stephanie Rubio; and my friends: Becky Elliott, Rima Mullins, Sue Skees, Kelly Askew, Elizabeth Bedart, Terese Booth, Colleen Vetter, Shelagh Davis, Sue Kellett, Mary Adams, and Kathy Randall.

My parents, Stephen and Frances Hanlon, raised me and my two brothers to think that family and social justice were of one piece. My in-laws Hector and Marilyn Rubio instilled in their nine children a similar sense of familial responsibility for the most vulnerable. My husband, Marty, and I both come from what we call "missionary families," and for that we are both very grateful. I am most grateful, though, for the love and support Marty has given me over the last very full five years of writing, teaching, and caring for our boys. His fathering has allowed me to be both mother and theologian, a gift I cannot measure or repay. I dedicate the book to my sons, Stephen, Thomas, and Dominic, for all they have done and will do to love and challenge me and their future families.

PART ONE

FOUNDATIONS

– ONE –

Family or Families?
The Problems of Parenting
in a Postmodern Age

What Is a Family?

Books like this one used to speak about "the family." Nowadays, many people feel that it is less and less appropriate to use this monolithic term. Instead, they talk about a diversity of "families." Close your eyes for a moment and think about the word "family." Focus on the images that come to mind immediately. What do those images look like? Do you see a middle-class mom and dad picnicking with their two children? A long table filled with noisy relatives who have come to celebrate a major holiday? If so, you are not alone — many Americans visualize some version of the nuclear family (mom, dad, and kids) or its extended-family incarnation and see these models as normal or at least desirable. Yet most of us know many families that do not look like this. Some of us might associate family with pictures of a single mom and her baby or a blended family that combines parts of two families through remarriage. Because of our diverse experiences of family life, we have begun to visualize different family models. No one single model seems adequate.

The popular media, too, have begun to give us a diverse set of images of families. We only have to look at the early example of *The Brady Bunch* (which told the story of a blended family) or the more recent examples of *Toy Story* (which centered — without comment — on a single-parent family) and *Mrs. Doubtfire* (which dealt with the problem of divorce). Robin Williams's Mrs. Doubtfire celebrates the growing diversity of family forms. The moral of this movie, spoken by

Williams's character at the very end, is that there are lots of different types of families, and they are all equally good. In other words, children ought not to worry if their family does not look like the image of "the family" that we have come to see as the norm. The popular children's TV show *Barney* echoes this theme every time its star child actors sing a favorite song about families. Each child sings a verse describing a different kind of family, and they all join in the refrain, "Families are different . . . and mine's just right for me. Yeah, mine's just right for me."

Most Americans are comfortable with the diversity of families exemplified in and advocated by the media. When people are asked to define family, they say, by a ratio of three to one, that a family is simply "a group of people who love and care for each other."[1] Even if they begin thinking about family with that image of two parents and their children, they do not stop there. They know what they are supposed to say and how things are supposed to be, but they know that this is not "reality" anymore. They do not want to impose the ideal (even if it is in fact their own personal preference) on others. They want to affirm peoples' right to live and love in the families of their choosing. They do not want to define "the family" one way. Instead, they want to speak in the plural, without judgment, about "families."

Some question the wisdom of tolerating so much diversity in family life. They argue that the image that comes to so many of us first is, in fact, the correct one. They want to preserve the ideal of "the family" and, they claim, the culture itself. In their view, the prevalent cultural idea that all families are equally good is destructive to "the family." They want to hold on to that powerful image of the picnicking parents and their children. It is not beneficial, in their eyes, to focus on the diversity of family life in the United States. It would be better to talk more about the way "the family" is supposed to be.

This disagreement, which is rooted in conflicting images of the family, can be characterized as a debate between those who speak of "the family" and those who speak about "families." It is a symptom of a larger cultural disagreement between postmodernists and modernists. Postmodernists, in this case those who want to speak about many different kinds of families, seem to be more prevalent, for we live in a time when uniform notions about most things are questioned.

What is "postmodern"? It begins with a recognition and acceptance of difference.

One of the marks of our age is diversity. We look around us and see many different ethnicities, cultures, religions, and ways of life. People seem to disagree about almost everything. They are more and more reluctant to claim that their religion is the one true religion, that their values are the only correct values, or that their way of life is the only way to live. Philosophers like Alasdair MacIntyre tell us that we are living in "a new dark ages"[2] in which we are unable to talk to each other about anything that matters because our basic moral commitments are so very different. People are reluctant to claim that Truth with a capital "T" exists. Instead, they say, we have many truths held by many different people and no way to sort through them all. Truth and morality seem to be relative things. Answers to life's biggest questions seem elusive. This does not stop most people from seeking, believing, and living their own truths, but it does mean that most people muddle through alone, figuring things out for themselves and trying their best to be faithful to what they have found to be true. This diversity (or confusion) is what characterizes the postmodern age. We are post-Truth, post-black and white, post-universal, and post-certainty.

Things were not always this way. Not so long ago, philosophers and ordinary people were much more optimistic about their ability to seek and find the Truth. In what is usually called the Modern era, science gave people confidence that they could figure out the way things were supposed to be and live accordingly. For example, John Locke thought he could discern what the best form of government was. America's founders believed in John Locke's vision, and their confidence is revealed in our own Declaration of Independence, in which they declare, without qualification, that God has created all men equal (the exclusionary "men" is appropriate here), and government derives its power from the people who decide to cede some of their powers to it. Thus if government violates the rights of the people, the people have the right to overthrow it. There is nothing here about the need to recognize a diversity of good forms of government, including those in which a monarch had total power over his subjects. The founders were sure that their vision of government was the correct one.

Today most Americans believe in this same vision, but debates over how much the United States should intervene in the politics of other nations reveal that we are much less certain than Locke was that we have found the only right way to govern. How can we claim that China is violating human rights, some ask? Aren't we simply imposing our own ideas about what human rights are on another culture? Where do these rights come from anyway? Do we really know? We cannot claim to share the certainty of our very modern founders, because we are living in a postmodern age. This does not mean that modernity is dead. Certainly, many believe that postmodern philosophers have gone too far, and many others, secure in their modernist worldview, have never grappled with postmodern questions.

Still, most people have been touched in some way by postmodern skepticism concerning the validity of universal moral principles. My students, for example, are often perplexed when I ask them to give their point of view on a case study about a family who cannot decide whether it is moral to spend money on a vacation cabin. They are similarly perplexed when I ask them to discuss their views on when sex is a moral choice. "How can we say?" they ask. "It's a personal choice," they protest. "It's reality — everybody does it." I try to explain that I am not asking them to judge people. Rather, we are trying to evaluate various moral arguments. Somewhat reluctantly, they agree to participate in the discussion, and often we get to a point at which we can make distinctions between moral and immoral actions, but these kinds of discussions are foreign to many of my students. They are uncomfortable with the language of moral norms, and their discomfort mirrors the problems many adults today have with what they see as the imposing of morality on others. They and the culture are postmodern when it comes to ethics.

The modernist-postmodernist conflict materializes in American political debates on family issues in the guise of the liberal-conservative divide. Liberals are those who are most likely to approach these issues with an emphasis on diversity. They will speak of "families" and of the importance of valuing families in their diversity (including single-parent, divorced, blended, and sometimes gay families). Conservatives, on the other hand, are more likely to refer to "the family," and to the need to return to "family values," by which they mean lifelong fidelity between heterosexual spouses, a certain authority of parents over children, and gendered division of labor in home.

This division was a significant source of tension at the Republican and Democratic conventions in 1996. At the climax of the Republican convention, presidential nominee Bob Dole told the American people that Hillary Clinton, who had recently published a book entitled *It Takes a Village to Raise a Family*, was wrong about families. He said, "We are told that it takes a village — that is, the collective, and thus the state — to raise a child. . . . I am here to tell you, it does not take a village to raise a child. It takes a family." His claim was a statement of the Republican party's idea of family values: if government would just let families alone, they would be better able to do what they are supposed to do. A few weeks later at the Democratic convention, Hillary Clinton responded, telling Dole and everyone watching at home that "it takes a village and a president" to raise children in the 1990s. This is the Democrats' version of family values: society (or government) must enable families to do what they are supposed to do.

However, government involvement is not the only important issue in the "village" debate. The traditional family is also a key concern. For when Dole asserts that it takes a family to raise a family, he is probably engaging in criticism of families who rely on day care and thus do not raise their children alone. His claim seems to echo a question I frequently hear stay-at-home moms ask, "Why have kids if you're going to let somebody else raise them?" Dole's implicit support for the traditional twentieth-century American or modern family ideal of a breadwinner dad and homemaker mom is at odds with Clinton's explicit support for postmodern single-parent and dual-career families.[3] Dole is upholding "the family," while Clinton is offering support for "families."

Recent day care debates have only extended this very basic conflict. *Los Angeles Times* columnist Katherine Dowling, writing in the spring of 1998, for instance, takes Hillary Clinton to task for advocating increased government spending on day care. She begins her critique by stating that Clinton gives us a hint of her disdain for the uniqueness of the maternal vocation in the very title of her bestseller, *It Takes a Village*. For this columnist, the assertion that parents, particularly mothers, need assistance with child rearing is demeaning. Clearly, the modern notion of a nuclear family with a breadwinner dad and a child-rearing mom is important to Dowling, for she paints Clinton's quest for funding as a quest for disruption of what to her is a sacred model:

> If you buy into the first lady's notion that standardized day care is the best place to raise children, then you must also accept the premise that the average mother is somehow inferior to a federally regulated facility where trained "child care providers... promote early learning and healthy child development." That the breast milk a mom provides her infant can be replaced by formula. That a 21-year-old childcare trainee will be as excited about a baby's first steps as that child's parents would be. In fact, were one to conceive of a plan to slowly dissolve the latticework of the family, it would be hard to come up with anything more effective than the promotion of duel [sic] parental employment, using the lures of feminine self-actualization and lowered taxes.[4]

Dowling's concern, clearly, is that "the family" is under attack. Clinton's concern, clearly, is that the diversity of postmodern families should not only be recognized, but also helped along by government. Dowling is probably right to assume that Clinton's lack of support for traditional families is deliberate, for the first lady most likely sees more to celebrate in dual-career families like her own. So what we see emerging underneath the day care debate is competing notions of family.

The very fact that those promoting "families" are the ones with political power and more civility in their discourse (a reflection of power status) should indicate that "the family" side is losing ground. Even if public debates on family issues seem like even battles (or battles in which "the family" side is winning), it is doubtful that Americans really yearn for the days when moms could stay home with their kids and dads were home for dinner and on the weekends. Consider Arlie Hochschild's recent work, *The Time Bind,* which chronicles the problems of employees at a Fortune 500 company who are trying to balance work and family. Hochschild reveals that despite the fact that a majority of Americans say they want more time with their families, even a relatively family-friendly company like the one she studied does not easily lure postmodern parents away from their jobs. They are unwilling to trade the family-like friendly atmosphere they have found at the office for the un-family-like atmosphere of their ever more stress-ful home lives. Few adults want to stay home with the kids and do the housework. Being home feels too much like work. It seems bet-ter to stay at work, where one can count on breathing space, order, and companionship. Hochschild's work questions the nostalgia many Americans seem to have for "the family," and suggests that for most, these feelings about the old way being better do not go very far. Few are willing to give up work at the office or factory for time at home.[5] Despite all the talk about family values, most are comfortable with the trade-offs they have made. At least they are not uncomfortable enough to change.

The comments of students in my undergraduate courses bear this out. When we talk about what family is, they typically say that they support the ideal of a working dad and homemaking mom to a point, but they claim that it is irrelevant because it is unrealistic to think that anyone could pull this off today. They are convinced that a family needs two incomes to survive. When I present testimonies from families who are making it just fine on the national median income of $30,000–$50,000 a year (either from one salary or a combination of two part-time salaries), and insist that a few such families are alive and well and living on my street, they express disbelief. When pushed, they acknowledge that by "making it," they mean not just being able to feed, clothe, shelter, and educate their family, but also to take their family out to dinner, on vacation, and to the mall. But even then, they do not back down from their position that "the family" is unrealistic. They simply counter that the claims of those who live on small incomes are unrealistic. What's really going on here is that my students have accepted in the ideal form what the participants in Hochschild's study have accepted in their everyday lives: postmodern family forms that are flexible according to the perceived financial and emotional needs of the adult individuals involved. The ideal form of "the family" is no longer capable of exerting a powerful influence over their choices in this area.

On the other hand, recent acrimonious exchanges over domestic partner legislation, the guilt working mothers continue to report, and the strength of conservative Catholic and Evangelical Christian pro-family forces in Washington all suggest that the fight for recognition of all kinds of families is far from over. It will surely continue for some time, because there is so much at stake and so much remains unresolved.

In the rest of this chapter, we will attempt to focus in on what is underneath this basic conflict between "the family" and families by looking more closely at how scholars have reflected upon these two differing points of view. This will prepare us to ask the questions that will be central to this book, with its focus on Catholic views on marriage and family: Where does Catholic thought situate itself with respect to this cultural debate? How does the Catholic magisterium view families today? How can Catholic parents begin to understand what they are supposed to do in a world in which the very meaning of family is so debated?

Feminist Questioning of the Family

Sociologist Barrie Thorne summarizes several decades of feminist work on the family in her introduction to a volume of essays entitled *Rethinking the Family: Some Feminist Questions*. Thorne begins with the claim that feminists have challenged the very idea that one kind of family did exist, does exist, or should exist.[6] They have shown that family arrangements have varied according to needs throughout history and across cultures. In contrast to well-known male anthropologists like Bronislaw Malinowski who studied other cultures and found a family similar to that which was the norm in their own societies, feminists have tended to see diversity and note that even when structures seem similar, they may have different meanings. For instance, one group of researchers states:

> An outside observer...may be able to delimit family boundaries in any and all societies by identifying the children of one woman and that woman's associated mate, but natives may not be interested in making such distinctions. In other words, natives may not be concerned to distinguish family members from outsiders, as Malinowski imagined natives should be when he argued that units of parents and children have to have clear boundaries in order for childrearing responsibilities to be assigned efficiently.

Many languages, for example, have no word to identify the unit of parents and children that English speakers call a "family."[7]

These authors claim that family has meant different things to different people at different times, and it continues to do so. The problem, according to Thorne, is the privileging of one kind of family over others. Like many feminists, Thorne would like to see a diversity of family forms accepted. She notes that "only seven percent of households fit the pattern of bread-winning father, full-time mother, and at least one child under age eighteen." Only 7 percent fit the ideal vision. Thorne puts this figure in perspective by noting that the most common household is that of the dual-career married couple with or without kids, so the nuclear family is not obsolete.[8] Still, she emphasizes the sociological data that shows a diversity of family forms, criticizes conservatives who seek a return to what she calls "an idealized, middle-class, patriarchal family," and is more comfortable dealing with families than "the family."[9]

Judith Stacey, another feminist sociologist, did in-depth case-study analysis of working-class families in California's Silicon Valley in the mid-1980s. She began with two assumptions: that upper-middle-class families were the ones experiencing the most upheaval, and that working-class families were the last stronghold of the modern nuclear family. Instead, she found that the working-class was leading the way in transforming the family in radically new ways.[10]

Stacey's research showed that working-class families had more working wives, better developed extended kin networks (including relationships that continued despite family break-ups), more shared housework when men remained in the households, more resource-swapping among families, and more family break-up than upper-middle-class families.[11] In sum, working-class families are nothing like the picnic-family ideal that so many Americans share. Instead, according to Stacey, the time when "family gathering" means a married couple, their children from previous marriages, ex-spouses, ex-in-laws, friends of ex-spouses and in-laws, friends who are just like family, and assorted "regular" relatives is here. The nuclear family form that was prevalent in the modern era is crumbling, and working-class families are developing new ways of being family in a postmodern age.

Like Thorne, Stacey decries attempts to define family in one way and asserts that "an ideological concept that imposes mythical homogeneity on the diverse means by which people organize their intimate relationships" (i.e., "the family") "distorts and devalues this rich variety of kinship stories."[12] She is interested in telling the diverse stories of postmodern families because she wants to show the falseness of attempts to define family one way and encourage acceptance of the multiplicity of ways in which Americans come together in families.

We have seen that feminists question the existence of "the family" in the past and present, in this culture and other cultures. They also question the desirability of the nuclear family model. Thorne, for instance, argues that "the family" is both an ideology and an institution, and that as an ideology, it has been oppressive for women. That is, because women have been given the duty of raising children and doing housework in the relative isolation of the home and have been prevented from achieving economic independence and vocational fulfillment outside it, they have suffered from the prevalence of the ideal of the nuclear family.[13]

Other feminists have questioned the idea, first promoted by author Christopher Lasch, that the family is a "haven in a heartless world." They have asked, "For whom is family a haven?" Sociologist Arlie Hochschild, notably, raised questions about the role home plays in the lives of working women and men whom, she shows, do not share housework equally. She claims that on average, women work an extra two hours a day, or an extra month a year. This is due to the fact that when most women return from work, they have to do a "second shift" of work at home. They are the ones who do the grocery shopping, make the evening meal, wash the dishes, pick up the house, make the children's lunches, and make a mental list of things to be done the following day.[14] Thus even though the families she studies are dual-career and thus not examples of "the family," her research reveals that the ideal of "the family" is making home life more difficult for women. Even though they are working outside the home, they are still expected (and still expecting themselves) to fulfill the traditional role. Meanwhile, their husbands are expected (and expecting) to maintain their traditional role. Hochschild's research shows both that "the family" is not very prevalent anymore in the concrete, and that "the family" as ideology can function negatively in women's lives.[15] It shows that while families as they exist in America are exceptionally diverse, and while "the family" is no longer as powerful an ideal as it once was, Americans are still conflicted about family. They cannot quite rid themselves of the vision of that picnicking family of four, and so they continue to debate within themselves and among themselves: "the family" or families, which should it be?

Christian Theology: Family or Families?

Liberals Embracing Families

Liberal Christian theologians, like many feminist theorists, often approach family issues with a broad definition of family. Well-known Catholic marriage scholar Michael Lawler, for instance, chose to call his new book *Family: American and Christian*, but he did so not to celebrate "the family" but to call it into question.[16] Lawler argues that "the family" "was never as common in reality in the United States as it was in the 1950s' television shows and in contemporary nostalgia," that it no longer exists, and that it makes more sense to speak about families in their diverse incarnations.[17] Healthy processes or ways of functioning are far more important to him than particular forms or structures. Lawler claims that "diversity . . . and not demise, is the work for the future of the American family.[18] By this he means that hyperbolic discussions that assume that the family is dead are limited because they assume that "the family" is historical as well as ideal. Once one realizes that family forms have varied historically, that family forms do vary enormously today, and that family values and success transcend family form, then, according to Lawler, one is free to discuss American families in all their diversity without getting hung up on questions of which form is superior. Lawler's theology thus takes as its starting point a postmodern understanding of family.[19]

Other liberal theologians, like Lisa Sowle Cahill, are more interested in showing how the new empirical research on gender correlates with recent interpretations of Genesis, allowing a Christian scholar to affirm gender equality from squarely within the Christian tradition. As she reads Genesis and the best new research on gender, male and female are distinct human forms, but these distinctions are not overwhelmingly significant. Thus:

> The exclusion of either sex from all but a few professions that require certain clear gender-related physical capacities should not be an issue. In particular, neither empirical evidence nor the scriptural accounts of creation support the thesis that the exclusive role for which women, and women alone, are suited is a domestic one, or that domestic and parental roles are intrinsically less valuable than public political and economic ones. Most human roles (as distinct from traits or capacities) can be fulfilled in a variety of styles.[20]

Cahill's position is that men and women are more similar than different by nature. She advocates flexibility in gender roles, and in doing so, she shows her preference for a less rigid model of family life. She is comfortable with variety in family structure. She is talking about families, not "the family." Many other liberal theologians, both Protestant and Catholic, work from similar assumptions.[21] However, there are other, more conservative Christian scholars who proceed with a more traditional or modern understanding of family.[22]

Conservative Defenders of "the Family"

Popular author, radio commentator, and head of the very influential Focus on the Family organization, James Dobson is a a good representative of conservative Christian thinking on the family. Dobson's books have sold well since the 1970s, in part because of his down-home, practical advice for parents, and in part because he assumes and upholds traditional family values. Dobson's early work, *Dare to Discipline*, is a case in point.[23] In this short book, Dobson attempts to convince parents that current permissive ideas about child rearing are misguided. Instead of relying on love and eschewing the use of parental authority and force, parents should, according to Dobson, dare to demand respect, by employing physical punishment when appropriate. In his discussion, Dobson addresses parents, but his text assumes that mothers will do most of the day-to-day disciplining because they are the ones at home.[24] He rarely appeals to religion, but when he does, he reveals himself to be a strict theological conservative, one who believes that "God, in His infinite wisdom, created and ordained the family as the basic unit of procreation and companionship."[25] Dobson, like most conservative Christians, sees "the family" as an institution whose form is given to human beings by God. His books are written to counter postmodern challengers to "the family," that is, those who suggest that parent-child relations should be more democratic, that traditional values are not absolute, or that gender relations should be more equal, less structured around perceived gender differences than around individual preferences. In response to postmodern questions, he tells Christians that their traditional ideas about family are correct.

Outside the evangelical Christian community, these kinds of simple affirmations of "the family" are rarer. Still, many writers hold to a modified form of Dobson's vision. Episcopal theologian Stephen Post, for instance, author of the 1994 work *Spheres of Love: Toward a New Ethics of the Family*, is careful to place himself on the side of those who value gender equity in the home. So in this aspect of his thinking, he does not uphold the traditional model. Still, Post wants to advocate what he calls a "new nuclear familialism" that is "consistent with gender role equality and the gains of women, as well as with the truth that families often need significant social support."[26]

These affirmations of women's rights and some government help for families may seem liberal, but Post himself claims that his updated modern family is in fact the ideal family (the new norm), so he puts himself on the conservative side of the family divide. Interestingly enough, he uses both sociology and philosophy to support his claim. First, he quotes the National Commission of Children's 1991 report, which states that "families formed by marriage — where two caring adults are committed to one another and to their children — provide the best environment for bringing children into the world and supporting their growth and development."[27] Post is careful to say that he does not mean to use his claim to denigrate single-parent or gay families, but his (liberalized) assumptions about marriage are closer to Dobson's claims than to those of postmodernists who want to accept everyone without distinctions. He states, "I accept no definition of family, so wide, for example, as 'any caring relationship,' nor do I think that there are any effective substitutes for the social arrangement of the nuclear family in which fathers and mothers together create a stable life for their children."[28]

With these words, Post lets his readers know that his discussion of family ethics will take as its foundation not families but "the family."

Protestant theologian Max Stackhouse offers historical and scriptural arguments for a similarly conservative position.[29] He begins by asserting that while American marriages vary in the particulars, "they always and everywhere involve a holy bond of social, emotional and sexual commitment rooted in the very condition of being human, in the sense of love as a gift, and in the potential to participate in the creation of new life."[30] Right from the start, Stackhouse reveals himself as a scholar who sees and affirms more unity than diversity. He is not blind to diversity, but he sees it as incidental to the general agreement about what marriage is, and he is interested in furthering discussions of how to support the traditional ideal in a world that has lost its way.

Those who want to expand the boundaries of marriage and family by emphasizing and welcoming diversity are, according to Stackhouse, on the fringes of American society and the American church. Specifically, he argues, those who want to include in their definition of family families founded on the marriage of two men or two women are misguided. Stackhouse turns to the first two books of Genesis for his defense of "the family." Here he finds three important truths: the existence of a moral order to which human beings are called to be faithful, gender differences between males and females that are the basis for marriage, and the specific structure of the nuclear family. Stackhouse maintains that most Christians believe that this is what marriage is about, and they should, because "these stories reveal the way sexuality is at its deepest level, and thus how it ought to be when life is not distorted."[31]

According to Stackhouse, what Scripture reveals, in traditional Protestant terms, is an ordinance of God, or a timeless institution that God has given to human beings because it will help them to realize their human dignity. It is also what "most" people believe to be true. If this is the norm, "all other options are properly seen as adjustments, exceptions, compromises, or relative approximations."[32] Those who want to bless homosexual marriages are thus "false prophets" who seek to legitimize what is properly called sin.[33]

Stackhouse's analysis is notable for its straightforward approach to the biblical text. He asserts the timeless truths of Scripture without qualification. This makes his argument rather conservative, for liberal theologians like Lisa Cahill tend to approach the text with more caution. They tend to believe that every time contemporary believers approach Scripture, they see it through the lenses of their culture. Thus, for liberals, interpretations of Scripture are never pure (and neither, for that matter, is Scripture itself). Rather, Christians interact with the text in a complex process, hoping to find some connection between their truth and the truth of biblical writers. Cahill claims that the Bible

> is the original and primary standard, but its very perception as authoritative standard is contingent upon the continuing life of the church that it engenders; comprehension of the actual human situation to which it speaks; and some innately human capacity to criticize that situation and envision a standard of "humanity" that transcends it.[34]

Liberals like Cahill would not turn to Genesis to seek pure and timeless truths. They would be suspect of assertions like Stackhouse's that we find in the Genesis texts exactly the family we all believe in (or should believe in) today. Viewed from a liberal perspective, Stackhouse's analysis is too easy. There is too little room left for the mutual criticism that a recognition of different perspectives engenders. The move from a notion of what the text means to a condemnation of those who question some aspects of traditional Christian teaching on family issues because they read and appropriate Scripture differently is, finally, too quick. Liberals seek more recognition of the possibility that truth can be found in many places, when it can be found at all.

Stackhouse, like many conservatives, implicitly and explicitly rejects the liberal idea that it is difficult to know what God intended for human beings. He asserts that we can know what Scripture meant, and that we can know what we are supposed to do about it. We can know, then, what God intended for "the family," so, according to Stackhouse, there is no need to speak of families and celebrate their diverse incarnations, like Michael Fahey does when he writes about the healthy diversity of families in the United States today. It is much more important for Stackhouse to uphold the timeless structure and value of "the family" that God revealed to humankind in the biblical text.

Liberals (postmodernists) and conservatives (modernists) approach family issues in very different ways. Liberals are concerned with showing that families have been and continue to be diverse. The ethical imperative for them is valuing, supporting, and uplifting families as they are. Conservatives, on the other hand, are concerned with showing that family structure has been fairly consistently lived out by people across time and culture and affirmed in religious traditions. The ethical imperative for them is conforming to the model of "the family" and pointing out that those who desire more diversity are moving in an immoral direction. The next logical question for Catholic readers is, "Where does the Catholic magisterium stand on the question of family?" In a postmodern age, in an age in which there is much more talk of families than "the family," how do church leaders approach the issue?

Magisterial Views of Family

As we begin to look at what the relevant church documents say about marriage and family, it is important to understand a little bit about how to read these writings. Papal documents and episcopal documents (the writings of the American bishops in our case) have different functions and different audiences. Papal documents (including encyclical letters and less authoritative apostolic exhortations) attempt to set out the basic outlines of Catholic thinking on general issues. They provide theological justification for various positions by using Scripture, the teachings of previous popes, as well as their own ideas to reflect on broad topics. In recent years, for instance, Pope John Paul II has produced letters on work, social concern, women, the family, the social teachings of the church, and evangelization, among others. He rarely speaks of particular moral situations or public policy issues. Rather, he is concerned with the broader picture. He writes of the ideals to which Catholic Christians are called.

To whom does the pope speak? Most of his letters are officially addressed to the Catholic bishops, clergy, and laity throughout the world. Some are also addressed to "all people of good will." In reality, few lay persons, aside from theologians and students of theology, read papal documents. They are just too dense for the average lay person to plow through, too laden with assumptions that only theologically sophisticated readers will understand. The true audience for most papal documents is a select group of very educated bishops, clergy, and lay theologians. It makes sense then, that the pope is not overly concerned with working out the details that are relevant to the complicated lives of most lay persons. Rather, he is a like a painter who designs a beautiful picture of the way things ought to be.

The U.S. Catholic bishops, on the other hand, have quite different concerns and write for a quite different audience. The bishops attempt to translate papal teaching into language Catholic lay people can understand. They write to their people, not to theologians. Their letters (on subjects like the economy, peace, domestic violence, and families) are attempts to apply Catholic ideals to specific situations that American Catholics face every day. One might say that when it comes to marriage and family, the pope writes about "the family," while the bishops write about and to families. What, then, are Catholics to make of this?

In some ways, Pope John Paul II seems to be very much a modernist, or a conservative. The pope's opening claim that "willed by God in the very act of creation, marriage and family are interiorly ordained to fulfillment in Christ and have need of his graces in order to be healed from the wounds of sin and restored to their 'beginning,' that is to full understanding and the full realization of God's plan,"[35] says a great deal about where he stands. With this statement, the pope reveals himself to be on the side of those who believe that God has ordained or instituted "the family" in its specific form. He also indicates, with references to the "beginning," that he finds this truth in the book of Genesis.[36] The bulk of his letter on family is a fleshing out of God's plan for marriage, in which he argues that the primary vocation of human beings is to love, that the marriage covenant is the primary structure given by God for the living out of this love, that children are the greatest gift of marriage, and a family is a communion of persons devoted to living the Christian life.[37]

The pope writes as if there were only one kind of family, one way of being family. He is concerned with defining the ideal. While he is, of course, aware that not all families live up to the ideal, he asks them to strive for it. The very language he uses to say this reveals his focus on the ideal. He asks simply, "Family, become what you are."[38] Note his use of the monolithic term "family" and the paradox inherent in the idea that families must "become" what they "are." The pope never steps out of the ideal realm to touch the reality of individual families. From his perspective, it is only necessary to call all families (by referring to them as one) to be what they are meant to be, what they "are" in their core, at their best, when they are living the truth. He believes that all families "are" truly communions of love, thus they can become loving communities that make present God's love. He calls them to realize themselves, to be all that they can be — which is all God intends them to be.

Despite this high-minded focus on the ideal family, John Paul II does not ignore the obvious contradictions between what he proposes and what exists in reality. He sees his letter as an offering for a world that has been led astray, in that it has forgotten what "the family" is, or should be. He acknowledges that in order to be effective as a messenger, he must understand the contemporary situation and be able to speak to families where they really live:

> It is, in fact, to the families of our times that the church must bring the unchangeable and ever new gospel of Jesus Christ, just as it is the families involved in the present conditions of the world that are called to accept and to live the plan of God that pertains to them. Moreover, the call and demands of the spirit resound in the very events of history, and so that church can also be guided to a more profound understanding of the inexhaustible mystery of marriage and the family by the circumstances, the questions and the anxieties and the hopes of the young people, married couples and parents of today.[39]

Here the pope is showing the humility of the magisterium in its approach to teaching the Catholic faithful. He is saying that the magisterium must present both the timeless message of the Gospel and its eternal newness, which suggests that contemporary Christians may interpret the Gospel in new ways. He also implies that scriptural reflection is not something that is done once and for all. Rather, it is an ongoing task, through which believers may find new ideas (otherwise there would be no need to keep writing new encyclicals!). So the task of the Christian is not simply recognition of the eternal truths of the Gospel, but also appreciation of new truths that may be found there.

Christian families are here acknowledged as the primary interpreters of the Gospel and magisterial teaching on the family. They are called to accept and live out those aspects of God's plan that apply to them. They have to apply the ideal to their everyday lives, adapt it to their situation, and make it work in practice. The pope cannot do this for them. Moreover, their questions, anxieties, and insights, which are born of experience, may lead the teachers of the church to more profound reflections on the ideals themselves. Not that experience will always trump traditional teaching — the pope clearly believes he has a duty to evangelize a world in great need of wisdom[40] — but he also recognizes that those who are married and have children bring something to a discussion of family ideals that he, as a celibate cleric, cannot. Thus while he does not focus on the application of ideals or the incorporation of the insights of married persons into higher level reflections on "the family," he does acknowledge that this work needs to be done.

It is the U.S. bishops who begin to do this work in earnest. In their 1993 document "Follow the Way of Love," the bishops of the United States identify families, not "the family" as their starting point, and they structure their reflections as a set of responses to the concerns and insights of a diverse set of Christian families. These are followed by questions designed to encourage families who read the document to engage in even more reflection on what they are called to do. Unlike the pope in his letter, the bishops use a dialogical model of reflection that allows them to truly speak to the concrete realities of the families they serve.

The bishops show their concern and respect for a diversity of families early on in their letter by quoting from their discussions with Catholic lay people. Their deliberate use of quotes from Catholics who live in many different kinds of families (i.e., extended, nuclear, divorced, etc.) indicates that they have respect for diverse family models.[41] The bishops respond to this diversity by stating that love is at the core of family life and affirming that "in every family God is revealed uniquely and personally, for God is love and those who live in love, live in God and God dwells in them (1 John 4:16)."[42] Note the emphasis on function rather than form. The bishops would never agree with the most liberal advocates of family freedom who define any group of people united by love as a family, but they are more concerned than John

Paul II with letting families know that God is with them in whatever family form they find themselves. The bishops, in their role as pastors, write to make Catholic teaching intelligible to average Catholics, to dialogue with families, and to offer their support to families as they are.

This is not to say that the bishops have no interest in using their reflection on family to call families to something more, but they begin by trying to show families the holiness of much of what they are already doing. To do this, they use the image of family as domestic church. This is an image revived at Vatican II, pulled from the writings of early church fathers like John of Chrysostom.[43] It simply means that families, as small communities of Christians, like the smallest parishes, are not just part of the larger church, but actual manifestations of the church. Just as parishes "do" church by having liturgies, sponsoring socials, and sending volunteers to soup kitchens, so too families "do" church (and thus are church) when they do what Christians are called to do. The bishops want all families to realize that, according to Catholic teaching, their life together is very important.

So they tell families that they *are* the church in their home because they come together in loving ways, and when they do, God is present. They tell families that they are church when they believe in God, love each other, share themselves, teach their faith, educate each other, pray together, serve one another, forgive each other, celebrate together, welcome others into their home (especially the needy), work for justice in their communities, affirm the value of life, and raise up vocations for the church.[44] The bishops teach that all families are holy, no matter how imperfect their form.

The bishops then ask families to judge themselves by the very standards that, to some degree, they already embody. They encourage families to live more faithfully, to be life-giving within the family and as a family, to grow in mutuality (moving "beyond gender stereotypes"), and to take the time they need to develop strong relationships.[45] In each area, families are given an ideal and asked to judge themselves by it. The bishops do not judge. Instead, after offering challenges, they pledge their support in specific ways. In sum, this document shows the dialogical nature of the bishops' approach to marriage and family.

Listening to Families;
Talking about "the Family"

Pasting together the visions of the pope and the U.S. bishops yields an approach to family issues that combines respect for the traditional family as an ideal with a commitment to listening to the experiences of different types of families. The Catholic magisterium falls somewhere in between the postmodernists and the modernists, the liberals and the conservatives. The highest teachers in the Catholic Church seek to engage in a true dialogue, one with opportunities both to transform the world and be transformed by it. The magisterium speaks both about "the family" and to and with families. It attempts to give families both the affirmation they need to keep going and the moral ideals that will push them to work even harder at their task.

What does this mean for Christian families, especially for Christian parents today? It means that if they look to church teaching for guidance, they will find a general set of ideals to guide them and a call to involve themselves in the process of the church's theological reflection on marriage and family. The church does not give them a blueprint of how to conduct their family life. The church's teachers have enough wisdom to know that producing such a blueprint is impossible. Instead, they present their reflections on what families are called to be and ask families themselves to do the important work of discerning how they are to live out this calling. They present a moral vision; it is up to families to fill in the details.

When families attempt to do this, they will want to mine the Christian tradition for anything that can help them. They might begin by turning to the marriage liturgy. They will need to know what Scripture scholars and church historians say about family in the Bible and the Christian tradition. They will want to understand the work of social scientists who study family. They will want to look to the constructive work of theologians who attempt to think through the relationship between faith and family today. The pages that follow cover all of these topics. This book attempts to encourage a serious conversation among lay Christians about the relationship between theology and family; it attempts to fill in some of the details.

Discussion Questions

1. What are examples of current controversies that illustrate the divide between those who speak about "the family" and those who advocate for families? Which side appears to have more power?

2. How do you define family? Is your definition one with which most people would agree?

3. What kinds of challenges do feminists put to "the family"? Are these challenges legitimate?

4. Are liberal theologians watering down the Christian tradition on family? Are conservative theologians too inflexible?

5. Do you prefer the approach of John Paul II or that of the U.S. bishops? What is more problematic: too much dialogue or too much discussion of ideals? Do you agree with Rubio's claim that the church balances talking and listening, or is there a need for more of one or the other?

- TWO -

The Catholic
Marriage Liturgy:
A Different Vision
of Marriage

Weddings are as much a part of American summers as vacations and swimming pools. Many of us know the experience of traveling hundreds of miles to attend the wedding of a distant cousin or the joy of celebrating with good friends in our hometowns. We also probably carry in our heads pictures of weddings we know only from the mass media — TV show and movie weddings, and news coverage of weddings of famous people. From these weddings and those of friends and relatives, most of us derive our earliest ideas about marriage.

Rather than reading philosophical or theological treatises on marriage, we attend weddings or watch them on TV, and these weddings become an important "text" for our thinking on the subject. It is important for us to "read" the texts of different wedding ceremonies in order to better understand what we think and feel about marriage. When we do this, we will find that the popular text of the wedding differs from the Catholic text in significant ways. Reading the Catholic wedding as a text will give us the basics of Catholic theological thinking on marriage. Thus attentiveness to the particulars of ceremonies and celebrations will enable us to see the beginnings of the Catholic vision for marriage. Reflecting back on the popular vision will enable us to ask if Catholics have listened attentively to voices in today's world.

Reading the Popular Wedding

Visualize a wedding you have recently seen or attended. Think about the invitation, the locations of the wedding ceremony and the reception, the clothing worn by the wedding party, the music played and sung, the decorations used, the rituals incorporated into the day, the photographs taken. What was central on this day? What were the priorities of the people planning the day? How did you feel when you left the celebration? What, in your eyes, was this wedding really about?

Most American families see weddings primarily as celebrations of a couple's love for each other. We often say that it is "their day," or even "her day." Invitations are printed on thick paper and sealed with "Love" stamps. They ask the invitees to celebrate the joining of a couple in the bonds of matrimony. The etiquette of wedding invitations is drawn (still) from etiquette books like those of Emily Post, and getting the wording right is important to preserving the grandness of the occasion. Often, arguments over the guest list dominate early conversations about the wedding. Families find it hard to find the right balance of extended family, friends of the couple, friends of the parents, co-workers of the couple, and business associates of the parents. Weddings are parties as well as ceremonies, and the guest list has to work.

Ceremonies on "the big day" are held in churches and synagogues, but also in gardens, parks, and homes — places where the romantic ideals of the couple's relationship will be celebrated. Sometimes contemporary weddings are very short — sometimes only fifteen minutes or so — because no one wants to have a long, boring ceremony. Couples focus on the vows that will unite them. These days, traditional vows ("I, _____, take you, _____, to be my wedded husband/wife, for richer for poorer, in sickness and in health, in good times and bad, till death do us part") are sometimes set aside, and personal vows substituted. The old vows do not seem to capture the passion that many couples want to celebrate on their day. They write vows that give voice to the depth of their feelings for each other and thereby personalize the ancient rite of marriage, making it special.

Music during the ceremony is often sung by a soloist or played on organ or harp. Musical selections include anything from "Here Comes the Bride" to love songs from classical musicians, old musicals, or current movies. The contemporary focus is on personalizing the ceremony by choosing music significant to the couple.

A lot of time and energy goes into choosing and clothing attendants for the bride and groom. Originally, attendants dressed like the bride and groom to ward off evil spirits who might be searching for the bride and groom. Today we continue the custom, in order to include friends and relatives who are important to us and honor them with special dress — at least this is the intention. Typically, bridesmaids walk in a procession and meet groomsmen who stand, waiting, at the front of the church. A bridesmaid and a groomsman are paired together for the day — a reflection of the bride and groom. We speak of attendants as those "in" the wedding. They are central players with key roles in the ritual.

In most weddings, the bride proceeds in after her bridesmaids. Most often, her father or a male relative accompanies her. Traditionally, she wears an elaborate white or off-white dress. Her costume for the day is the finest and most expensive of all. When she comes in, the music changes, and everyone stands. This is a key moment in the ritual. Everyone watches as the bride makes this most important walk. Why is her walk so important? Why does no one watch the groom walk? The emphasis on the bride is not accidental. It signifies the popular perception that this is the bride's day. Something momentous is happening to her, even more so than to her groom. Her life will radically change. It is the most important day of her life and the reason we lavish so much time and expense on her dress, shoes, hair, and makeup. For a woman, our ceremony says, getting married is a very big deal, so it makes sense that, as her walk indicates, she has the central role.

What is she walking into? In Roman times, a wedding was viewed as a life cycle ritual in which the bride moved from her father's home and control to her husband's. She walked in with her father because he was responsible for her. She wore a veil, because when marriages were arranged, often the groom did not meet or even see the bride before the ceremony. To avoid the possibility that the groom would see the bride and change his mind about the transaction, the bride's face was covered until the very last moment. Finally, bride and groom met, the father gave the bride's hand to the groom, and the bride and groom proceeded to walk up the aisle together. Today most people do not see the wedding as a transaction between groom and father of the bride, and few men even ask their future fathers-in-law for their daughter's hand. Still, versions of the old customs persist, and their very persistence shows that vestiges of the old way of thinking continue. Reading this ritual tells us that in our culture, weddings are different for women than for men. Weddings are more important to women, women are more central actors in them, and women are understood to be the ones making the bigger change, moving from the love and care of one man to another.

During the ceremony, many different smaller rituals accompany the main ritual of the exchange of vows. Many secular and religious weddings include the lighting of a unity candle. This ritual provides a way for mothers of the bride and groom to have a role in the ceremony. The mothers light two side candles on a three-candle candelabra. Later, the bride and groom approach and together they light a middle candle, which symbolizes their new life together. The side candles are extinguished, because they are moving on. This ritual captures for many people the coming together as one that lies at the heart of the wedding ceremony. Many ethnic customs, like the tying of ropes around the couple, have similar intents. Others, like the modern Catholic custom of the bride taking roses to place in front of a statue of the Virgin Mary or the Jewish custom of breaking a glass are more personal expressions of thanks for the happy occasion.

Pictures taken before, after, and during the ceremony also reflect cultural understandings of marriage. A frequent complaint is that weddings and especially wedding receptions are structured around pictures. With so many moments to capture, receptions seem to move from one picture taking opportunity to another. We want to remember the first dance, the best man's toast, the bride and groom's kisses in response to knives tapping on glasses, the cutting of the cake, the removal of the garter, the throwing of the bouquet, the farewell wave of the couple. All of these moments honor the couple and their romantic relationship. On this day, they stand before their family and friends and offer their love as an inspiration. As the crowd gathers around to watch the bride and groom dance to "their song," older relatives cry, younger siblings and cousins look on wistfully, and friends smile knowingly — they are all privileged to be able to look upon this young love and hope that it will last forever. At the same time, they hope that the marriages that they have already begun or have yet to contemplate will be equally passionate and long lasting.

The pictures on which so much money is lavished and to which so much attention is devoted speak to the desire to remember this reality. They also reveal once again that the day is centered on the bride. She is the only one who has her picture taken alone. In the endless group photos, she stands out, for her dress is different. The groom may have a slight difference in his costume, but he looks much more like his groomsmen than the bride looks like her bridesmaids. It is no surprise that she is the one who has been given the expensive and beautiful engagement ring to symbolize their engagement. This celebration of romance is thought to be much more hers than his.

In sum, the wedding as most of us know it can be read as a celebration of many things. Primarily, it is a tribute to the romantic love of a particular couple, attended by their family, friends, and associates, who come to wish them well. If much time and money are devoted to the ceremony, we can understand this as evidence of a desire to recognize the importance of this moment in the life of the bride, first, and then the groom. The ceremony is personalized out of a desire to celebrate the unique individuals involved in this particular relationship. Their unity is the main focus. Those invited come to watch, celebrate, and be inspired.

Limitations of the Popular Wedding

There is much to admire in the contemporary wedding. In particular, the focus on the foundational relationship of the couple provides a good alternative to the transactional focus of the older ceremony. On the other hand, a Catholic wedding has a somewhat different focus, which, if read correctly, yields a theology of marriage built on relationship but rooted in and oriented toward God and community. The couple is celebrated not simply as a romantic unit, but as a new Christian community with responsibilities to and grounding in the larger Christian community. This may not sound appealing at first. After all, what's wrong with weddings celebrating romantic relationships? Isn't this what marriage is about?

At the most basic level, of course, contemporary marriage is about relationship. Our culture frowns upon arranged marriages precisely because most of us believe that the search for a lifelong soulmate of one kind or another is valuable. We choose our mates and are chosen by them because of love. The classic 1970s movie *Love Story* exemplifies this focus on relationship. Oliver and Jennifer marry over the strenuous objections of his wealthy WASP family and the anxiety of her Italian Catholic working-class father. Oliver's family disowns and disinherits him, but Jennifer's father opts to attend their wedding and accept the couple. Still, the wedding does not reflect his values; it reflects theirs. They stand before a small group of friends and speak their very beautiful and literary vows to each other. A minister presides over the ceremony, but they marry each other. The Catholic wedding that Jennifer's mother and father would want is passed over in favor of what Jennifer's father calls a "do-it-yourself-er." As the wedding proceeds, the camera swirls around Jennifer and Oliver, for the "story" of the wedding (as of the novel) is their love.

The novel and movie were tremendously popular because they celebrate the courtship and marriage of a young couple who were truly in love. As a young girl, I remember reading the novel time and time again. Only later did I come to believe that a wedding (or a marriage) that was only about two people lacked something. Later, I read the text of Oliver and Jennifer's wedding and found it disturbing because of what was not said or recognized in ritual. This wedding seemed empty to me, because it neglected the community that surrounded and supported Oliver and Jennifer.

The popular Marriage Encounter movement, which offers Catholic couples the opportunity to spend a weekend working on their marriages, is a real-life conceptualization of some of the values that *Love Story* portrays so well. Here, couples minister to couples, so that deeper, more satisfying marriages are possible for more people. Chuck Gallagher, S.J., one of the movement's founders, writes about the importance of the communication techniques at the heart of Marriage Encounter weekend:

> Dialogue is a reminder of what marriage is all about — *us.* Marriage is not an institution, not a bastion of society. It is not a baby carriage, a service organization or social security for a woman and

comfort and convenience for a man. It is the fullest, richest, most wonderful, most imaginative, most exhilarating possibility that life has to offer, *us* in relationship with another.[1]

This is the heart of a movement that has had wide-ranging influence on a great many American Catholics. Its strength comes from its strong focus on "coupleship" in a church that has historically had not enough to say about what love has to do with marriage. However, in Gallagher's zeal to uphold the relationship of the couple, he claims too much for marriage. His vision somewhat over-romanticizes and over-emphasizes couple-love at the expense of the full vocation of Christian persons. Marriage need not be, and probably often is not, the deepest, most intense, most exhilarating thing in life, surpassing all else that we do. Although there is much to celebrate in the Marriage Encounter movement's turn to the everyday lives of married couples in love, the idea that "real life begins with that relationship, and not in the factory or the conference room"[2] limits human beings who have real experiences and encounters at work and in their communities, as well as in their families. It is especially limiting to Christians who are called to something more than this when they marry. Their real lives exist in the extended family, in neighborhoods, in work places, and in the parish as well. So the Marriage Encounter emphasis on "us" is overdone, because marriage has a broader context when it takes place within the church. It begins with "coupleship" but moves beyond this. From a Catholic perspective, then, a marriage ceremony that centers so intently on the individual married couple is misguided. This is not to say that the popular marriage ceremony can be read as a lie, because Catholics certainly believe that the love of the married couple is the fundamental reality of their marriage. However, Catholics add to this ideal of romantic love a broader context. For them, a wedding is not simply "her day" or even "their day." It is, rather, a day of celebration for the whole community surrounding the couple.

A Brief History of the Christian Wedding

In fact, marriage was not always a liturgical event, even for Christians. In the first thousand years of the church's existence, marriage was a civil affair. Seen as a contract between families, the main event was the transfer of the bride from her father's house to her groom's home. Christians simply followed the local customs with regard to marriage. The earliest Christian writers had little to say about it. Those who did refer to it in a positive way encouraged Christians to marry other Christians and warned them not to get drunk at wedding feasts.[3] From the fourth century on, a bishop or priest would sometimes offer a blessing on the marriage at the feast that followed the wedding, in the wedding chamber, or at a mass after the wedding, but the blessing was not essential.[4] Over time, parts of the wedding ceremony were celebrated near or just outside a church building, so that the couple could be blessed right afterward.[5] In the eleventh century, more bishops began to require that marriages be blessed by priests. Gradually the ceremony moved inside the churches, and the secular ritual was transformed into an ecclesial ritual.[6] The twelfth century saw the establishment of an official ritual presided over by a priest, though the details still varied according to local custom.[7] Finally, at the Council of Trent in 1563, the church declared that all Christians who wished to have a valid and sacramental marriage must marry in the presence of a priest and two witnesses.[8] The marriage liturgy remained essentially the same for hundreds of years.

New guidelines for the marriage liturgy issued in 1969 emphasized the new theology of Vatican II, especially the importance of the relationship of the couple and the active role they play in the sacramental aspect of wedding liturgy.[9] In 1990, a second edition of the 1963 guidelines was issued, and it included new developments in liturgical thinking that emerged from Vatican II.[10] There the dominant image used to talk about the church was "people of God." The emphasis on the people had implications for many areas of Catholic life. In the liturgy, it meant that the congregation became increasingly important. The bishops of Vatican II wanted people to recognize mass as a celebration of God's people, presided over or led by a priest. The emphasis on the congregation, which became significant in the weekly mass, carried over into the marriage liturgy. Theologians began to think about why marriage in particular demanded a focus on participation of the congregation, and some wrote popular books explaining the new guidelines to engaged Catholic couples.

Reading the New Catholic Guidelines for Weddings

If a Catholic couple follows the guidelines now available in a number of popular wedding guides, they will put together a wedding that looks very different from the popular version so familiar to us. They will begin by inviting not only their family and friends, but also the people in the parish in which they will marry. This way, the wedding can be celebrated as an event of the church community rather than as an isolated event in the lives of an individual man and woman. They might upset popular custom on their wedding day by standing at the door of the church to greet, welcome, and introduce their family and friends, performing what is known and practiced in many parishes as the ministry of hospitality. The hope is that having family and friends meet one another before the ceremony will help couples "shape a worshipping assembly out of the many individuals who will be at [their] wedding."[11]

The procession into the church will look different, too. It will bear greater similarity to the regular Sunday procession, beginning with an usher carrying a processional cross, a reader carrying the Scriptures, the priest, groomsmen accompanied by bridesmaids, the groom accompanied by his parents, and the bride accompanied by her parents. How might we read this procession? The more traditional bride-with-father meeting the groom procession is gone, as are the sexist connotations that inevitably accompany it. Instead, the religious nature of the ceremony, the equal nature of the man's and woman's experience of their wedding day, and the important roles played by the families of both bride and groom in the marriage ceremony receive emphasis. Rather than encouraging an exclusive focus on the bride and her father, this procession highlights the relationships of both bride and groom with their parents for a brief, important moment. It seems both contemporary (in its equal treatment of men and women) and ancient (in its inclusion of all four parents) at the same time. In fact, it is notable for its symbolization of the significant relationships between the bride and groom and their parents, which will be forever altered, but not left behind, after the wedding ceremony.

What happens, then, to the role of bridesmaids and groomsmen? Is their role diminished when the procession downplays their importance?

It should not be, for the new guidelines emphasize the roles of the attendants as witnesses to the marriage. This is, after all, what they are supposed to be. Their dress is less important than their support as friends. So in this new ceremony, the witnesses (one or more pairs of a man and a woman) sit on the altar with the bride and groom. They serve as symbolic representations of the couple who will wed. Their important role consists of being there for the couple and witnessing their vows.

The ceremony itself has as its main liturgical goal the participation of the assembly — the gathering of family and friends who have come to witness the marriage of a couple. As witnesses, they are called to an active role in ceremony. They are participants rather than audience members. To encourage wedding guests to own this role, couples are asked to print up a program that includes the music to be sung at the wedding. The hope is that most musical selections will be sung by all — just like in a regular Sunday mass. So after the greeting and procession, an entrance hymn might be sung. Later, the assembly would be encouraged to join in singing the songs for the preparation of the gifts, communion, other parts of the mass, and a closing hymn. When it is time to pronounce a final blessing on the couple, the assembly might be asked to raise one hand toward the couple and read the blessing (printed in their programs) along with the priest. This way, their role as witnesses and blessers of the marriage will be made clear.

The assembly, in the new Catholic guidelines, is also asked to make an offering, as Catholics are asked to do every Sunday when they attend mass, but rarely when they attend weddings. The idea here is that a collection can be taken for a specific charity close to the hearts of the couple. A note in the wedding program may simply state, "On a day when we are blessed with so much abundance, the church asks us not to forget those who have little. Today we will be taking up a collection for _____, a group we know and respect." This way, the bride and groom model their concern for the less fortunate of their community to all those who make up their wedding assembly, and the assembly has an opportunity to participate in an act of charity with the bride and groom. Thus the meaning of the wedding will extend beyond the couple, symbolizing that the marriage will as well.

All of this may sound hopelessly foreign, but many Catholic couples have found that following these guidelines shaped their wedding in positive ways. It can be powerful for couples to hear the singing of family and friends and to look out and see loved ones extending their hands in blessing. Many guests travel hundreds of miles to come to a wedding, and many do not know each other, yet they can make themselves into an assembly and show the couple by their involvement in the wedding that they care about their marriage. As one writer of a marriage preparation guide explains,

> When you exchange your vows, you offer a visible sign of God's presence and love to the parish in which your wedding is celebrated. You create a new family within that community. At the same time, the church, and, in particular, the local parish, promise to be there for you in times of joy and in times of need. You are making a commitment to each other and to the church. In turn, the church is making a commitment to you.[12]

The guidelines make clear the public nature of the Catholic wedding ceremony. When a man and a woman get married, they do not do so alone, with others looking on. Instead, they celebrate with a community of people whom they love. Asking members of that community to participate in the wedding mass makes that idea concrete.

Because participation is a high priority, and because the mass itself is the central vehicle by which couples are to emphasize the unity between the couple and between them and their family and friends, many other customs more central in popular weddings are not central in the weddings of couples using the new guidelines. These couples are less concerned with personalizing their vows because they see the vows as public declarations of their long-lasting commitment to each other. So, like millions of couples before them, they simply promise to be faithful for better or worse and to love and honor each other all the days of their lives. They do not substitute secular music or readings, but instead choose religious songs and scriptural readings that underline both the love they feel for each other and the strong ties they feel to family, friends, and church community. Brides do not offer a bouquet of flowers to Mary, as so many Catholic brides do today, because they learn by reading the new guidelines that this is a relatively recent ritual that is more private than public, and thus not particularly appropriate to a wedding ceremony. Ironically, they leave out many popular Catholic devotions in order to emphasize the religious nature of the ceremony and the important role of the assembly in the sacrament.

One Catholic writer who speaks powerfully of the importance of community involvement in the wedding ceremony is Jo McGowan. She describes her marriage to her Hindu husband, Ravi:

> We wanted our wedding to be a celebration of our love, naturally, but also for the community who had come to share our joy.
>
> And it was. What a diversity of talents went into that day — from the wedding invitations and programs we designed . . . to the wedding clothes made by Ravi's cousin and the wedding cake made by my father and a close friend. Ravi's mother performed the Hindu wedding ceremony; two priest friends witnessed the Catholic ceremony. . . . Two nuns who had taught me in high school provided their oceanside convent for the day. The vegetarian banquet . . . was entirely prepared by friends who arrived a few days early to cook . . . and best of all were the children, everywhere, behaving exactly as children should behave, especially at a wedding.
>
> It seemed to us then, and it seems even more so now, that our wedding was a symbol of the way we want to live our lives: surrounded by family and friends; giving and receiving the gifts of time, laughter, advice, and help; sharing food, work, prayer, and celebration; creating a world where children are free and full of joy.
>
> But marriage is a community event. It expresses, in its ideal form, a belief in the goodness of community, a belief in the beauty of two people who love each other coming together to live in communion.[13]

This community emphasis makes sense to some couples at an intuitive level: of course, when they marry their life will be about much more than themselves. It will be about their relationship as a couple, and their extended family, their careers, their future children, their neighborhood, their community, and their parish. They make a commitment that day to love each other deeply, but also to be a force for good together in the world around them. They look forward to that at least as much as to what they hope will be a lifelong romance. But this model of a wedding ceremony and a marriage does not make sense to many, perhaps most, young Catholic couples. It will be important, then, to clarify the theology that underlies the new wedding guidelines to show why contemporary liturgists are so justly concerned with revising the marriage liturgy.

Theology behind the New Marriage Liturgy

Why does the new Catholic liturgy, when read as a "text," seem to center itself on a vision of marriage that is quite different from the popular model? Why isn't the ideal of passionate and abiding love between a woman and a man enough? Think about what it would mean to see marriage only as a relationship of two. For how long does it make sense to concentrate on just these two? Think of a marriage you know well. Is it possible to limit your understanding of the marriage to the couple themselves? Isn't it more reasonable to think of the couple you know with their three children, the soccer and baseball leagues they are involved in, the schools where their children learn and they volunteer, the workplaces where they each have a network of friends as well as students or clients with whom they interact daily, the neighborhood where they are in charge of the annual block party, and the front yard where they sit outside on summer evenings watching their children run around with their neighbors' children, the shelter where they volunteer once a month, the friends (some of his and some of hers) whom they invite to dinner parties and birthday parties, the parish where they meet the same families week after week over coffee and doughnuts, and on and on? When a man and a woman marry, they do not just start a relationship; they start a family. Their success as a married couple extends not just to their own relationship but to their partnership in a whole series of interlocking communities.

As theologian Francis Schüssler Fiorenza puts it, in marriage, "one develops a relationship not simply as an intimate relation with a private other, but rather as a community of intersecting relationships and interests."[14] Theologically speaking, then, "marriage should be understood as a sign and symbol of the church precisely insofar as it is a sign of the community brought about by the Spirit of God and Christ. A marriage between two individuals is the beginning of a new community, a community of equal disciples and partners under the impact and power of the Spirit."[15] For this reason the new liturgical guidelines ask couples to situate the celebration of their marriage within the context of a participating community of family and friends gathered as one family in the church. If marriage is about more than two, the liturgy must be as well. This applies especially to the liturgy of the Eucharist, the church's sacrament of unity, where the community comes together (in each parish) to reenact the last supper Jesus ate with his community of disciples and thus remembers that it (the church) is a community of disciples centered upon the risen Christ. The marriage liturgy, then, is a time for the church community to gather as it always does to celebrate its unity in Christ, as well as a time for a particular community of Christian families and friends to gather and witness the union of a particular couple. This particular union of a man and a woman symbolizes the broader unity of the church. In theological terms, those who witness a wedding ceremony are privileged to draw near to a concrete, loving union of two Christians — a community of disciples — that gives a taste of the spiritual communion among all Christians united in Christ.

A marriage that strives to be a community of disciples provides a service of sorts to the community. Not just by serving the community directly, but simply by being united (being a community) a married couple can have an impact on the people around them. One theologian, writing in a book of prayers for engaged couples, asks young men and women to consider the public nature of their approaching marriage. He asks them to reflect on the idea that when they marry, "others should be able to count on [them] for love, for fidelity, to see the light and taste the salt of God's presence in [their] community."[16] In Fleming's view, marriage consists not simply or even primarily of a personal relationship. Rather, it crystallizes the love of the larger church community. The couple is not just two-in-one, but two together within the whole, with specific responsibility for the whole. They must be strong, because the community needs their strength. They must persevere in love, because the community needs to see God's love actualized among God's people, and this is precisely what people see when they know an outward-focused loving couple. The man and woman who are alone staring into each other's eyes cannot offer their love to the community in a comparable way.

Another problem with the ideal of marriage as a commitment to a romantic relationship of lifelong lovers is that it heightens our expectations and sets us up for disappointment when passion fades or shifts forms.[17] After all, if a couple's marriage is only about them, then when the intensity of their passion settles into the rhythms of married love, if it becomes somehow boring in comparison to the young love everywhere around them, if they question their desires to spend so much of their time together, what remains of their marriage? It seems to be over. The contemporary focus on relationship has put a great deal of stress on married couples. They focus more on the quality of their love, and though there are some important positive implications that come out of this focus (like the growing understanding that relationships require work), there are also negative implications (like the stark increase in the divorce rate since the 1960s). Today, "for the first time in American history, official statistics showed that more marriages ended by divorce than by death."[18] As Lisa Cahill argues,

> Once marriage becomes focused exclusively on personal fulfillment and dependent on romantic love, it is also cut off from social and kinship supports and purposes which augment the resources of the couple to sustain their relationship through times of difficulty. Hence an alarming incidence of divorce and the perilous situation in which the inner-directed and isolated nuclear family currently finds itself.[19]

If the contemporary era has been an experience with the relationship model of marriage, it seems that we have failed on at least one important measure: we have failed to keep marriages together. Perhaps romantic relationship is a pressure that marriage as an institution cannot bear. Perhaps this indicates that marriage is meant to be about more than just the two. Perhaps it is impossible to create a strong relationship if we ignore the community in which the relationship lives and grows. Theologians like Cahill advocate a renewed understanding of "the marital commitment [as] a commitment to a whole framework of life, which sustains the love of the partners, but which also must be construed in terms of family, community, church, and wider society."[20] This is exactly what the new liturgy tries to do.

Focusing on the whole way of life that a marriage brings into being may be a more practical as well as more realistic way of thinking. Fiorenza argues that "in a marriage commitment is primarily to a community."[21] This may sound a lot less appealing than marriage as a commitment to a particular person whom I love more than life itself, but once again, if we think about how the long-term marriages we know really are centers of communities, and about how short-lived marriages often are weak in community grounding or support, this model might make more sense.

Thinking of marriage as a small community does not necessarily imply the death of passionate love, though it does imply a reformation of that love. Instead of inward turning, it will be outward looking. If we were to image this love, we would not think of it as two lovers gazing into each other's eyes. We would think of it instead as two lovers walking along the beach hand in hand, talking excitedly about their plans for themselves, their children, their work, and their neighbors and friends.

The Catholic emphasis on the "big picture" of marriage questions the secular romantic ideal not because it says the wrong thing, but because it does not say enough. As Fiorenza argues, the passion of a married couple is not an end in itself; it expands into shared passion for public work/action.[22] Consider the example of a couple, both high school teachers, who share a passion for education. They derive great pleasure from leading their students in discussions on "the big questions," and in mentoring those who come to them for guidance. Each supports the other's work and draws energy from it. They stand united in their commitment to make meaningful work (and to them that means work with social significance) central in their lives. Their relationship does not draw them away from that work; it brings them together so that they are capable of even more. Their marriage seems to reflect what the bishops at Vatican II had in mind when they called marriage an "intimate partnership of life and love."[23] The bishops speak of an intimate relationship, and this is often what strikes people when they read the text for the first time. The Catholic understanding of marriage is not limited to couples and their duty to procreate. Rather, it begins with intimacy between husband and wife. And yet, by speaking of a "partnership of life and love," the bishops reveal their belief that married couples are involved in something larger than themselves. They are partners in bringing something else about. Partners do not play alone; they play or work with and for others. Partnership begins with intimacy but does not end there. The partnership of marriage, in the Catholic understanding, is oriented toward something more.

Theologian Karl Rahner speaks of this particularly Catholic vision of marriage when he says:

> Marriage is not the act in which two individuals come together to form a "we," a relationship in which they set themselves apart from the "all" and close themselves against this. Rather it is the act in which a "we" is constituted which opens itself lovingly precisely to the ALL. This aspect of the basic essence of such love "appears" already in the very fact that those united by married love themselves already come from a community. In their love they do not abandon this — indeed they must not abandon it.[24]

Rahner describes the communal context of marriage to which our reading of the liturgy has pointed. He claims that the two who become one flesh in marriage do not break up community. Rather, they unite and build up community. His vision is particularly and essentially Catholic in its refusal to limit marriage to the personal realm of individual couples. His theology provides a way to understand why a couple would ask their parents to accompany them as they walk down the aisle, why they would elect to greet their community of family and friends at the door of the church and ask them to join in singing and blessing them on their special day, and why liturgists would be concerned that weddings be at least as memorable for what they do to bring a community together as they are for the reception.

Rahner's theology, like Fiorenza's, also helps us understand why the marriage ceremony usually includes a celebration of the Eucharist. Christians are said to be one body in Christ, and they celebrate this truth in the sacrament of unity — the Eucharist. In the celebration of the Eucharist, the church community reenacts the last supper and thus actualizes or creates itself as the community of disciples of Jesus Christ. It is only fitting to celebrate marriage (which celebrates the union of a man and a woman and is thus the other sacrament of unity) in the context of the Eucharist. It only makes sense that a marriage liturgy would include the whole body of the assembly in its ritual, for the sacrament of two of its members is also the sacrament of all of its members. Marriage deepens and extends the original unity. The presider prays in the liturgy, "Lord, in your love you have given us this Eucharist to unite us with one another and with you. As you have made [this couple] one in this sacrament of marriage and in the sharing of the one bread and the one cup, so now make them one in love for each other."[25]

Marriage is founded in the church community, sacramentalized within its assembly, graced by the community, and given the task of gracing that community in return by becoming a living example of community. In their love, and in their participation in communal and ecclesial activities, the married couple actualizes in a very human way what the church is called to be. Their relationship is not, according to Catholic thinking, simply about "creating a world which only two can share," in the words of an old popular song.[26] Theologians like Karl Rahner believe that Catholic couples are called to more.

Rahner reminds couples that they come from somewhere when they get married. They come from families with connections in schools, churches, sports leagues, civic organizations, and neighborhoods. He encourages men and women to think of their marriage as more than a couple-ship. They should see themselves as a new "body" with existing connections to the families and communities, new connections to a new set of communities just beginning to take shape. Their passion for each other is not an end in itself. The couple brings their passion to its fullness by sharing it with others.

How could this vision be actualized? Let me give an example of a couple that attempted to share their union with others. Theologians Mark Chmiel and Mev Puleo married after Mev wrestled with the desire to join a religious community. She finally came to say, "I am part of a community, a community of two!" In an article that celebrates the sacrament of their life together (which ended tragically when Mev died of a brain tumor in 1996), Mark Chmiel tells of how their marriage was a community-building relationship:

The doors to our homes in Cambridge, Berkeley, Oakland, and St. Louis were regularly being opened. From the time I met her in 1988, Mev was a spirited impresario, an extroverted instigator and a welcoming hostess. She often would invite friends to a favorite ice cream parlor. And she loved throwing dinner parties for fellow students, taking pride in making fresh pesto. Friends in the apartment complex would be invited to snack with us on the front porch after a run to a nearby deli. Haitians would meet Brazilians, and activists would meet academics, and old friends would meet neighbors at our Sunday evening potlucks with slide shows on current events. We also hosted friends and neighbors at weekly prayer and meditation sessions on Wednesday mornings.[27]

Later, when Mev was very sick, they opened their home once again. Friends and family tended to Mev and supported Mark around the clock. Mark later wrote, paraphrasing Dorothy Day, "We have all known the long loneliness and we know that the only solution is love and that love comes with community. It all happened while Mev was lying there dying and it is still going on."[28] Mev Puleo and Mark Chmiel's marriage was extraordinary, but there are many couples who reach beyond themselves without sacrificing their relationship, because they find their own relationship strengthened by people outside their family. Couples choose to bring the energy they create together to a whole new set of communities. This is what Catholic marriage is all about and why the Catholic marriage liturgy reads so differently from the text of the contemporary secular wedding that is only about the romance of two.

Discussion Questions

1. Do you agree with Rubio's analysis of the popular wedding? How would you "read" a wedding you've recently attended?

2. Does knowing that the church has not always had a wedding liturgy make a difference?

3. Rubio shows that the new guidelines for the marriage liturgy emphasize participation. Does this emphasis appeal to you? What else would you emphasize in your marriage liturgy?

4. Use the new guidelines to plan your own hypothetical wedding. Incorporate those new options that appeal to you. Choose readings that reflect your understanding of marriage. How does your ceremony compare to those of others in your group? What is the source of the differences?

THREE

New Testament Vision

What Will We Read?

As I was preparing to write this chapter, my sister-in-law called to ask my advice. Her best friend was getting married that weekend, and they needed readings. She did not want anything sexist ("none of that submission stuff"), and she was not too excited about the traditional passage in Corinthians that speaks of a seemingly unearthly love that is always patient, kind, and giving either. What else was there, she wanted to know. I pulled out my marriage planning books and made some suggestions: Jesus' affirmation of marriage in the Gospel of Mark, the passages in 1 John and the Gospel of John about love, the traditional wedding at Cana story, the first creation story in Genesis 1, and the Song of Songs. I was struck, as I remember being when I planned my own wedding, by how little there was to choose from. Those who are searching for an inspiring passage about the joys of love between husband and wife and the delights of parenting should look elsewhere. As I told my sister-in-law, "It just isn't there."

From our twenty-first-century perspective, the New Testament is remarkable for its lack of attention to realities we take as central. Most contemporary Christians, like most contemporary Americans, would probably agree that putting family first is the moral thing to do. People often say things like, "No one on his deathbed said, 'I should have spent more time at the office.'" They praise those who manage to prioritize and make time for their families. They say that if they had the choice, they would work less and spend more time with their families.[1] They affirm that practicing love in one's family is what life is ultimately about. Of course, reality proves more complicated than this, as studies show that family members in fact spend less and less time together because women, men, and teens work more and children spend longer days in day care or school. Sociologist Arlie Hochschild has argued that even when working Americans have the opportunity to take time off from work, they generally refuse to do so.[2] Still, pro-family ideals remain forceful, and they are implicated in the many daily decisions we make to put family first (as when we spend money on take-out food or movies, but turn down the charitable appeals that fill our mailboxes).

It should not surprise us then that Christians who have entered the public debate on family values have most often done so as advocates for the family. Conservative Christian organizations such as Focus on the Family, the Christian Coalition, and Promise Keepers have all called mothers and fathers back to the home, and few Christians would question their assumption that being a good Christian means being committed to the family.

Family, however, is not a central idea in the New Testament. In fact, it hardly mentions family at all. Moreover, in those few passages in which the New Testament writers do take up the subject of marriage, their words are often more disabling than affirming. Followers of Jesus are told to hate their families, leave them behind, put service to the kingdom first. The earliest Christian sources point away from the primacy of family duty. Jesus, the model for all humans who call themselves Christian, was an itinerant celibate preacher for whom family ties were unimportant. Discipleship with this Jesus, according to the Gospel writers, asks people to decentralize family, not focus on it.

The questions that arise, then, are these: What exactly does the New Testament tell us about how to live as Christians in families? What did Jesus do? Why wasn't he married? What did Jesus tell the people gathered around him about family? What did he want people to do in response? How did members of the Jesus movement respond to conflicts between the demands of their families and the demands of discipleship with Jesus of Nazareth? What do contemporary Christians do with texts that seem to be so opposed to what we believe today? How can we, in our very different situation, remain faithful to the essence of this message?

Reading the New Testament

Before moving to the New Testament texts, some background is necessary. The New Testament Gospels (Mark, Matthew, Luke, and John) were probably written sometime around 70–100 c.e. by second- and third-generation Christians, none of whom knew Jesus. They worked, most New Testament scholars believe, with oral traditions that had been passed down through the early church communities. Luke and Matthew, it is thought, also had access to a written source of Jesus' sayings (usually called "Q"). Each writer compiled his story of Jesus in a different way, in part because the community for which each wrote had its own unique perspective on Jesus, unique concerns, and unique ideas about discipleship. Still, there is a significant amount of overlap, especially in the synoptic Gospels (Mark, Matthew, Luke).

Biblical scholars have varying amounts of trust in the factual truth of the Gospels but generally agree that a man named Jesus lived, taught, and was crucified, that his followers believed he was resurrected, and that a community of believers quickly formed in his name. There is a lot of argument about the rest, but many respectable scholars believe that we can get a reasonable, if partial, picture of Jesus' ministry from each Gospel writer. In addition, there is a general belief that the evangelists wrote the truth as they saw it and did not try to deceive or make something up. The difficulty comes when modern Christians living some two thousand years later try to understand what they wrote. The Gospel writers were writing in Hebrew or Greek, so we read their words in translation. Additionally, these writers addressed a radically different time and culture, so we also read their ideas, to a large extent, in translation. We attempt to understand their words and ideas by making analogies to what we know. Only then can we begin the equally arduous task of applying them to our own, very different, lives. All of this means that we need a degree of humility when approaching New Testament texts. It will not be easy to decipher their meaning. Still, those who wish to understand and/or practice Christianity must plunge in.[3]

In doing so, one must avoid thinking that once we have understood what a particular text says, we know exactly what to do. The New Testament writings represent the witness of different groups of early Christians. The witness of these groups offers us models, but not easy answers, because our time, culture, and situation are greatly different from theirs. Thus we can look to them as prototypes — important, primary models of Christian discipleship — but not archetypes. We take up the challenges they pose, even if we are not able to do things exactly as they did.[4]

Jesus as Model: Leaving Family Behind

The Gospel of Mark provides an example of a conflict between family and discipleship in Jesus' own life. Jesus is teaching a large crowd that follows him everywhere he goes. His mother and brother,[5] hear about this and go to find and "restrain" him (Mark 3:31). When the crowd tells him that his family has come to see him, he says, " 'Who are my mother and my brothers?' And looking at those who sat around him, he said, 'Here are my mother and my brothers! Whoever does the will of God is my brother and sister and mother' " (Mark 3:33–35). Jesus rejects his family's attempt to take him away from his disciples. He might have simply told his family that he had pressing work to do. Instead, he uses his rejection of their request to call the whole nature of the kinship bond into question. He says very plainly that those he has gathered around him are his new family, and he seems to deny all loyalty or duty to his family of origin. The Anchor Bible commentary claims that this statement "exemplifies the radical demand of Jesus upon those who are set in a new framework in which bonds of fellowship in a common obedience to God are placed above the bonds of kinship."[6] Another commentator simply says that Jesus tells his disciples here that "spiritual kinship surpasses the accidents of birth."[7]

When confronted with the demands of his family, Jesus proposes a new radical moral standard that threatens the most basic family loyalties and engenders the most difficult conflicts between family and religious commitment. Jesus continues his mission despite the protests of his family. He refuses even to talk to them, asserting that the people gathered around him are more important. He will not be deterred from his decision to preach the Gospel.

In one of the other passages showing a similar kind of conflict, the young Jesus is found in the temple by his parents, who think he has been lost, and a similar kind of "resolution" occurs. According to the story, Jesus goes to the temple without his parents' permission and without concern that they might be worried about him. When they finally find him, after three days of searching, he does not apologize, but says only, "Did you not know that I must be in my Father's house?" (Luke 2:49). The story concludes with the affirmation that he returned home and was obedient to his parents. Children's Bibles often use it to make an example of Jesus' obedience. Still, despite the young Jesus' decision to go home with and be respectful toward his parents, what seems really significant here is Jesus' original separation from his parents and his affirmation that God's house, not theirs, is where he truly belongs. This sets up the later refusal to see and submit to his family. Clearly, according to Luke, when Jesus is older, his calling to preach a new Gospel overrides the duty to submit to family. Calling, then, is ultimately separate from and more important than family for Jesus. These two stories in Luke's Gospel give a strong indication of Jesus' own family-denying ethic. His later ministry, in which he was known as an itinerant, celibate preacher, simply confirms this picture. While not denying that Jesus could have experienced sexual temptation or even desired marriage, especially in his twenties (a period on which we have no information), as an adult he confronts Christians with a life of celibacy, not marriage.[8] Answers to the question "Why?" are found in his teachings.

Jesus' Message: Questioning the Primacy of Family Ties

In the Gospel of Luke, Jesus tells a man who wants to follow him that he must not stop to bury his dead father. "Let the dead bury their own dead," Jesus says, "but as for you, go and proclaim the kingdom of God" (Luke 9:60, parallel in Matt 8:21–22). In this passage Luke shows Jesus asking for devotion to the work of the kingdom of God, understanding that his command will call into question even ordinary family affection. Jesus knows "that the demands of the kingdom are bound to rupture even ordinary family life."[9]

Once again, we have a passage that grates against our most basic moral sensibilities. What can Jesus possibly have meant by this? It seems that he can't have been speaking literally. But even a figurative inter-pretation leaves us with an extreme family-denying ethic. Perhaps, some have argued, Jesus is speaking only to those with a special calling to leave everything for him. Or perhaps this and other similar passages date from early strains of the oral traditions (usually called "Q" and "proto-Mark" by biblical scholars) that were gathered and edited by the wandering charismatics who made up the core of the Jesus movement.[10] However, it seems more likely that this saying of Jesus is not a literal command addressed to a special group (there is no indication that it is), but rather a command pregnant with symbolism that is intended to address a general need for disciples of Jesus to place their commitment to Jesus above their commitments to their families. New Testament scholar Richard Horsley makes precisely this point and further claims that Jesus' radical anti-family message was rooted in his commitment to his mission: "the revitalization of local community life."[11] This mission required some to leave their families and spread the word, while others opened and restructured their families at home. The goal, according to Horsley, was a society in which people treated each other with compassion, forgave each other's debts, shared their property, and refused to lord power over each other. A radical rejection of the traditional family was necessary in order to move toward the goal of a renewed and restructured family and community life in which discipleship had priority for all.

One major part of this reconstruction was the dismantling of the patriarchal family. After all, if everyone was to share property and power, traditional hierarchical relations between men and women would be impossible to maintain. Jesus' own preaching is the justification for the change in thinking about gender roles. Jesus evidentially did not share the reverence for women's maternal role that was popular in his time. In the Gospel of Luke, for instance, we are told of an instance in which Jesus is speaking to a group of people, and a woman calls out, "Blessed is the womb that bore you and the breasts that nursed you!" Jesus answers, "Blessed rather are those who hear the word of God and obey it" (Luke 11:27–28). Here Jesus refuses to uphold the cultural priority on mother-nurturing. He places the work of the Gospel above this nurturing work, suggesting that nurturing is not to be the primary form of God's work for women who follow him. As Harvard biblical scholar Elisabeth Schüssler Fiorenza puts it, "Faithful discipleship, not biological motherhood, is the eschatological calling of women."[12] Thus Jesus is to be understood, according to Schüssler Fiorenza and others, as someone who asked women to do something more than bear and care for children. Women who seek to follow him, then, must be prepared to "hear the word of God and keep it" in other ways.

Jesus also calls into question the role of fathers. For instance, Mark's Gospel includes a story in which Jesus is talking about the coming kingdom. He says, "There is no one who has left house or brothers or sisters or mother or father or children or fields, for my sake and for the sake of the good news, who will not receive a hundredfold now in this age — houses, brothers and sisters, mothers and children, and fields..." (Mark 10:29–30). Fathers are the only group that is left behind in the new kingdom. Why? Elisabeth Schüssler Fiorenza has convincingly argued against the traditional reading of this passage that fathers are not included because only men are being addressed here. She notes that wives are only included in the list of those left behind in Luke's version of this passage, not in the earlier version in "Q." So in the original version, she believes, men and women are asked to leave family behind, and both are promised a new family: the community of those who are disciples of Jesus. "This new 'family' of equal discipleship, however, has no room for 'fathers.'"[13] The absence of fathers in the lists of those who will inhabit the new kingdom is an indication, in Schüssler Fiorenza's view, that the patriarchal privilege of fathers is rejected, that hierarchy cannot be a part of new life in Christ. So men and women are included, but privileged and powerful fathers are not. Similarly, Schüssler Fiorenza points out, Jesus tells his followers to "call no one your father" (Matt 23:9), indicating that no one in the new Christian community will have this kind of power over others.[14] These, then, are signs that Jesus is concerned with the creation of new forms of family and community that move beyond the problems of the traditional patriarchal model.

Schüssler Fiorenza's interpretations allow us to make some sense of the most difficult of the anti-family passages. When Jesus asks his followers to leave family behind, he is talking about a particular kind of family: the patriarchal family in which men held nearly absolute power over women.[15] It is this family that Jesus finds objectionable. It is this family that has no place in the Christian community.

It is tempting to believe that this concern about sexism is all there is to the anti-family strain in the message of Jesus of Nazareth. After all, this would mean that our own family-focused values were not so far off the mark. If sexism is the problem, and we no longer practice sexism, then maybe Jesus' message cannot properly be called "anti-family." However, patriarchy in the family is not Jesus' only concern. As many of his sayings show, family itself is the problem. The strongest of the anti-family sayings, for example, Luke 14:26 ("Whoever comes to me and does not hate father and mother, wife and children, brothers and sisters, yes, even life itself, cannot be my disciple") seems to indicate that separation from family is essential to discipleship.[16] If we follow Horsley's assumption that the anti-family demands are meant to apply to all those who would follow Jesus, it is clear that, at some level, Christians must confront a Jesus who is radically questioning much of what we value most highly.

We have to wonder what could have inspired such concerns. What was Jesus so worried about? Why did he see family as such a significant stumbling block for believers? We have to look to the culture within which Jesus preached in order to begin to understand his profound mistrust of strong family bonds. There were two primary cultural milieus in first-century Palestine: the Greco-Roman culture of those who occupied Palestine, and the traditional Jewish culture of those who were living under Roman occupation. Both are significant backdrops against which Jesus' sayings can be measured.

In the Greco-Roman world in which the Jews lived, family was a weighty matter. It was the primary reality, more important than individuals certainly, and significant in its relation to the state, for in it more citizens for the Roman Empire were created.[17] For this reason, the early Christians were derided and even persecuted for their anti-family views.[18] Greco-Roman ideals of marriage in Jesus' time emphasized the ethical duty to marry. Marriages came into existence via private compacts between two persons who intended to become husband and wife.[19] However, children were a crucial part of marriage. In fact, "procreation was regarded as a civic duty, and all citizens of marriageable age were expected to contribute."[20] Because life expectancies were so short and the survival of the society was so crucial, through law and social pressure "young men and women were discreetly mobilized to use their bodies for reproduction."[21]

Those who did not fulfill their civic obligations were considered immoral. Historian Peter Brown notes that those early Christians who elected to remain celibate were often criticized. For example, in the fictional account of one fifth-century Christian writer, St. Paul is brought before local authorities and taken to task because, he "denigrates marriage: yes, marriage, which you might say is the beginning, root and fountainhead of our nature. From it springs fathers, mothers, children and families. Cities, villages and cultivation have appeared because of it."[22] This is but one instance of cultural and ethical conflict between the Romans, who believed the family to be sacred, and the early Christians, who often did not. In another example, the Acts of Paul and Thecla, an early Christian text, portrays Thecla as a heroine, because she leaves her fiancé to preach the Gospel with Paul.[23] She and other early Christian celibates contributed to the Christians' reputation in Palestine as " 'homewreckers,' initiators of a message not of household order but disorder."[24]

The contrast with Judaism could not be starker. "In Judaism," Peter Brown tells us, "the Law rested equally on every aspect of the human person. It required reverent attention to those things which all human beings were held to share — food, time, and marriage."[25] Judaism, much more than Christianity, then, can be considered a pro-family religion in which family is a primary place where the good life can be lived.

Among the Palestinian Jews, marriage was expected as a matter of course.[26] If one reads the Hebrew Bible, one is presented with "a religious community built upon the patriarchal family."[27] Unlike Roman society, in which family loyalty is linked to state and cult, then, in Jewish culture the family is directly tied to the faith. The Jews as a people have a covenant with God, and each Jew becomes a part of the covenant in and through the family. Marriage went largely unquestioned in the lives of Palestinian Jews, until Jesus of Nazareth came onto the scene.[28]

The marriage ideals of both Jewish and Roman cultures were sweeping in scope and demanding in expectations. It is not difficult to understand that Jesus of Nazareth, who, like other radicals of his time, wanted to give himself totally to God, questioned the marital ethos of the time. The demand for so much loyalty to family seemed to him idolatrous. He did not want family to function as an idol in his life, or in the lives of his followers, so he asked them to go against the cultural mores of their time and put God first.[29]

However, Jesus himself does not reject marriage altogether. Rather, in his refusal to sanction divorce, he reaffirms the importance of the marital commitment in the lives of the people he has gathered around him. He recalls the myth of Genesis and claims that "from the beginning of creation, 'God made them male and female.' 'For this reason a man shall leave his father and mother and be joined to his wife, and the two shall become one flesh.' So they are no longer two, but one flesh. Therefore what God has joined together, let no one separate" (Mark 10:6–9). This saying is widely viewed as support for marriage as a holy union. It should allay any fears that "marriage or the nuclear family [was] rejected or even devalued."[30]

So if marriage is not rejected altogether, what is? Certainly, the patriarchal structure of the family—both the absence of fathers in the new kingdom and Jesus' admonition to "call no one your father" (Matt 23:9) attest to this. But it is difficult to deny a more far-reaching anti-kinship message in this crucial set of Jesus' sayings, for he does not simply target fathers. Mothers, children, and siblings are implicated as well. It is the bond of kinship itself and all the ethical priority that comes with it that is being called into question, because the Jesus of the Gospels preaches that family, like money and power, can be dangerous to the person who is trying to live a holy life. He taught that those who would serve God must resist the temptation to make care of their own their only mission in life, and the early Christians heard this message.

Early Christian Practice: A New Kind of Family

One good way to understand the change in family ethos that was evident among the early Christians is to look at the practice of adoption. Stephen Post recently studied the Christian tradition on adoption and concluded:

> Christianity challenges the increasingly prevalent cultural assumption that the only real kinship is based on birth, biology, and blood. Indeed, Christian ethics suggests that even if blood is thicker than

water, it is not thicker than agape, which informs the altruistic imagination underlying the historical Christian theology of relinquishment and adoption.[31]

How does Post come to the conclusion that for the early Christians love is more important than kinship? He looks at Christian practice and sees that although the first assumption is that birth parents will rear their own children, if the best interests of the children require that others rear them, adoption is a welcome alternative. In fact, early Christians affirmed the morality of adoption by referring to their own adoption as children of God in baptism.[32] Post uses his conclusions about Christian thought and practice to challenge current American cultural mores that seem to him to question the legitimacy of adoption by privileging biological parenthood. He suggests that the Christian ideal — love extends beyond biological connections — is the better one.

What Post shows is that the early Christians did not limit their love or duty to the family sphere. They did not believe that their responsibilities to their families were their only ethical responsibilities. They did not limit their understanding of family by thinking of it as only biological. Rather, because they saw beyond nuclear family, they had an enlarged sense of what life required of them. It is this ethical sense, exemplified in the Christian practice of adoption, that is rooted in the radical family-denying ethic of Jesus of Nazareth, who called his followers to reject nuclear family-idolatry and embrace a larger family of all God's children.

What, then, would the new family that Jesus preaches look like? First, Jesus called his followers to a new kind of relationship in community with others who sought to do the will of God. The first Christians can be seen as a people who wanted to actualize Jesus' vision of the kingdom. Horsley claims that "even if we allow for considerable exaggeration in Luke's nostalgic and romanticizing summaries (e.g., [Acts] 2:41–47; 4:32–37; 5:42), we can still imagine a group excitedly celebrating table fellowship, sharing resources, and energetically preaching and healing in the Temple area."[33] This group would have heard Jesus' message about the dangers of all-encompassing family loyalty. They would have been attempting to live in a new kind of family-community in which all those who were disciples of Jesus would be better able to focus on what was really important: teaching and living the good news. The Jesus of the Gospels used radical anti-family sayings to shake up his family-devoted listeners, shake them loose from the ties that kept them from being true servants of God. And they, in response, changed the ways they thought about family and, more significantly, the way they lived as family. In this Christian family-community, four important changes are evident.

The De-Centering of Children

First, children are included, but they are not as central to the meaning and mission of the family as they would have been in the Greco-Roman context. One indication of this decentering of children and procreation is the paucity of New Testament material on the subject of children. The few passages we do have are often taken out of context. The account of Jesus calling the little children to his side over the protest of the disciples in Mark 10:14–16, for instance, is sometimes offered as testimony to the New Testament's valuing of children.[34] However, most New Testament scholars view the passage as one that uses children as a model of what a Jesus-follower should be like without commenting on the value of children per se.[35] Somewhat more promising is the passage that reads, "Then he took a little child and put it among them; and taking it in his arms, he said to them, 'Whoever welcomes one such child in my name welcomes me, and whoever welcomes me welcomes not me but the one who sent me'" (Mark 9:36–37). Schüssler Fiorenza argues that the Gospel writer is trying to say that "Jesus himself is present to the community in those children whom the community has accepted in baptism ('in my name')."[36] She claims that the passage may indicate not only that children were seen as gifts to the community (rather than the family) but also that children were actually cared for by people in the community (as well as by the family). This may be assuming too much, but certainly, there is an affirmation of children as gifts of God or, better, as bearers of God's spirit, which suggests that the anti-family ethos in Jesus' sayings is not any more anti-children than it is anti-marriage. The relationships of love and care that exist between parents and children or husbands and wives are not the problem. Rather, the structure of the family and its preeminence in the lives of many is problematic.

Still, we do not find here the child-centric language that is common in our own culture and the later Christian tradition. Children are not the reason early Christians get married. They marry, if at all, to work together in service of the kingdom of God.

The Movement toward Equality

The marriage itself, however, is different at its core. Unlike the patriarchal Jewish and Roman marriages, early Christian marriages were notable for their emerging egalitarianism. While it would be anachronistic to claim that these Christians were feminists or that they believed in the kind of equality many envision today, it is fair to say that the first Christians responded to Jesus' message and practice by trying to reshape their marriages so that they would be more equal. Jesus, many feminist scholars have shown, was unique in his behavior toward women. While other teachers or priests would not speak to women in public, allow women to become students or followers, or allow themselves to be touched by women, Jesus welcomed women, spoke with them, was touched by them, and invited them to be his followers. In many New Testament stories, we see Jesus breaking with the social mores of his time through his inclusive ministry. One well-known example is the story of Martha and Mary in Luke 10:38–42. When Martha complains to Jesus that Mary is listening to him teach instead of helping her prepare food for those who have gathered at their home, Jesus gently rebukes her, saying, "Martha, Martha, you are worried and distracted by many things; there is need of only one thing. Mary has chosen the better part, which will not be taken away from her." Jesus affirms Mary's right to hear his message and be a part of those who come to him for his teaching.[37] He separates himself from the traditions of his culture and faith, which exclude women from education and public religious life. His ministry is inclusive in a radically new way.

Jesus' followers respond to this new vision in different ways that are, of course, partial. Patriarchy does not end overnight. Rather, we can see gradual transformation taking place. For instance, in the well-known passage in the Letter to the Ephesians (5:21–26), written by a follower of St. Paul, the husband and wife are compared to Christ and the church. The writer says that the husband must love his wife as Christ loves the community of faith that gathers in his name, and that the wife must submit to her husband, as to Christ. This does not sound too progressive to our ears because of the obvious differentiation of roles. Despite the strong, sacrificial love required of the husband, it is still the wife who is asked to submit to her spouse. However, it is important not to overlook the beginning sentence in the passage, which reads, "Be subject to one another out of reverence for Christ" (5:21). This sounds more like the mutual sacrifice that Christians might speak of today. What happens to the equal call to submission later in the passage? According to some scholars, it gets muddled because the strong gender codes of the culture are only partially overcome. Thus, while the early Christians are striving for the egalitarian vision to which they feel Jesus called them, they are not quite able to free themselves from the ideas of patriarchal marriage that are pervasive in their culture. What we see is a transformation in progress.[38] From this passage, as well as from research on the social world of the early Christians, we know that the families in the young Jesus movement were distinct in their emerging egalitarian ethic.

The Rejection of Hierarchy

The families of the first Christians were also unique in their rejection of the hierarchical relations that were central to marriage in first-century Palestine. When these Christians rejected marriage, as they often did, they also rejected the upper-class status that came with marriage. Unlike those who married into respectability, many Christians called the community of faith their family and rejoiced that there they could say to others, "If you desire a friend who supplies goods not of this world, I am your friend. If you desire a father for those who are rejected on earth, I am your father. If you desire a legitimate brother to set you apart from bastard brothers, I am your brother."[39] The Apocryphal Acts of the Apostles is full of similar stories of young men who leave behind possessions, of young women who sneak out of their husbands' marriage beds into other bedrooms where Christian worship is taking place, of disciples of Christ who come together despite diverse backgrounds,[40] of women who give up their high status as wives to embrace the life of a "slave of God."[41] In sum, Christians who turned away from marriage did so, at least in part, because they rejected the upper-class status that marriage would bring them. Instead, they identified with a small Christian community that included people from all walks of life, and they called this community their family.

Eventually, most Christians would marry, and, of course, many Christians did marry even in the beginning. It is reasonable to assume that these marrying Christians also found ways to reform their relationships and make them more inclusive. We know, at least, that the baptism of adult Christians in these times included the formula found in Galatians 3:27–28, You have "clothed yourselves with Christ. There is no longer Jew or Greek, there is no longer slave or free, there is no longer male and female, for all of you are one in Christ Jesus." Many scholars have come to believe that this formula was understood by the earliest Christians not just spiritually, but concretely.[42] To be baptized, then, was to affirm that all socially important distinctions were no longer significant. A Christian was brother or sister to all. Christian communities included both the very poor and very rich, both former slaves and former nobles. Christian families, too, crossed class lines, and in doing so, repudiated ideas that often went unquestioned in their time.[43]

The Inclusion of All

The final characteristic that set early Christian families apart from the typical Roman and Jewish families is at the heart of all else we have been discussing so far. It is the idea that the early Christians' families were not limited by biology. We know that Jesus' message included the claim that his real family was the Christian community, not his mother and his brothers. We know that others noticed that the Christians sometimes left their biological families for their new Christian families. And we know that the Christians were often seen as unpatriotic and immoral, as family-wreckers, because they sometimes refused to give in to what was expected of them. However, we also know that Christianity began in households where communities were led by married couples (for example, Prisca and Aquila in Acts 18:18 and 18:25; 1 Cor 16:18; Rom 16:2).[44] These first Christians used family language with reverence in speaking about their own communities, which were not limited by biological ties. According to New Testament scholars, they "saw themselves as extended families. This is clear from such evidence as the title of brothers and sisters commonly given to believers, burial in common cemeteries, and conscious modeling of community leadership on that of the household. The vision of church was that of a community that was inclusive of all."[45] All of this means that family to the first Christians was an expansive term that referenced not just the household, but, more importantly, the community of disciples of Christ. Within this community, some married and lived out the call to discipleship within marriage, while others remained celibate, devoting their lives wholly to the work of the kingdom.

Thus it seems that relationships of love and care that characterize families were not what Jesus was trying to eliminate. Rather, the structure of families, and their preeminence, was problematic, and this is what the first followers of Jesus tried to do something about. They allowed his anti-family sayings to shake them up, and they took pains to cut themselves loose from those family ties that would keep them from being true servants of God. Sometimes this meant leaving one family and embracing another, and sometimes it meant rejecting biological family life all together, but either way, the point was to try to live life focused on what really mattered: working to spread the message of Jesus.

Why Celibacy?

What might still be distressing to contemporary Christians is that in the early Christian literature, it often seems as though celibacy is seen as the highest Christian calling. It seems as if the way to be really, truly holy is to give up marriage altogether. Is this so? When Paul says that it is better to marry than to burn (1 Cor 7:8–10), is he remembering Jesus' negative comments on the family and interpreting them as Jesus would have wanted? Actually, compared with the radical Christians in Corinth to whom he is writing, Paul is very much the preserver of marriage. Over against the Corinthian idea that "only by dissolving the household was it possible to achieve the priceless transparency associated with a new creation," an idea promulgated by the more radical of Jesus' followers who took his anti-family and anti-money statements more literally, Paul stands with those Christians who stayed with their families, approving marriage for ordinary Christians.[46] Still, even he is ambivalent, because he fears that those who are married will not be able to serve God with their whole heart and mind (1 Cor 7:32–40). Why was this ambivalence so strong?

According to Peter Brown, whose important work *The Body and Society* has added a great deal to our knowledge of the early Christian world, singleness of heart is the key moral virtue in first-century morality.[47] So marrying is problematic for early Christians like Paul because it divides the heart between God and home. Moreover, this is most likely what lies behind the most radical of Jesus' anti-family sayings. However, from the beginning, Jesus' followers respond to the command to be single-hearted in discipleship in different ways. Some, like Paul, acknowledge the reality that most people will marry. Though he (unlike Jesus) upholds celibacy as the superior option and recommends it, he knows that the majority will marry and simply encourages them to be vigilant lest they lose their lives in worrying about the wrong things. Others of Jesus' followers, like the Corinthians, are more convinced that celibacy is the only way to realize Jesus' vision. It is important to remember that even the more conservative Paul is not a cheerleader for marriage. "It is not, he insists, a sin, but neither is it, or the establishment of a Christian family, a positive contribution to the creation or preservation of the Christian tradition."[48] Why the pessimism?

Most of the earliest Christians have reservations about the traditional family, even if they ultimately approve of it, because they see that it "is a distraction from the preparation for the imminently expected end of time."[49] This is crucial. The anti-family strains in the thinking of the early Christians have some relation to their beliefs that the world would end (and Jesus would return) in their lifetimes. Some theologians would argue that these eschatological beliefs explain most if not all of the concern about family and free contemporary Christians who do not believe the world will end any time soon to embrace family life without hesitation. However, this argument minimizes the importance of the anti-family strain in early Christian thought. While the influence of eschatology cannot be denied, I find it hard to believe that eschatology explains everything. Often in Christian theology, eschatology has been used to explain away or soften the radicality of the New Testament in other areas.[50] It is easy to say that Gospel injunctions to give up money or family are not to be taken seriously because the New Testament writers would never have said such things if they had known the world would be around for another two thousand years. However, it seems more likely that while believing that the end of world was not near might lead the early Christians to feel more confident that they could live out Jesus' calling within families as well as outside them, it would not cause them to give up their concerns about family altogether. Responding to the message of Jesus would have to mean rethinking the structures and values that dominated their everyday lives, and that would have to include family. A disciple of Jesus of Nazareth would have to come to terms with the root of the message: "the way of life, ethical priorities, and passions to which you are accustomed are no longer to go unquestioned. Turn to me and away from all that leads you astray." One need not believe that the world is ending soon to understand that family loyalties must be lessened if discipleship is to truly rule the heart.

Return to Family?

And yet, in the writings of the second generation of Christians, in Paul's followers in particular, there is something altogether new that calls this interpretation into question. In Ephesians 5:21–23 (discussed above), we have an analogy between Christ and the church and the husband and his wife. We have codes of conduct that parallel the household codes of the Greeks (wives are to submit to husbands, children to parents, slaves to masters). In short, here is an assertion of the holiness of the marital relationship that seems to fly in the face of the spirit of Jesus' anti-family ethic. And in some ways, it does. Yet scholars tell us that the presence of the codes in the text indicates that the practice in the Christian communities was very different from the codes. That is, if everyone were doing it, it would not need to be said. The writer of the text is then seeking to modify or overturn the new structures of family and community that have come to the fore among the early Christians.[51] The radicalism of the early days is being modified by the assertion that family could be holy in itself.

Still, it is interesting that even in this passage, it is primarily the spousal relationship that is raised up as holy. Children are mentioned, along with slaves, almost as a secondary concern of the writer. It is the duties of husbands and wives that are described in detail. The primary intent is to uphold the Christ-centered marriage relationship, not to promote a vision of a loving, Christ-centered family. This text represents the strain of the tradition that recalls those brief but significant biblical affirmations of marriage (Genesis 1 and 2; Mark 10:6–9). This strain upholds the life experience of the majority of Christians who did and do marry and have children. It blesses the intense, giving, and respectful love that two people can have for each other. There were early Christians who glorified marriage in this way. But even they, like Paul in his warnings to the Corinthians, claim that marriage makes one anxious. Like Paul's follower, who fails to fully include children in his attempt to raise up marriage, they all fall short in their attempts.

Moreover, there were also Christians who, seeking a more radical way of life, recognized the other and, in New Testament terms, more significant strain of the tradition, which calls all of this glorification into question. The tension between living out the call to discipleship through one's family versus answering a call that requires one to decentralize family continues throughout the history of the church. According to Peter Brown, the more radical vision of a transformed household that has the potential to transform society "is the great hope which, in all the future centuries, would continue to flicker disquietingly along the edges of the Christian Church."[52]

It is this disquieting hope that must be kept in mind by all Christians who want to be loyal disciples of Jesus of Nazareth. Although affirmations of marriage and family life are also a part of the early Christian tradition, they are less significant in comparison. What is truly distinctive about the early Christian message is the call to question family ties, structure, and values. It is this message that Christians are called to wrestle with.

Of course, it is important to remember our discussion at the beginning of the chapter about how to read the New Testament. We look to the Scriptures for accounts of how the first Christians responded to the call to discipleship. Their responses are for us prototype rather than archetype. This means that contemporary Christians should not automatically run off and leave family or forgo marriage. On the other hand, we should listen attentively to the radical witness of the first

Christians, making sure that we do not miss the truth in what they say and do. The next step is figuring out how to respond to that truth, for the New Testament is not the end of the story. It is only the beginning. In the next chapter we begin to look at the different ways Christians thought about marriage and family, and it will quickly bring us to the present day, where our own reflections must necessarily begin.

Discussion Questions

1. How significant is Jesus' own celibacy for contemporary disciples?

2. Do you see a "far-reaching anti-kinship message" in the teachings of Jesus?

3. What four key changes did the early Christians make with regard to their families? Are these practices part of contemporary Christian family life? Should they be?

4. What are contemporary Christians to make of the tension between celibacy and married life in early Christian writings? Is the quest for single-heartedness valid today?

Traditional Ways of Speaking about Marriage

Domus

In a class on religious and ethnic diversity in America, I had my students read about Italian American immigrants who came to Harlem in the late 1800s.[1] We talked about how this group believed that being a good Christian meant doing right by your family. The "domus," or extended family, meant everything to them. Honoring the domus meant caring for your family, being loyal to your family, sacrificing for your family, and respecting the family elders. Families had much more control over the personal life of individuals than they do now. When young people wanted to marry, female relatives on both sides checked up on the prospective spouse before they gave, or did not give, their approval. If adults received job offers that would take them away from the neighborhood, they were expected to turn down the offers. Sunday dinner with the family was the week's most important commitment, more important than Sunday mass. A person who failed to live up to demands of the domus was a *cafone*, or an uncaring human being for whom nothing was sacred.

In our discussions of the book, we talked about how contemporary American Christians are both like and unlike the Italian Catholics of Harlem. On the one hand, contemporary Christians value their freedom, and so they are less willing to sacrifice their own happiness for the good of the family. On the other hand, a commitment to family is still a very important component of being a good person. Though my students pointed out that one should not take family dinners more seriously than church (this seemed idolatrous), they admired to a great extent and shared in part the family values of the immigrant Italians. Though they thought the Italians had gone a bit overboard, they thought that this community was essentially on target in the way it linked family values and Christian values. Like most American Christians, my students understood their own commitments to their families as a fundamental part of their faith. This assumption is so ingrained and widespread that it makes up part of the worldview of most contemporary American Christians.

As we have seen, however, some of the earliest Christians believed that celibacy was the appropriate way to devote one's life to God, and others believed a new kind of family could provide a context for living a holy life. What happened between then and now? Why do most Christians today believe that family life is godly, holy, a calling, even? How did Christians go from being highly suspicious of the family to embracing it as a privileged arena for Christian living?

This chapter briefly explores the early history of Christian thinking on marriage and the movement from suspicion to ambivalence. It discusses four different ways that Christians since that time have looked at marriage: sacrament, covenant, relationship, and communion. In each case, Christian theologians struggled to honor the state of life in which most Christians found themselves even as they tried with varying degrees of success to preserve the biblical sense that marriage could make single-minded devotion to God more difficult.

The Legacy of the First Christians

Historian Peter Brown characterizes early Christian thinking on sex and marriage as a divided legacy. In the ancient world, the virtue of singleness of heart was sought by all but achieved in different ways. Some chose the way of total renunciation of sex and marriage. Jewish observers like Philo and Josephus saw colonies of celibate males in first-century Palestine as alternative communities that allowed their members to avoid "the seductive wiles of women and the disruptive effect of the claims that women made upon men as the bearers of their children and the sharers of their bed."[2] These groups sought to realize the radical Gospel call to leave everything behind for Jesus. They were particularly concerned that women would distract them from concentrating on their Christian mission. Note that Jewish and

Greek Christians saw women as problematic both because of their lust (which makes it difficult for men to suppress their own lesser lust) and because of their desire for children (who make additional claims upon men's resources of time, energy, and money). Women and children, they believed, make it difficult for Christian men to live the simple life in community to which they are called.

Most Christians admired this radical witness but few emulated it. The majority of Christians remained married but sought to reform marriage by emphasizing sexual purity.[3] Wandering preachers and celibate community dwellers comprised the radical though not insignificant minority, while the "silent majority of those who awaited the coming of the kingdom were careworn and decent householders."[4] Jewish Christians in particular brought with them a tradition that proclaimed the holiness of all aspects of human existence. Jewish rabbis of the era continued to uphold the holiness of marriage. Non-Jewish Christians also supported marriage. So most Christians did not leave marriage behind; they reformed it, especially in the area of sexuality. The commitment to purity was not simply a rejection of sex but also a "commitment to communal solidarity and a rejection of the hierarchical and state-controlled functions of the patriarchal family."[5] The early Christians rejected class and gender privileges, and the government control that came with marriage, and so they created new forms of marriage that allowed for greater inclusivity and mutuality. Still, they had strong suspicions about sexuality, and those suspicions, coupled with a profound recognition of the worries that spouses and children brought to Christian men and women, made marriage second best.[6]

Early Christian writers more tied to communities of families tended to emphasize the redeeming qualities of a well-ordered, or moral, marriage.[7] They found ways to make peace with the common moral standards of the times. The silent majority and their defenders developed the side of the New Testament witness that testified to the goodness of marriage. However, the radical witness of communities like the Essenes and the Corinthians (which challenged traditional ideas of marriage) continued to contribute to tensions among the early Christians. The tension between two different modes of living out the message of Jesus would only deepen in centuries to come.

In the second century, for instance, Clement of Alexandria defended marriage against the strong criticisms of gnostic and Encratite sects who taught that "only by rejecting marital intercourse and procreation... could people be restored to their original spiritual condition intended by God the Creator."[8] In response, Clement wrote of the married Christian who "becomes the image of God, by cooperating in the creation of another human being," and spoke of marriage as an arena for ministry. He redefined celibacy, arguing that a married man can be celibate if he replaces his intemperate desire for his wife with love. Both the married and the unmarried can serve God through their self-control, and the married man, who has the tougher task, may also serve through care for his wife and children.[9]

Clement, one of the early apologists for marriage, attempted to counter the spreading influence of gnostic communities that saw the renunciation of marriage as the only true way to follow Christ. His defense of the marital calling is notable for its lack of ambiguity and its failure to question the structure of the family or the importance of marriage. In this second-century writer, we see the beginnings of a real departure from the early Christian dis-ease with marriage and family. As the Christian community continued to grow in experience, some, like Clement, used that experience (including that of the spiritual fruitfulness of marriage) to develop a positive Christian theology of marriage. Still, finding this tradition in the writings of the early church fathers is quite a task. Historian Carol Harrison, who makes a valiant attempt to mine the fathers for writings like Clement's, admits, "I have dwelt on these very positive notes usually drowned out by exhortations to virginity; they are most definitely there when the Fathers come face to face either with their own wives...or with their married congregations."[10] Harrison admits that, as opposed to highlighting the best of a broad-based pro-marriage tradition, she is sifting through a tradition enamored of virginity and pouncing on anything that points in another direction. This material exists, but it is not dominant.

Moreover, the radical anti-marriage tradition continued to gain strength. Many defenders of marriage were less convinced than Clement about the positive qualities of marriage. Clement's contemporary Tertullian, for instance, is less emphatic in his praise. In a letter to his wife, he urges her to adopt a celibate way of life if he dies, but admits that marriage "has been blessed by God to be the seedbed of the human race."[11] He brings out the full force of Paul's reluctance to sanction marriage ("It is better to marry than to burn") when he exclaims to his wife, "How much better it is neither to marry nor to burn!"[12] Yet he manages to praise marriage in the words of great eloquence in another place in the very same piece of writing, saying, "What a bond is this: two believers who share one hope, one desire, one discipline, the same service! The two are brother and sister, fellow servants. There is no distinction of spirit or flesh, but truly they are two in one flesh."[13]

How can we understand such sublime praise from one with such a strong suspicion of marriage? Most likely in this passage Tertullian refers to a celibate marriage.[14] According to Tertullian, only when marriage is freed from its distractions (sex and children) can it function as a supportive community for two committed Christians. He celebrates the same partnership that the writer of the letter to the Ephesians upholds, with the understanding that this is a new kind of marriage. Indeed, it is the only kind Tertullian could envision as a vehicle for living out the single-minded devotion to God required of Christians. Not all Christians who sought to reform the family thought that leaving out sex proved the best way to do so, but many did. The kinds of reforms that took hold among the first Christians (who desired greater inclusivity) were apparently short-lived.

In the third century, the tendency toward asceticism among radicals, such as the writer of the Acts of Thomas, increased. The writer tells a story of an apostle named Jude Thomas, who is asked to bless a newly married couple. In his blessing, the apostle tries to encourage the couple to keep their marriage pure, saying, "Know that if you refrain from this filthy intercourse, you will become holy temples, pure, free of trials and difficulties, known and unknown, and you will not be drowned in the cares of life and of children, who lead only to ruin."[15] With this amazing description, which includes much more information on how children can corrupt the Christian husband and wife, the apostle convinces the couple to dedicate themselves to the Lord instead of each other. Although extreme in his discussion, the writer of the Acts of Thomas speaks convincingly to his contemporaries of the distraction of family life and superiority of a life totally dedicated to Christ.

Many other writers spoke to women about the superiority of virginity in discourses that emphasized what Carol Harrison calls "the horrors of marriage," including:

> the shame and sorrow of infertility, the discomforts of pregnancy, the risks of childbirth, worry about one's children, the drudgery of childrearing and housework, problems with servants, family quarrels, the death of family members, abusive, violent, jealous husbands, constant worry about a husband's fidelity, his health and safety, and finally, widowhood.[16]

Other dedicated Christians in the third century could speak more positively of marriage because they believed that Christians have two possible callings — one to celibacy and one to marriage. One was clearly higher, but both were holy and had unique fruits. Writers like Methodius and Lactanius, for instance, upheld the primacy of celibacy but permitted marriage, largely because it created more Christians, some of whom might become martyrs for the church.[17] Once again, the defense of marriage, while consistent, is notably weak and ambiguous. It is as if these writers cannot see a way around acknowledging marriage as a part of God's plan for human beings (because of the crucial texts in Genesis, Jesus' support for marriage, and the experience of "the silent majority"), so they find a way to support it even when their hearts are not in it. Moreover, even in their defenses of marriage, they warn their readers of the difficulty of fulfilling their Christian vocations in the married state. They remain convinced that maintaining one's Christian identity in marriage would require a great deal of vigilance.

The fourth century gives us several important writers who pay sustained attention to the marriage question and begin to develop a real theology of marriage, but the tension between supporters and detractors of marriage continues. Jovinian describes marriage and celibacy as essentially equal vocations, but his ideas are bitterly denounced by Jerome, who gives the traditional weak defense of marriage as a lesser calling before recommending celibacy to all men who want to avoid the annoyance of being married to women who "want many things, costly dresses, gold jewels, great outlay, maid-servants, all kinds of furniture, litters and gilded coaches. Then come the curtain-lectures the live-long night. To support a poor wife, is hard. To put up with a rich one, is torture."[18] Though he found a first marriage understandable, he had less enthusiasm for second marriages, which he regarded as "one step from the brothel, like a dog returning to its vomit."[19] In defending views that many of his contemporaries found extreme, he compared marriage to wood and pottery. Useful and necessary as they are, they do not compare to silver and gold.[20] This proved the best Jerome could do in upholding the idea of the acceptability of marriage, and it is his theology, not Jovinian's, that the church ultimately adopted.

John Chrysostom, also a fourth-century writer, though from the East, writes much less disparagingly of marriage, especially the sexual relationship between husbands and wives, which he considers to be "the highest form of human love."[21] However, he has concerns about the tendency of Christian adults to forget their Christian calling in their zeal to provide for their children. He writes "An Address on the Vainglory and the Right Way for Parents to Bring Up Their Children" in order to warn parents about the dangers of family life. He worries that when a child is born, parents are too concerned about buying clothes for him and not concerned enough at all about teaching him the importance of sexual morality, sobriety, and the dangers of wealth and fame.[22] He exhorts parents to ignore the expectations of the world regarding children and, instead, "raise up an athlete for Christ."[23] To do this, fathers, especially, must help their sons avoid temptation. John's mission consists of getting those who marry to stay on track. He knows the real pressures of living in a family and sees the tendency of married people to value the wrong things, especially material things, which do not ultimately matter. So he urges Christian fathers to remain true to their calling by approaching family life as a school for Christian virtue. If the family does not commit itself primarily to the business of raising up disciples for Christ, John cannot see it as a moral entity. But if it does, he supports it, though he continues to worry about the strength of its commitments.

Even Augustine, whose theology of marriage remains central to Catholic thinking, worries of its corrupting power. He clearly delineates the goods of marriage: children, fidelity, and sacrament. Like many defenders of marriage, he believes that bringing sexual morality to the relationship will save it. The goods of marriage depend on sexual morality. Children provide justification for sex and marriage itself.

Sex is limited to husband and wife. The spouses make a lifelong commitment to each other — a sign of God's fidelity to his people. Thus marriage can be good if it respects sexual morality. Still, celibacy is a higher and clearly preferable state in a world with enough people, where the need to be fruitful and multiply no longer exists. Augustine claims that "surely it is better and holier in the present time not to seek after offspring in the flesh and thereby to keep oneself perpetually free, as it were, from all this activity and to be subject in a spiritual way to the one man Christ."[24]

Augustine makes his best effort to give marriage a theological justification, and in doing so, he provides the basics for the church's theology of marriage for centuries to come. Still, in his defense one finds little of the joy or wonder that people like ourselves bring to our discussions of family. Though Harrison says of Augustine's view of Paradise, "there is probably no better defence of marriage and the family or higher evaluation of it, than this,"[25] Augustine's description of sex without passion, childbirth without pregnancy or labor, spirits without bodies, and children without need for their parents seems about as far removed from most Christians' experience of family as one can get. Most people who read this "praise" for marriage would, I believe, leave with the distinct impression that Augustine, like most of his predecessors, is reaching here, trying in vain to justify something that his reading of the Christian sources and his own sensibilities tell him is simply an inferior way of life.

No doubt Augustine and others were limited in their writing by a sense, widely shared in their time, that everything bodily was inferior to everything spiritual.[26] These writers simply could not see anything related to sex as truly good. However, the fathers do not see sex as the only problem in marriage; they also think of the distraction of spouses and children as weights on the Christian striving for a godly life. Moreover, one can trace a suspicion of marriage and family life back to the Gospels and, more importantly, to the earliest strands of the sayings of Jesus. The early Christians were not crazy to think it difficult to reconcile traditional marriage and family life with a commitment to Christ; many of Jesus' contemporaries thought the same thing. Aside from sex, the distracting qualities of living in a passionate relationship, raising children, and dealing with the material needs and demands of family make these early followers of Jesus fear the family. Far from justifying the contemporary Christian equation of family values and Christian values, they call into question that moral priority we give to family. This leaves us, then, with a divided legacy from the early years. On the one hand, the celibate communities continue to thrive and defenders of celibacy develop their family-denying theology. On the other hand, defenders of marriage increase, but with a few exceptions their defenses prove not nearly as strong as contemporary defenses would be, and the worry about what family can do to a Christian continues.

From Contract to Sacrament

If so many early Christians approached marriage with ambivalence, how did it come to be thought of as a sacrament, a channel of God's grace? A gradual transformation, which we can review only briefly here, occurred over a period of sixteen centuries of Christian life. Marriage as a secular reality only gradually, and with difficulty, came to be seen as a sacred part of Christian life.

In the first three centuries, marriage was regulated by secular laws, and marriage ceremonies followed local customs. Sometimes, a priest or bishop would bless the married couple after the ceremony, but this practice was not widespread. In the writings of the early church fathers, marriage is not a major concern. After all, at this time, there are no liturgical ceremonies to talk about and no major doctrinal issues to dispute. When bishops did speak of marriage, they tended to express pastoral concern, "affirming the goodness of marriage, urging Christians to marry within their own community, and warning them not to get drunk and unruly at wedding feasts."[27] Most Christian writers agreed that marriage was a holy institution to which Jesus gave his blessing, but they saw it mostly as a mundane matter, not something in need of theological sanction.

In the year 380 C.E., Christianity became the official religion of the Roman Empire, which presented the opportunity to recast secular laws. However, no major changes in the marriage laws occurred right away. Christians continued to marry each other according to the ceremonies and laws of their culture. Priests or bishops received more frequent invitations to bless the married couple at the end of the ceremony or at a later eucharistic celebration. Sometimes they were asked to place a veil over the couple to symbolize their unity. Around 400 C.E., according to papal decree, priests and deacons were required to have their marriages blessed by a priest, but lay Christians continued to vary in their practice.

St. Augustine was the first to speak of marriage as a sacrament. For him, the bond between husband and wife was sacred because it symbolized the bond between Christ and the church. It was a holy promise, parallel to baptism in that it marked the beginning of a new way of life in Christ.[28] Historian John Witte notes that, from a modern perspective, Augustine's theology looks "presacramental," in that he believed that the symbolic stability of the marriage was sacramental but did not treat the sacramentality of the relationship in its fullness.[29] Augustine began to think about marriage as a sacrament but did not work out a systematic sacramental theology of marriage. Most of his contemporaries thought him radical for daring to assert that marriage, an institution that they saw as secular, sexual, and economic in nature, bore any resemblance to baptism or Eucharist.

Although Augustine's theological understanding of marriage was not widespread, marriage increased in importance in the church during this period for other reasons. During the second half of the first millennium, with civil authority collapsing, the clergy stepped into the power void in many areas, including the regulation of marriage. While marriage remained primarily a secular reality, clergy increasingly controlled it, simply because they took control of most aspects of public life.

In the eleventh century this began to change. The blessing of a priest became a required part of a marriage between Christians. First, weddings were held near churches, so that a couple could obtain a blessing soon afterward. Gradually, the ceremony moved right to the church door and was followed by a nuptial mass inside the church. Finally, by the twelfth century, the church established a wedding ceremony at which clergy officiated and assumed control of many functions that were previously the responsibility of parents.[30] It rediscovered Augustine's writings on sacrament, as well as those of Peter Lombard, an important medieval theologian who wrote about marriage as a sacrament in his *Sentences*. Many theologians remained skeptical, seeing marriage as a secular institution that existed before the time of Christ, a financial arrangement between the father and husband of the bride, and a sexual relationship between a man and a woman.[31] They found it especially difficult to believe in marriage as a sacrament, as a way to holiness. At this time, most considered celibacy the primary path to holiness and marriage as a means for people who could not live the truly holy life to curb their desire.

Gradually, however, in deference to the experience of the silent majority and thanks to the creativity of theologians, the notion took hold, and debate focused not so much on whether marriage was a sacrament, but on what the sacrament was. Eventually, Thomas Aquinas's idea that the sacrament in marriage was not just the consent or promise between the man and woman, but the marriage itself, took hold.[32]

At the Council of Trent in the sixteenth century, the church defined many of its doctrines more completely than ever before. The Protestant Reformation in the fifteenth century had been a major inspiration. For instance, because Martin Luther and his followers declared that marriage was not a sacrament (they did not agree that Jesus instituted it, seeing it rather as a secular reality), the Catholic Church had to reaffirm and defend its view that it was. So at Trent, the church defined marriage as a sacrament, claimed the right to regulate it, declared that the presence of a priest and two witnesses was necessary for a valid marriage, and claimed that a validly contracted marriage could not be dissolved for any reason.[33] This sacramental theology was refined and developed over the next few centuries without any major changes.

Protestant Models: Social Estate and Covenant

While Catholics worked out their sacramental theology, Protestant Christians thought through their own ideas about marriage. Two models dominated the discussion: social estate and covenant. In each, theologians combined a sense of marriage as a holy calling second to none with a reluctance to call marriage a sacrament. Thus Protestant images said both more and less about marriage than Catholic images.

Social Estate

Martin Luther, the Catholic priest who started the Protestant Reformation, believed that the world was divided into two realms: the earthly kingdom and the heavenly kingdom. Marriage, Luther taught, belonged to the earthly kingdom. It was good, but not a sacrament. Luther did not see celibacy as a higher calling, and thus did not consider marriage second best. However, because it had always existed and was not particularly Christian, Luther did not see it as a sacrament. Convinced of the seriousness of human beings' tendency toward lust, Luther believed that marriage provided a necessary remedy to keep people from sin. He understood marriage as a "natural, created institution subject to godly law," but not as holy. Luther analyzed marriage as a social institution under the authority of the government, not the church. It proved useful to society, in that it cut down on sexual sins (prostitution and fornication), reminded human beings of their tendency to sin, and taught human beings love, self-control, and virtue. As a social estate, marriage provided a way of life for most Christians, but not a channel of God's grace.[34]

When Luther spoke of marriage he rejoiced in its goods and called domestic duties godly work. He also warned of the difficulties of married life, especially the difficulties men suffered when they took wives. Writing of a Christian wife, he says

> We can hardly speak of her without a feeling of shame, and surely we cannot make use of her without shame. The reason is sin. In Paradise that union would have taken place without any bashfulness accompanied by a noble delight.... Now, alas, it is so hideous and frightful a pleasure that physicians compare it with epilepsy or falling sickness. Thus an actual disease is linked with the very activity of procreation. We are in the state of sin and of death; therefore we also undergo this punishment, that we cannot make use of woman without the horrible passion of lust, and, so to speak, without epilepsy.[35]

Although Luther very clearly did not denigrate marriage in relation to celibacy, he saw sex within marriage as inherently sinful (though excused by children and the need to avoid sexual sin) and women as less than equal Christians. Thus, although he advocated marriage and saw himself as a defender of marriage over against Catholics who prized celibacy, his writing shows much of the same ambivalence about marriage that permeated the work of most Catholic authors. By relegating marriage to the social realm, even as he tried to uphold it, Luther para-doxically revealed his own discomfort with marriage. This may be why few contemporary Lutherans use the language of estate in their discussions of marriage. The Calvinist language of covenant has proved more enduring.

Covenant

John Calvin, who carried on the work of the Reformation in Switzerland, began with much the same theology as Luther, but later came to value marriage as a covenant with goods of its own. While the early Calvin thought of marriage only as a remedy for incontinence, the later Calvin wrote of God's role in marriage. He upheld the traditional Protestant idea that marriage had three purposes: love, children, and the avoidance of sexual sin. However, he went further in insisting that God participated in the marriage ritual (through the presence of the minister, parents, witnesses, and government officials) and the marriage covenant itself. Calvin came to speak of marriage as holy and claimed that "God reigns in a little household, even one in dire poverty, when the husband and the wife dedicate themselves to their duties to each other. Here there is a holiness greater and nearer the kingdom of God than there is even in a cloister."[36] While not rejecting Luther's two kingdoms theory out of hand, he added his understanding of marriage as a holy covenant and saw to it that marriage and divorce laws in Geneva reflected that understanding in their strictness. Yet in his reluctance to call marriage a sacrament, in his discomfort with sexuality, and in his deficient understanding of women, Calvin reveals the same ambivalence as Luther and the earlier Protestant reformers.

Contemporary writers in the covenant tradition fall into two camps. Some, like Max Stackhouse, develop the biblical idea of covenant, beginning with Genesis, and emphasize the link between covenant and law.[37] This leads them to an understanding of marriage as a timeless institution governed by strict rules. Like the early church fathers, they see marriage redeemed or purified by strict sexual morality. Liberal writers in the covenant tradition, like James Nelson, emphasize instead the love that binds in marriage covenants. Nelson asks the radical question, "Are there limits to human covenants?," and answers in the negative.

All rules, he believes, are human and subject to revision. Thus he enter-
tains the possibility that two Christians may decide to allow each other
multiple sexual partners, if such an arrangement contributed to the
growth and development of each, separately and together. Christian
marriages of the future, he claims,

> will be enduring covenants — pledges of ongoing faithfulness to
> the well-being and growth of each partner. They will be covenants
> of intimacy in which eros is undergirded, infused, and transformed
> by agape. They will be sacramental covenants, whether or not offi-
> cially sacraments, of the church.... And they will be covenants
> that in one way or another, genuinely enlarge the partners' capac-
> ity for communion with others and expand their willingness to be
> part of God's work of giving new life and renewal to the world.[38]

For Nelson, and other liberal Protestant writers, the relationship
proves central to the covenant, so central that the very rules that
ensured the holiness of the covenant for people like John Calvin no
longer apply. The bottom line is the quality of relationship and the
personal growth of the partners. Relationship is no longer viewed sus-
piciously at all. This trend in covenant theology has its parallel in the
Roman Catholic turn to thinking about marriage as relationship. Both
seem to leave the scriptural warnings about the dangers of relationships
behind.

Marriage as Relationship

The official Catholic teaching represented in the 1917 Code of Canon
Law held that a sacramental marriage was a contract, that each spouse
in such a marriage had a right to the body of the other, and that procreation was the primary purpose of the marriage. In its legalism and focus
on children, this formulation reflected the ongoing ambivalence about
marriage.[39] Only with proper form and the promise of children could
intimate relationships between Christians be holy. Many theologians
found this understanding of sacramental marriage to be unnecessarily
narrow, and they began writing about marriage relationships instead of
exploring the implications of marriage as sacrament.

Ethicist Margaret Farley exemplifies this new school of thought. Farley writes about marriage as one of many important personal commitments a Christian may make in her life. She tries to think through the implications of a promise to another person and the limits of that promise. Ultimately, for Farley, commitments to others are good insofar as the resulting relationships are good for the persons involved.[40] Commitments that move persons away from God or make it more difficult for persons to be in relationship with God are not binding. Promises that we make are not holy in themselves; their holiness must be judged by the relationships they bring into being. Farley has moved far away from the theological debates over whether consent during the marriage ritual or sex on the wedding night sealed the sacramental bond between husbands and wives. She has left behind not only the legalistic debates, but also the sacramental language itself. The reality of relationships is what she finds holy, and her lack of attention to sacrament indicates that she does not find sacramental imagery a helpful tool in her quest to get to the heart of marriage.

Christine Gudorf is another Catholic theologian who has written a great deal about relationships, but not much about sacrament. In her most recent exploration of sexual theology and ethics, Gudorf attempts to place pleasure in a central place, alongside procreation and union, the two traditional ends of sexuality in Catholic thinking.[41] Gudorf admits that pleasure has not played a large part in traditional thinking on sexuality (though she does retrieve some little known sources in the tradition that do affirm the goodness of sexual pleasure), but she argues that the contemporary emphasis on relationships makes a strong affirmation of the centrality and goodness of pleasure in sexual unions imperative. Her work moves away from the traditional Catholic understanding of sexuality, and even toward an openness to nonmarital forms of relationships. She does not find in sacramental theology an adequate model for the sorts of relationships in which contemporary Christians find themselves.

The work of theologians like Farley and Gudorf is somewhat radical, and some of their writings prove difficult to reconcile with mainstream Catholic marriage theology. However, while not giving up on sacramental theology and permanent marriage commitments, many theologians have gradually responded to developments in the cultural understanding of marriage. As they have come to see marriage more and more as a relationship of love between a man and a woman rather than an agreement between two families that allows young men and women to fulfill their social responsibility to procreate, Catholic theologians have sought new ways to speak about the sacramental bond of marriage. Many theologians turned to personalist philosophy, which emphasized the experiences, needs, desires, and commitments of persons, as a source for renewing Catholic thinking on marriage. Personalists wanted to talk about the importance of the marriage relationship and about the growth and development of that relationship over time. They "tried to move away from a legalistic theology of marriage and sex toward one that was more scriptural, more personal, and more related to contemporary married life."[42] In addition, they spoke of marriage less as a contract and more as a relationship of self-giving in which both partners gave themselves in love to the other.[43]

Their work proved difficult for two reasons. First, the magisterium worried that personalist reforms would dilute elements of the traditional teaching, such as children as the primary good of marriage and the indissolubility of the marital bond. So the work of personalist theologians met with little enthusiasm when it first appeared. The second reason for the difficulty lies in the nature of the sacramental model itself. Despite the insistence of many that the sacrament in marriage is the marriage as a whole, official church teachings and the popular Catholic imagination often focus on the wedding ceremony and particularly on the words of consent spoken by the bride and the groom. The sacramental language has tended toward legalism, especially in discussions of why marriage must remain indissoluble. There has also been a proclivity to think about the sacrament of marriage as a special grace that will help Christian spouses overcome difficulties they may face during the course of their marriage. The language seems to describe something added to marriage rather than the marriage itself.

Why? The magisterium did not develop the idea of the relationship as sacrament because of a lingering ambivalence about calling marriage holy. Many ordinary Christians do not think of their marriages as sacraments for much the same reason. Most find that the sacramental language hinders rather than helps them in seeing their relationships as holy, and they are simply not ready to think of their families as sacramental. The significance of the sacramental symbol is lost on most people. As much as priests and theologians might want people to see the beauty of marriage as a sacramental reality, the term has little real meaning for most of the laity, except in its connection to holiness or churchliness. The link between the love of the man and woman for each other and God's love for the church as well as the key role played by the couple themselves in becoming sacrament escape them. Referring to marriage as a sacrament tends to spiritualize it and separate it from passionate, concrete Christian communities and everyday life. For this reason many contemporary theologians, like Farley and Gudorf, have abandoned sacramental language entirely and turned to relationship language to describe marriage.

However, other theologians have tried to revisualize the sacramental language by thinking about real-life marriage relationships as sacraments in themselves. They have tried to bring the best of both models together. Michael Lawler, for instance, argues that at Vatican II and in the 1983 Code of Canon Law, the church moved away from the contractual language of the 1917 Code of Canon Law and spoke of marriage as a covenant, a "partnership of life and love," a relationship of mutual self-giving that had as its twin purposes love between the spouses and the procreation and raising of children.[44] In his own work, he makes the theology concrete by talking about the marriage of a couple he calls Will and Wilma, and claiming that their "mutual love... their passionate desire to be best friends forever [is]... the very essence of marriage. It is, therefore, equally the essence of the sacrament of marriage."[45] This kind of down-to-earth language brings sacramental theology much closer to contemporary thinking about relationships.

Theologian Bernard Cooke is even more explicit on this point. He says that the problem with classical sacramental theology is its reliance on older thinking about grace. In its crude form, it thinks of grace as a resource in a spiritual "bank." When people get married, the old theology seems to say, they get extra grace from the bank to help them through difficult times. The first problem with this idea is that Catholic married couples have just as many difficult marriages as everyone else. The second and more important issue for Cooke is the understanding of grace it communicates. According to contemporary theology, grace is not a magical added something that helps people out, but God's self-emptying love constantly communicated to us. Once we understand grace this way, we can more easily understand marriage as a sacrament of friendship in which we can experience God's love for us through the experience of being loved by another.[46]

If this seems too radical, Cooke explains that he is only building on what we know. Love is the most profound human experience. We experience love in friendship, and marriage is the paradigm of friendship and perhaps the most intimate and complete friendship. We know God in relationship and experience God's love and care for us. It makes sense then that God communicates God's self to us in marriage through the love of another, and that this is the sacrament. In relationship with another, we know God's goodness intimately. For Cooke, committed and close friendship is not separate from the marriage sacrament; it *is* the marriage sacrament.

The contemporary writer who has perhaps done the most to elevate the marriage relationship and link it to sacrament is John Paul II. The pope's writings on the theology of the body leave behind the worries of early Christian fathers about relationships and the difficulty of remaining single-hearted within them. He sees relationships of total self-giving as the point of human existence; it becomes ridiculous to worry that this kind of mutual love would lead one away from God. Rather, the woman "finds herself again in the very act of giving herself," and the man receives her gift of self, taking her to his heart.[47] When they come together in relationship, men and women do not move away from God. "Man and woman, uniting with each other (in the conjugal act) so closely as to become 'one flesh,' rediscover, so to speak, every time and in a special way, the mystery of creation."[48] In drawing close to one another, men and women draw close to God. With their hearts and with their bodies, they recall the "original unity" of the first couple who found their true selves when they gave themselves to each other. Their marriages are sacraments because their relationships signify God's loving covenant with human beings, and because in their lifelong struggle to overcome concupiscence (or lust) and use sexuality correctly, men and women participate in the mystery of the redemption of the body.[49] The sacrament is their relationship, as sign and lived reality.

One can find this exalted understanding of relationship throughout the pope's speeches on the theology of the body, surprising many who expect to find more suspicion of the body and sexual relations, even marital ones. Some of the pope's critics argue that while he celebrates marital love and sexual union, he does so in a way that seems to spiritualize the body, perhaps because his theology is not grounded in experience. Theologian Ronald Modras argues, for instance, that most lay Catholics would not connect with the pope's focus on self-control, his distrust of erotic desire, or his assertion that anyone involved in a sexual relationship that is not heterosexual, noncontraceptive, and marital is "using" another person.[50] He claims that "the greatest challenge to the pope's theology of the body and its sexuality is people's experience. What the Pope approaches from the outside and calls lust, they live on the inside and call love."[51] For Modras and others, the pope's attempt to lift up sexual relationship does not go far enough, because it relies on a desire-less form of sexuality in which persons are required to give of themselves but not to receive from their partners. It is as if the pope has purified sexuality by focusing on the giving (surely an important part of the whole experience) while leaving out the desiring and the receiving (which are at least as important).

Like Augustine, who theorized that sex in the Garden of Eden would have been free of the sounds and movements of physical desire, the pope cleanses sexual union and detaches it from the lived sexual experience of the great majority of Christians. Unlike Augustine, however, he raises up his spiritualized version of marital sexuality as any good Christian can experience it, and in doing so, goes much further than Augustine in celebrating the goodness of marriage. Although the pope can certainly be criticized as insufficiently attentive to the potential goodness of sexual desire, clearly he goes much further than the early fathers who likened a second marriage to a dog returning to his vomit, counseled virgins to escape the cares of family life, or challenged married couples to remain celibate. More importantly, he certainly cannot be accused of underappreciating the one-heart one-flesh unity of marriage relationships. This pope celebrates relationship to a new degree and reshapes the Christian tradition in the process. Those who have criticized the tradition for its lack of appreciation of relationships have much to be thankful for.

However, the problem with the focus on relationships, whether in the more conservative work of the pope or the more liberal work of Farley, Gudorf, and Lawler, is that a Christian marriage is a relationship and more. The New Testament writers had concerns that marriage relationships, however giving and spiritual, would take energy away from the public work of discipleship. Jesus' admonition to leave a dead father unburied starkly challenges those followers fully engaged in their family relationships. His affirmation of the indissolubility of marriage reminds us that he did not ask celibacy of everyone, but neither did he make marriage and family the center or limit of Christian discipleship. Being true to the challenge of Jesus means living faithfully within the relationships we choose and moving outside those relationships to give faithfully to others. Children, usually, are the first "others," others curiously absent from the sacrament as relationship model. Speaking of marriage as a relationship says too little about the kind of marriages to which Christians are called.

Marriage as Communion

The pope himself moves beyond the relationship language that dominated his earlier writings on the theology of the body to speaking of family as a communion of love. This language reconciles the suspicion of marriage in the early Christian tradition not by eliminating or spiritualizing sexuality, but by understanding families as small Christian communities notable for their giving inside and outside their boundaries. Marriage is "the covenant of conjugal love freely and consciously chosen, whereby man and woman accept the intimate community of life and love willed by God himself."[52] The foundation of the communion is still the relationship revealed in the book of Genesis. The communion is to be intimate, sexual, and loving. Their union symbolizes God's covenant with his people and Jesus' love for humanity, not just for the husband and wife but for the whole world.[53] As a symbol, the communion has a significance beyond itself:

> Spouses are therefore the permanent reminder to the church of what happened on the cross; they are for one another and for the children witnesses to the salvation in which the sacrament makes them sharers. Of this salvation event marriage, like every sacrament, is a memorial, actuation, and prophecy.[54]

Conjugal life "finds its crowning" in children, or, if procreation proves impossible, "other important services to the life of the human person."[55] Married love spills over, then, in giving to others. The family, with or without children, becomes a communion of persons dedicated to the church and the human family.[56] The pope's writing still indicates that celibacy is a better choice, but it does not denigrate marriage. It only recognizes how good marriage is and how hard it is to give it up. For the pope, both marriage and celibacy provide ways to serve God, in that both require fidelity, fruitfulness (spiritual and/or physical), and service.[57]

In the family communion God's love is known and symbolized; Christians learn to love each other deeply and serve the church and world together. By speaking of the family as a Christian community, John Paul II has retrieved the best of the New Testament vision where family is valued but not idolized, so that discipleship inside and out may flourish.

Discussion Questions

1. Is a commitment to family an important part of Christian life, as you understand it? Why?

2. The ambivalent views of the first Christians on sex and marriage are very different from those of contemporary Christians. How seriously should these views be taken today? Does historical context explain much of the ambivalence?

3. Is it surprising to find that the Catholic sacramental theology of marriage is fully affirmed only in the sixteenth century? Is this finding significant?

4. Are Protestant models of social estate or covenant more appealing than the Catholic sacramental idea? What do you think of liberal Protestant attempts to update covenant theology?

5. Why is Rubio suspicious of relationship language and affirming of communion language? Could one argue that the relationship model is the better one?

PART TWO

APPLICATIONS

The Dual Vocation
of Christian Parents

The last chapter traced the development of Christian theology on marriage and family from the New Testament to the present, ending with John Paul II's theology of the body. This chapter explores the question of how parents as parents, rather than spouses, ought to live. The Christian tradition has been both profoundly suspicious of marriage and deeply respectful of marriage. How should Christian parents in the twenty-first century respond to this tension, especially as they bring the Christian tradition into dialogue with their own needs and desires as well as the ethos of contemporary culture?

Lame Parents

Few literary critics read Flannery O'Connor's wonderful story "The Lame Shall Enter First" as a "family values" story, but ordinary readers like my students often hear it as a warning to parents who sacrifice their children for the sake of their work. In their eyes, this story calls out for a reexamination of parenthood. Sheppard, the father in the story, is a respectable middle-class widower, a city recreational director who volunteers as a counselor at a reform school for boys on the weekends. He has a burning desire to help disadvantaged children improve themselves, and he eventually invites a difficult boy named Rufus to come and live with him and his eleven-year-old son, Norton. Gradually, it becomes clear that Sheppard has become entranced with his own good mission to Rufus, so entranced that he allows his son to grieve his dead mother alone.

One morning at breakfast, in an attempt to inspire some compassion in his son, Norton, Sheppard tells him that he is lucky that his mother is not in the state penitentiary like Rufus's mother. Norton dissolves into tears, saying, "If she was in the penitentiary, I could go to seeeeee her."[1] His father tells him to stop being selfish and grow up. Throughout the story, Sheppard continues to put a great deal of effort into saving Rufus, while ignoring the silent grieving of Norton. Near the end of the story, when faced when Rufus's ultimate rejection, he claims, "I have nothing to reproach myself with. . . . I did more for him than I did for my own child,"[2] and fails to see the irony.

For the reader, the failure of a father to care for his own son is obvious. An eleven-year-old boy is left alone to make sense of his mother's death, another boy is brought into the house to take what is left of the father's attention away, and, at the end of the story, a father finds his son hanging in his room.

This story of an ordinary, fallen, or lame[3] human being perfectly illustrates Flannery O'Connor's famous pessimism about human nature. When my students read the story in class, they do not find it hard to understand. Many speak of parents (their own or others they know well) who put their children second, and their meetings, benefits, and social do-good-ing first. They know well the failures of parents to love their children. The anguish in their voices is unmistakable. Suicide may be an extreme response, but the pain that inspires it in O'Connor's story is, apparently, widespread.

Despite this emotional response, O'Connor did not intend to write a story about the importance of sacrificing social responsibilities for one's family. Rather, O'Connor tells a story about a man who fails to connect with two boys — one, his own, and one whom he tries to adopt. Ultimately, he can save neither boy. Like most of O'Connor's tragic characters, Sheppard is not a good Christian. Sheppard's sin is not failing to put his family first, but failing to see Jesus Christ in all those he loves. He ignores Rufus's concern with the state of his soul, forfeiting his trust, *and* fails to comfort his suffering son, forfeiting his life. He does not meet Christ or put on Christ at home or in the world.

If this interpretation is correct, why do my students often read the story as a cautionary tale for parents who fail their children? Perhaps something in our culture makes it easy to see Sheppard's failings as a parent and difficult to see his failings as a citizen. In America today, "family first" has become the closest thing we have to a sacred value. Most people agree that prioritizing family is the moral thing to do, and most people claim to do it. In her book *Ask the Children: What America's Children Really Think about Working Parents*, Ellen Galinsky of the Families and Work Institute published the results of a national survey of over a thousand third through twelfth graders and six hundred parents. Galinsky claims that most of the working parents she and her colleagues interviewed do put their families first. A small percentage of parents admit that they do not subscribe to this value, and the book makes it clear that these parents are more likely to have children who think their parents are not doing a good job.[4] The book holds that parents can avoid these sorts of problems by prioritizing family.

It is not always clear what this means. For the author of *Ask the Children*, it does not mean quitting work. Galinsky says that "it is not *that* we work, but *how* we work." The problem is not that parents have commitments other than their children, but that their commitment to their children does not claim top priority. Children, according to Galinsky, need to feel that their parents' work is not more important than they are. One girl wrote, "I think the thing that goes on with kids is: 'Wouldn't you rather be with me than do this other thing?' I want my mother to like her job, but not more than she loves me."[5] According to Galinsky, children are more likely to give their mothers high grades when they feel that they are managing the work-family balance successfully and putting their families before their jobs most of the time.[6] The book suggests that sacrificing everything for the sake of one's children is not necessary. One only has to put them first.

Of course, one could quite easily point out that Americans do not seem to practice the value they claim to hold, for they spend much of their most precious commodity — their time — away from their children. Even when parents are around, they are often not present. One of my students told a story in class about going out to a restaurant and watching a father try to eat dinner with his family as the two cell phones and one beeper at his side rang nonstop. This image powerfully illustrates how much Americans have allowed work to invade their family lives, making a mockery of the claim to prioritize family. It is also appropriate to point out that the U.S. government does not adequately fund programs such as day care, health care, and family leave that make the valuing of children concrete. It would be difficult to claim that America prioritizes family.

Still, as a Christian theologian, I am more interested in the ease with which Americans claim this value and in the suspicion that greets anyone who questions it. Even those who work the longest of hours rarely claim that family comes second in their lives. No other value seems worthy of the same reverence. The key to being a good parent today, it seems, is not being home all the time, but being the kind of person who professes a love for family and who will sacrifice work for family when it is important to do so. Yet even as parents profess this sort of confidence in their choices, they fear that they have not sacrificed enough for children. Americans want to have the kind of strong emotional ties to their children that will ensure enduring relationships; they do not want to end up like Sheppard. Thus the culture holds on to a family-focused ethic. However, the Christian tradition, exemplified by O'Connor (correctly read), points toward a dual vocation for Christian parents, one that calls parents to be Christians at home and in the world.

Sacrificing for Children

Certainly, no one would deny that sacrificing oneself comprises a large part of parenting. Pregnancy in particular provides in some ways a paradigmatic experience of sacrificial love, for the child takes over the mother's body (eating from her food, drinking from her drink, moving within her, causing her pain and discomfort, and distorting the shape of her body). If this is not self-sacrifice, what is? In addition, all parents know that sacrifice is a necessary part of raising kids. Believing this allows parents to go without sleep and change hundreds of diapers in the early years, to give up the leisurely Saturdays of their prechild existence in exchange for Saturdays spent watching youth athletic games and mowing the lawn, to give up relative tranquility for intense teenage years full of rebellion and challenge. Everyone knows that those unwilling to do some major sacrificing are not ready for parenting.

Moreover, most Christian parents probably feel that their children deserve all the time, energy, love, and sacrifice they have to give. Can this parental instinct be justified in ethical terms? To begin one might ask, "What are the implications of the natural connections between parents and children?"

It seems intuitively correct to say that children deserve parental care because of their physical connection to their parents. One Catholic theologian, for instance, argues that

> if we really believe bodies matter, and are prepared to follow this insight where it takes us, we cannot help but acknowledge the fact that a child is produced by the bodily union of its mother and father, that the mother carries it in her body for nine months, that the child usually shares many of its parents' bodily features and bears their genetic inheritance, is of enormous significance and provides a uniquely firm foundation for a relationship of love.[7]

Because children and parents are bodily connected, then, they have special commitments to each other. Most parents would readily agree that this commitment simply exists when a child is born; thus it seems a natural and good thing to fulfill.[8]

On the other hand, physical connection does not always lead to emotional connection. Stories of young women leaving newborn babies they never wanted in trashcans or hospitals give one indication that pregnancy is not always a bonding experience for women. Stories of the many men who leave women when they are pregnant indicate that genes are not enough to hold parents and children together. Writings by feminist mothers have revealed like nothing else the unnaturalness of the parental bond for many women. In Adrienne Rich's seminal text, *Of Woman Born*, for instance, she writes of how she broke out in a rash days before her first son's birth. The rash was diagnosed as "an allergic reaction to pregnancy."[9] A mother allergic to having children! Here, and throughout the book, Rich gives testimony to the difficulty she had embracing her role as mother, for being a mother required her to give up her vocation as a poet. Though she struggled to complete the sacrifice she knew she was supposed to make, she found herself incapable. This profound discomfort with the sacrifices of parenting compels Rich to begin and end her book with reflections on the true story of a mother of eight "who had recently murdered and decapitated her two youngest on her suburban front lawn."[10]

One can take this seriously as a warning that parental love is not always natural and yet still affirm that, though many parents would acknowledge moments of extreme anger with their children, most find that love and a profound desire to care for children in their vulnerable, dependent state win out. Theologian Sally Purvis speaks for many parents when she writes of how "the most sustained and trustworthy embodiment of agape in my life is my experience of being a mother to my two sons."[11] Like many, Purvis feels overwhelmed by how much she is capable of giving to her children. Over and against Kierkegaard's claim that love for the dead is the criterion for universal, disinterested Christian love, Purvis suggests the model of a mother who loves within an intense special relationship with her children.[12] She argues that mother-love is inclusive in that it extends to all of her children, no matter who they are as individuals, that it connects and focuses on the needs of others, and that it is unconditional.[13] She contends that her model better fits the scriptural stories that shape a Christian understanding of love. Purvis reminds us that Jesus told the story of the Good Samaritan (a story about love without limits) about a man who behaved not like a neighbor, but like a lover.[14] Mothers, too, act like lovers in that they care intensely for others, regardless of what they receive in return. It is this intensity to which Christians are both drawn and called.

Purvis's experience of mother-love led to a profound retrieval and reconceptualization of one of the most central demands in Christian life. Though aware of and sympathetic to feminist concerns about the complexity of the mothering experience,[15] Purvis contends that mother-love comprises a distinct and recognizable facet of her mothering experience, and this makes it worth upholding as a model. By being attentive to the natural love between a mother and her children, she claims, Christians can learn more about what it means to love.

Popular Christian writing also testifies to the importance of the parent-child relationship in the lives of Christian families.[16] For instance, many journals for pregnant women seek to help Christian women use their pregnancy as a way to deepen their understanding of God as parent. One author writes:

I'm giving up my old body; I'm giving up my old world. My world seems to revolve more and more around this child. When I bring this child into my life, my life will not be the same again. There is so much I'm giving up so I can receive this new life. But maybe I shouldn't be so surprised; that's what Jesus did for me, isn't it? He gave and gave until his body was changed almost beyond recognition — as it hung on the Cross. And finally he gave his very body and blood in order to bring me to spiritual birth.[17]

These are the words of a woman who gains insight into what it meant for Jesus to suffer and die on the cross by reflecting on the bodily reality of her own pregnancy. In her mind, the giving or self-sacrifice is very physical and yet also spiritual. The physical transformation has spiritual import. As she becomes a mother, she learns to give, and thus becomes more Christ-like. Like Sally Purvis, who came to understand agape by reflecting on her mothering, Carrie Heiman comes to understand the cross by reflecting on her pregnancy. Both women affirm the power of the experience of mothering and the connection between mother and child.

However, as theologian Bonnie Miller-McLemore points out, pregnancy constitutes one part of being and becoming a parent, but it is not something that limits or defines women. It is a profound experience, for,

in the pregnant body, the self and the other coexist. The other is both myself and not myself, hourly, daily becoming more separate, until that which was mine becomes irrevocably another. In the pregnancy moment, I am one but two.... As long as the woman has the womb that bears the child, we cannot ignore an initial biological inclination behind the heightened maternal investment.[18]

Nursing a child is also an illuminating experience, for "to lactate when another thirsts teaches a certain empathic, connected knowing."[19] Women's experience of having their milk "let down" when they hear the cry of an infant leads them to a deeper knowledge of the connection among human beings. The fact that women get pregnant and the fact that women nurse babies matter. These experiences teach women something about self-giving that fathers simply do not know naturally.

Still, self-giving is not learned or appropriated by all who become mothers, nor is it inaccessible to those who do not. According to Miller-McLemore, the knowledge women gain is not "privileged knowledge. It is knowledge that must be shared and appropriated by others who have not become mothers."[20] Because we are human beings who are not determined by biology, we experience things differently and learn in unique ways. If not all biological mothers learn connection and empathy from pregnancy, many fathers can and do. They, too, experience the pull of their children upon their energies. They, too, want to sacrifice for them and nurture them.

The Christian tradition testifies to the experience of contemporary Christian parents when it recognizes that most people come to know about love within family relationships. As noted in the last chapter, John Paul II in particular emphasizes the importance of the family as a communion of love.[21] This claim reflects the ongoing discernment of the Christian community, as its members reflect on their experiences and come to understand the import of their intense love for those closest to them. Clearly, sacrificial love for one's own makes up a crucial part of the Christian moral life.

Sacrificing for the World

However, this value does not provide an adequate basis for a full discussion of the Christian calling to parenthood. Historically, the Christian tradition has had more to say about family than this. In the Gospels, one finds a suspicion of the family, a concern that living a truly Christian life will prove difficult within the marriage bond. Ambivalence about the family continues throughout the Christian tradition. All of this suggests the necessity of rethinking the centrality of self-sacrifice in Christian moral discussions of the family.

Recall that Jesus defines himself in opposition to his family when he rejects his family's attempt to interfere with his preaching and identifies those who do God's will as his true family (Mark 3:31–35). His choice of public vocation over family of origin reveals that his primary mission is serving and sacrificing for the world, not caring for his family.

Jesus instructs his disciples to follow his lead. In his preaching, Jesus upholds the marriage covenant (Mark 10:6), indicating that his concern was not with marriage itself but rather with idolatry of family that can stand in the way of discipleship. Still, he challenges his hearers by calling them to "hate" their families (Luke 14:26) or leave their families behind for his sake (Mark 10:29–30). He promises them the riches of a new family of brothers and sisters united in God. The kinship bond and all the ethical priority that comes with it are called into question, because the Jesus of the Gospels preaches that family, like money and power, can be dangerous to the person who wants to live a holy life. He teaches that those who would serve God must resist the temptation to make caring for kin their only mission in life.

As we have seen, the earliest Christians heard this message and were called "homewreckers" by their critics because their faith often brought them into conflict with their families. Despite the fact that the New Testament includes significant affirmations of marriage (Eph 5:21–26), the dominant strain of early Christian thinking appears to have been suspicion of the value of family life when compared with the value of single-hearted discipleship.

While the more family-affirming tradition eventually won out, even today, respect for the more radical early strain that questions the possibility of harmoniously combining love for God (and its accompanying public vocation to spread the Gospel) with love for one's family mixes with celebration of the more private vocation of giving oneself in marriage. This respect for the radical family-questioning strain can be heard today in the Catholic Church's continued insistence that celibacy is a higher calling than marriage.[22] It can also be heard in the quiet lives of priests, monks, and women religious that say to married Christians, "There is more to life than family. God may be more deeply known and loved by those who are free from other passions." Every time the validity of the celibate life is recognized, the sacredness of family life is implicitly questioned, even if marriage is also recognized as a tremendous gift. The higher valuing of the nonmarried life constantly challenges the idea of marriage as a sacred calling for most. It recalls the life of Jesus and suggests that his sacrifice of family life for the sake of public mission should not be forgotten.

If Catholics take this tradition seriously, the self-sacrificial paradigm that privileges openness to children and parental sacrifice for children over the public vocations of men and women must be brought into question, for Jesus' followers are called first and foremost to discipleship in community. He tells them that discipleship with him means *not* putting their families first. He asks them to break out of traditional roles, especially traditional family roles, in order to realize the radical meaning of his message. The Christian tradition, at least in its early stages, is no more encouraging. Contemporary Christians who want to be true to their Scripture and tradition have to reckon with the centrality of the Christian's vocation in the world.

Dual Vocation

Is there a way to uphold both the primacy of discipleship testified to in the Gospels and the early Christian tradition and the deep valuing of children that comes from the experience of Christian parents? What would it mean to balance these two important values?

I would suggest that discipleship provides the appropriate framework in which to discuss the calling of a Christian parent. Discipleship is, after all, the primary ethical imperative asked of all Christians. But what does it mean to be a disciple of Christ? Should Christian parents abandon family for the monastery? Theologian William Spohn, whose recent book studies implications of discipleship for ethics, argues that the concept of discipleship is rooted in Jesus' command to "go and do likewise." Jesus, according to Spohn, does not ask his followers to do exactly as he does or to do whatever they want. They are not to imitate or ignore him, but rather follow him, to look to his life as their norm or standard. Their identity or character should reflect his identity. Their actions should be recognizably, and particularly, like his, even in their very different contexts and circumstances.[23] If this interpretation is correct, it must be possible for parents to be Christ-like even though they are not celibate pastors.

Still, the distinctiveness of Jesus' life as norm should not be lost. Richard Hays reminds us that for the early Christians, Jesus' obedience to God, which led him to the cross, is the essence of discipleship. For Hays, "the way of the cross is simply the way of obedience to the will of God, and discipleship requires following that way regardless of cost or consequences."[24] Popular piety, which suggests that mothers and fathers feed the hungry and clothe the naked when they care for their children, is off the mark. This and more is required of those who claim to be followers of Christ.[25]

Scripture scholars tell us that discipleship is the fundamental calling of Christians, and this presumes a public vocation. Certainly one can practice Christian virtue, keep many of the commandments of the Old and New Testaments, and obey God's will at home in one's family. Perhaps the Gospels and early tradition paid insufficient attention to this reality, which contemporary Christians know so well. However, one cannot, I would argue, fully realize the demands of discipleship to Jesus of Nazareth unless one also has a public vocation. The public nature of discipleship is evident in the life of Jesus. Jesus himself acknowledges the conflict between serving God (in his public preaching) and serving his family. His mission takes him to different places, puts him in contact with a great many people, and moves him to confront the local powers in such disturbing ways that they eventually crucify him (sentence him to the death of a political criminal). His earliest followers sought to continue his mission by traveling to spread his message, forming new kinds of radically inclusive families and refusing to participate in many mainstream political practices and institutions. Thus though the lines between public and private in Jesus' time surely differ from our own, Jesus' ministry was public in that it did not center on his family and in that it brought him into conflict with social institutions.[26] Discipleship to this Jesus, or "doing likewise," must, then, mean some form of public vocation.

Work

In fact, the Catholic tradition presumes that work constitutes an important aspect of one's public vocation. John Paul II writes in *Laborem Exercens* that "work is a fundamental dimension of man's existence on earth."[27] Work is not simply something one does to fill a day or what one has to do in order to eat. According to the pope, God commands work in Genesis 1:28 ("Be fruitful and multiply, and fill the earth and subdue it"), and therefore it must be fundamental to humanity. The subject of work is the human person.[28] Work is something persons choose. The work a person does must "serve to realize his humanity, to fulfill his calling to be a person that is his by reason of his very humanity."[29] A person's work is her vocation and a way she realizes herself as a person. Work comprises both an obligation and a right of all persons.[30] Through it human beings share in the work of the Creator.[31]

One can draw two important ethical implications from John Paul II's theology of work. First, all persons have a calling they must answer, an invitation to share in the shaping and molding of the world. Work is a right, not simply because all persons have a right to the basic necessities of life (though this is a part of it), but because all persons have something important to do in this world by which they will realize their very selves. Second, the work that persons do is crucially important. It is not something to be thought of lightly or as separate from one's Christian vocation. Work constitutes a fundamental part of the moral life. As the fathers of Vatican II write, Christians must not separate faith and life.[32] What people do is an important part of who they are. A Christian cannot choose to engage in work in a less than fully human way.

Nevertheless, no specific kind of work is ruled out. The pope claims that the person who works, not the work itself, is crucial.[33] This qualification affirms that people can work in a variety of jobs and live out their Christian vocation. However, it also acknowledges that people are easily persuaded not to look closely at what kind of work they do. Clearly, too, not all work can be considered Christian work.

Dorothy Day's insistence that work is prayer helps qualify the pope's general vision of work.[34] In her book *Loaves and Fishes*, Day speaks about the quiet commitment of a woman named Marie who sweeps the floor of the Catholic Worker house each night without complaint, seeing her work as a prayer.[35] The sweeping of this floor allows life to go on in a shelter for some of the most disadvantaged in the city. Surely it is important that she sweeps this floor and not another. Day, too, struggled to find work in accord with her faith. At a turning point in her journey, she "offered up a special prayer, a prayer which came with tears and with anguish, that some way would open up for me to use what talents I possessed for my fellow workers, for the poor."[36] Writing itself was not enough; she wanted to write and serve in a Christian community committed to the marginalized. In this context, sweeping and writing are both crucial. Day's example reminds us that all Christians are called to find significant work; only this work constitutes prayer.

Christian parents trying to live as disciples of Christ ought to see work as more than a means to an end, more than a way to support a family. It makes little sense to spend ten to fourteen hours a day getting ready for, getting to, doing, and getting home from something less than meaningful in order to make the other, more meaningful two to six hours of the day possible. It makes little sense to spend the majority of our time doing something unrelated to who we really are. If work is not what we are, then what are we? The pope's discourse forces this question, because it affirms that work is fundamental to the development and fulfillment of human beings and insists that human beings can and must choose humanizing work.

If work is all this, it does not seem that Christian parents can avoid the fulfillment of a public vocation during their parenting years. Work is a part of a Christian's commitment to live an ethical life. Parents cannot put it aside when children arrive, nor can they allow the needs of children to shift the focus of work from humanity to "providing the best." Still, being a parent does change one's situation. A parent does have the responsibility to provide and care for children. This limits the time and energy parents have available, unless the care of children can be considered "work" in John Paul II's understanding of the term.

Is Parenting Work?

On the one hand, the pope emphasizes the equal right of all persons to participate in their society. This could mean that women as well as men have a right to pursue a public vocation or to work in the public realm. However, John Paul II claims that women's family work is work and has social import because the love and nurture of children is crucial to society.[37] The pope rightly acknowledges that the work of parenting contributes to the good of society and is in that sense public work. However, if the church is to take up the call of Vatican II to read the signs of the times in light of the Gospel, it must listen to the women who do most of this family work, to those who so often speak of their experience of motherhood as a very private and even isolating experience. Many women who have strong commitments to parenting nonetheless speak about the need for work that involves them with individuals who are not their own. Many feminist mothers have expressed their frustration with the limitations of work that is concentrated in the home and involves a great many tasks that, while necessary and valuable, are also mundane, repetitive, and seemingly unconnected to the larger world. Feminist writers claim that many women need public work in order to be fulfilled as persons, and this claim fits nicely with Catholic teaching, which insists on the right and duty of public participation. Both Catholic thought and feminist thought affirm the importance of public vocation, while upholding the importance of the work of parenting.[38]

Feminist literature on mothering differs from the idealistic portraits of motherhood that appear in popular culture and even in academic writing. This literature seems unintelligible to many. For instance, in ethicist Stephen Post's discussion of parental love, Post criticizes a feminist essay entitled "Motherhood: The Annihilation of Women," claiming that, although in some extreme cases motherhood proves seriously problematic for women, "were most mothers asked whether motherhood has 'annihilated' them, they would find the question extreme and even peculiar."[39] However, in my own conversations with mothers, I have found that almost all of them speak in some way about losing themselves, having no lives, being constantly fatigued by their responsibilities to fulfill the needs of husbands and children, feeling guilty about taking any time for themselves, or putting all of their own plans on hold, perhaps until their children have grown. Almost every sustained conversation I have had with a group of young mothers eventually turns to this topic. Certainly, even more young women speak of their own mothers as having no identity of their own. Feminist mothering literature simply gives voice to the very real feeling of mothers, that parenting, while exhilarating and fulfilling in many ways, is not enough to fill a life.

In 1969, Betty Friedan called it "the problem with no name" and chronicled a generation of women's feelings of emptiness, lack of self-worth, and incompleteness.[40] Since then, feminist writers have struggled to explain the ambivalence of their experience of motherhood. Adrienne Rich is perhaps the best known and most articulate.

Rich writes in *Of Woman Born* that when she thought back upon her early mothering years, she "could remember little except anxiety, physical weariness, anger, self-blame, boredom, and division within myself: a division made more acute by the moments of passionate love, delight in my children's spirited bodies and minds, amazement at how they went on loving me in spite of my failures to love them wholly and selflessly."[41] Rich gave up her vocation as a writer in order to be with her children full-time. She writes that she struggled to have some life of her own and recalls that she "was fighting for my life through, against, and with the lives of my children.... I had been trying to give birth to myself."[42] She longed for more time for her work, for the realm of poetry, "where I lived as no one's mother, where I existed as myself."[43] Looking back, she mourned "the waste of myself during those years."[44] Out of this experience of suffering, Rich wrote a book examining the roots of motherhood as an institution. In the book she takes pains to establish that she has great hope for motherhood as an experience, but she believes that it must be freed from the trappings of the institution that makes it women's whole identity. Rich's poignant writing testifies to women's need to be something other than mothers, to women's need for public vocations.

Rich's work has richer analysis because of her feminist perspective, but feminist mothers are not the only ones frustrated with current paradigms of motherhood. My own sense of women's frustration (rooted in conversations with other mothers) is confirmed not only by feminist writers, but also by sociological studies of new parents. Cowan and Cowan's longitudinal study of first-time parents, for instance, shows that women who allow their mothering role to take over too much of their self-identity suffer from low self-esteem. The researchers used a pie-shaped diagram as a tool for measuring self-identity. They asked participants in the study to fill in a pie with the various parts of themselves (i.e., parent, partner, worker, etc.). Those women whose pies were dominated by the mother piece tended to have low self-esteem.[45] In contrast, in marriages where fathers were more invested in their parenting role, both the women and the men had higher self-esteem and were happier with their marriages.[46] This research seems to indicate that, for women, allowing parenting to consume self-identity (or annihilate the self) is both a real temptation and a dangerous choice.

Both feminist literature and the growing literature on parenting indicate that parenthood alone does not constitute a full life for most women. Some of the new work on fatherhood parallels this literature in its support for the notion that work is crucial to men's self-fulfillment. Pioneers in the field of fathering argue that men should not feel guilty about their work outside the home because work gives them a sense of accomplishment, emotional fulfillment, and a chance to make a difference.[47] Despite the fact that they encourage men to spend at least a little more time at home, the authors affirm men's efforts to care for their children by providing for them and let men know that their own happiness at work contributes to their children's quest for independence and success.[48] New writers on fatherhood advocate more interaction with children for men, while affirming the important, even crucial, place of public work in men's lives.

Even writers such as Robert Griswold, author of *Fatherhood in America*, who question the dominance of work in men's lives, do not suggest that men abandon work altogether. Griswold argues that women's entry into the labor force has changed all the rules for men. He asserts that "nothing has posed a greater challenge to the ideology of male breadwinning and traditional male prerogatives than this transformation in the household economy."[49] Griswold welcomes this challenge because he sees breadwinning as an inadequate platform around which to build a whole definition of fatherhood, let alone a whole identity. On the other hand, he speaks at several points about the "boring, repetitious, and vexing work of child care."[50] He closes his book with the hopeful claim that "clearly many fathers want to become genuine care givers; clearly many mothers want to be part of the work force. Surely in the years ahead social policies can be developed that will allow men and women to do both."[51]

Perhaps it is unremarkable that no one urges men to become full-time parents. When the average man spends so little time each day with his children, it may seem ridiculous to ask for more than additional "quality time" or, at most, a sharing of roles. Still, it is significant that most people know enough about the limitations of parenting work to understand that asking men to embrace that work full-time is not the best option. Men are not asked to become fathers in the same way that women have been mothers.

Thus fathering literature, in its insistence that men's public work is valuable for men, serves as the flip-side of the feminist mothering literature that insists that women's total investment in work in the home may be detrimental to them. Both sets of writings point toward the idea that persons have a need to participate in work that is in some important sense larger or more far-reaching than the work of parenting. Some characterize this need to engage in public work as a need for fulfillment, in opposition to the duty to sacrifice that grounds the work of parenting. However, this kind of dichotomizing seems inaccurate and unhelpful. In fact, many mothers speak with intensity about the joy of being with their children or with what seems like guilt about how much fun they have at home. Studies of stay-home mothers indicate that when women want to stay home, their experiences can be quite positive.[52] Thus, parenting is not wholly self-sacrificial and the desire to work is not wholly self-serving. Perhaps what women long for, and what men refuse to give up, is the very connection to the world, the very same vocation to serve, that the pope writes about. Perhaps parents are saying that they want to serve and enjoy life both at home and in the world. They want to be a central part of both realms of life — the private and the public. Perhaps this is the contemporary meaning of discipleship to the Jesus of Nazareth who upheld the sacredness of marriage even as he called men and women away from their families.

Family

If we conceptualize work as a public vocation, it becomes easier to understand why work has such importance for women and men, and easier to see how work fits into the demands of Christian discipleship. It is also important to think of family itself not simply as a private haven, but as a community with a mission that goes beyond itself, a part of the public vocation of Christian parents.

In John Paul II's *On the Family*, the pope does just this. The pope defines the family as "a community of life and love" that has four major tasks. Each of these has public dimensions. The first is the most obvious. The family must "guard, reveal and communicate love."[53] John Paul II distinguishes himself from earlier popes by the inspired way in which he describes married love and demands that it rise to the heights for which it is destined. His personalist language represents an attempt to take seriously the importance contemporary men and women give to spousal relationships. Love among family members is primary not because it is most important, but because it serves as the foundation for the rest of what the family does. This constitutes the beginning, not the end.

Second to love comes the task of "serving life." According to the pope, this means that parents have a responsibility to serve life by nurturing children *and* by bringing life to the world.[54] Having children comprises only the first step. Education is an important responsibility and includes the task of instilling in children "the essential values of human life," especially the idea that possessions do not make human beings what they are, and the responsibility to adopt a simple lifestyle.[55] The pope also affirms that when mothers and fathers teach their children about the Gospel, "they become fully parents, in that they are begetters not only of bodily life but also of the life that through the Spirit's renewal flows from the cross and resurrection of Christ."[56] This seems to indicate that passing on the Christian faith is even more important than the admittedly awesome process of passing on life. Here, as in the Gospel itself, the spiritual and public duty is placed above (but in relation to) the private duty. The pope makes this emphasis on the spiritual clear when he claims that families have a "spiritual fecundity" by which they share with others the self-giving love they nurture within.[57] Families are called to respond to all of God's children with compassion. Serving life means much more than having babies.

The third task to which the pope calls families further indicates that families are not simply oriented toward their own good. Families are called to participate in the development of society, for "far from being closed in on itself, the family is by its nature and vocation open to other families and to society and undertakes its social role."[58] This means that families "cannot stop short at procreation and education";[59] they have distinct and fundamental social and political duties.[60] Specifically, the pope asks families first to practice hospitality, opening their table and their home to those who are less fortunate, second, to become politically involved, assisting in the transformation of society, and third, to practice the preferential option for the poor, manifesting a "special concern for the hungry, the poor, the old, the sick, drug victims and those with no family."[61] All of this comprises part of the social mission of the family. It is neither optional nor an add-on that families are to perform after the really important tasks. It is a fundamental part of what families are and what they are called to do, a crucial part of the family's public vocation; it is what they do, as a community of love, in the world.

Finally, the pope uses the "domestic church" imagery, which received renewed attention at Vatican II, to suggest that families must serve the church as well as one another.[62] As a "church in miniature," the family evangelizes its members, witnesses to the world, uses its home as a sanctuary (for rituals of prayer, sacrament, and sacramentals), and serves the broader community; like the church, the family serves humanity.[63] Here again, the pope places emphasis on the public dimension of the family's calling.

At each point in his description of the ideal family, the pope implies that families are about more than themselves. They are communities of love, but not inwardly focused. They serve life by giving birth, physically and spiritually. They serve society, especially the poorest members. They are the church in their home and as such contribute to its ecclesial mission. The pope's emphasis on the social responsibilities of the family implies that Christian parenting requires something different of parents than focusing on the family. The genius of Catholic teaching on the family is that it refuses to limit families by telling them to just take care of their own. It calls into question any ethic of parenting that centers on the duty of parents to sacrifice for their children. The pope's definition of family seems to require instead that parents serve their children and the world.

Although here I will not attempt to develop models that would be true to this vision, I will offer a few illustrations. James and Kathleen McGinnis founded the Parenting for Peace and Justice Network, based in St. Louis. Their most basic and controversial assertion is that becoming a parent does not mean giving up the struggle for justice. They have shared the story of how they attempted to combine family life and public work in their book *Parenting for Peace and Justice: Ten Years Later.*[64] Their attempts to work for nonviolence at home and in public (through the practice and advocacy of nonviolent conflict resolution), for instance, are chronicled there. They represent a small but growing number of parents who see their family responsibilities as part of their public vocation. Family is not a retreat for the McGinnis parents, but a crucial piece of their commitment to Christian discipleship.

Jack Nelson-Pallmeyer's book *Families Valued* also attempts to link personal and social responsibilities, blurring the distinctions between the two. Nelson-Pallmeyer works part-time as a college professor and shares the care of his three daughters. He contends that one cannot value one's own family and not value the families of others. He begins his book with the story of his daughter's red tricycle, which neighborhood children destroyed one afternoon for no apparent reason. He claims that as a parent, he must ask not only how he can comfort and protect his daughter, but also how he can work to create a world in which children do not want to destroy tricycles.[65] He argues that all families are connected, and that we will stand or fall together. As a parent, he feels responsible not only for the safety of his own children, but for the safety of all children. His identity as a parent grounds his desire to make more children safe. Being a parent does not lead him to abandon the world; it inspires him to try to change it.

In both these cases, parents see themselves as Christians, or disciples of Jesus, first. They are involved parents, more involved than most parents today, but do not give up public work in order to care for children. Neither do they view their family life solely in private terms. Both at work and at home, they remember the public vocation of Christian parenthood.[66]

Dual Vocation with Caution

Because the Gospel and tradition witness to the primary obligation of adult Christians to discipleship *and* the goodness of marriage, while Christian parents testify to the importance of rearing their offspring *and* the significance of work, a Christian discussion of parenting will emphasize ethical obligations of men and women to realize their Christian calling both at home and in the world and develop practical models for the realization of this ideal. Christian parents have important public responsibilities inside and outside the boundaries of their families.

However, the idea of public vocation is not meant to justify high-paying or high-power jobs that do not allow for adequate time with children. Galinsky's *Ask the Children* provides powerful testimony from children themselves that some parents take their work commitment far too seriously. When asked what they want to tell the working parents of America, many children talk about time. They say, "You don't know how it hurts when you think your parents love their job more than you," or "I wish you would stop working so much and spend more time with us," or "Spend time with your children, because when you're gone, there is a big hole in our hearts that makes some or most of us want to cry."[67] A Christian understanding of the dual vocation of parenting must not contribute to the rationalizing of parents who do not spend enough time with their children.

Still, the Catholic tradition does point toward the notion of parenting as both a public and a private calling. The notion of public vocation implies that the full self-realization of a Christian requires involvement in public life. This understanding of the human person is assumed in Catholic teaching both on work and on the family. It sets Catholic theology of the family apart from other family-focused theologies.

Let me return to Flannery O'Connor's story, "The Lame Shall Enter First," with its portrait of a man who fails as a Christian in both his public and private vocations. In private, he denies his son's feelings and is crassly ignorant of his son's needs. He attempts to make his family life "public," but ends up failing to convince his son of the importance of unselfishness because he does not truly model it and because he has not provided an adequate base (a family that is a communion of love) from which it could flow forth. He fails in his public life because he tries to remake a boy in his own image instead of listening to what the boy truly needs. He is more in love with the idea of himself as savior than with the work and worker of salvation.

These failings should give pause to anyone who seeks to live out the public vocation of parenting, but they should not send us back to "focus on the family." Sheppard sins, finally, not because he fails to put family first, but because he, like all of Flannery O'Connor's characters, is finite or lame, limited by his very humanity in his quest to be a good parent and a good citizen. However, O'Connor did not write her gloomy stories to convince her readers to give up the struggle to go beyond limits. Instead, she hoped that they, whom she called "lame beasts slouching toward Bethlehem,"[68] would not fail to humbly take up the challenge of being Christ for others. Her story suggests, as any good Christian story would, the importance of doing this at home and in the world.

Discussion Questions

1. Is it possible that Christian parents will find in the call to dual vocation justification for too much devotion to work? Is it dangerous to argue against "family first" in today's society?

2. Is feminist questioning of the naturalness of parental love and sacrifice disturbing? How can Rubio accept the claims of feminists and still argue that "sacrificial love for one's own makes up a crucial part of the Christian moral life"?

3. Can one use the biblical and historical material to argue against putting family first?

4. Do you agree that disciples of Jesus must have some form of public vocation? Can you think of exceptions to this rule?

5. How might the pope respond to Rubio's idea that caring for children is not a public work?

6. Is the pope's vision of the family and its four tasks appealing? If not, what tasks do families have, in your view?

– S I X –

Mothering in Christian Families

Waiting in the Park

Many years before I became pregnant with my first child, I worried about what it would mean to be a mother. While a graduate student at Harvard, I watched mothers playing with their toddlers at local parks, and I wondered how they dealt with what seemed to me a monotonous routine. I thought I could see a "waiting" look in their eyes — as if they were waiting for naptime or bedtime or for when their children would be in school during the day. These women (often the wives of graduate students) — and most of the other mothers I knew — made me fear motherhood. They were wonderfully compassionate and giving, but most seemed to lack a sense of self. They were so unlike the strong, vibrant women I knew as students and professors in graduate school. I did not want to become like them. I did, however, want children. I liked children; I just didn't like what they did to women. I wanted to become a mother without losing myself.

Many women today share these same fears; even those who do not articulate the dilemma experience it in their everyday lives. When I had my first child and joined the moms in the parks, I heard many of them voice dissatisfaction with their mothering role, saying things like, "I have no time to myself," "I have no life," "I think I'll like the phase when they are in school a lot better." I heard those same mothers speak about the importance of their choice to stay home with their children, of the incredible love (surprising in its depths even to them) they have for their children, and of the selfishness they see in working mothers. These are not radical feminists. However, their discontent can be seen as part of an ongoing conversation that feminists began at least thirty-five years ago, when they began to respond to motherhood as a paradigm or institution that was, in many ways, oppressive.[1] In what ways is mothering oppressive? How does it call for the annihilation of the self? In what ways is motherhood enriching? How does it call for the empowerment of the self? And what does all of this have to do with theology? This chapter explores motherhood as theologians have reflected upon it, taking note of the ambivalent nature of the experience of most mothers. It will show that contemporary Christian theologians are often suspicious of traditional ways of conceiving motherhood and anxious to think about motherhood as something that does not swallow women whole, but rather leaves them able to give not only to their children but to themselves and to others whom they, as Christians, are called to serve.

This discussion of Christian motherhood begins with Pope John Paul II, for he has articulated the insights of the Christian tradition on motherhood and extended the tradition with his own theology of the body. Studying his thought reveals both the limits and potential of the tradition for contemporary Christian women who want to become mothers. It will help us discern how women in particular can understand their call to what Catholic teaching understands as the dual vocation of parenthood.

Mothering in the Thought of John Paul II

Sacrificing Oneself for One's Children

The pope believes all human persons are called to love other people deeply and profoundly, to give themselves away to others. Both men and women are to take their cue from the creation myth in the book of Genesis, which John Paul II interprets as a story of Adam searching for the perfect mate and finding her in God's gift of Eve. According to the pope, Eve finds herself in giving herself away to Adam, and Adam becomes who he is in receiving her and giving himself back to her.[2] Both are self-givers, lovers, and beloved. Both are asked to sacrifice for each other and for their children.[3]

This emphasis on self-sacrifice emerges again in John Paul II's argument against artificial contraception. He claims that birth control is never legitimate, even for a married couple, because sex acts as a sign that the spouses give themselves totally to each other. For the pope, total self-giving includes giving to your spouse the part of yourself that is a potential parent. Holding that part back, in a sense, denies your partner a fundamental part of yourself. Thus the contraceptive sexual act in which the physical actions of husband and wife "say" that they give themselves totally to one another while in reality they are holding back, is, in the pope's view, a lie. If a couple engages in the physical act that symbolizes total self-giving, then both husband and wife must be willing to give themselves as parents by being open to the possibility that conception might occur.[4]

Many Catholic theologians have raised questions about the pope's defense of church teaching against contraception,[5] but more interesting for us is the fact that openness to children receives such a high moral priority in the pope's thought. Assuming that methods of natural family planning are, in practice, somewhat less effective than artificial methods, couples are asked to put their own needs (for intimacy, time together, etc.) aside for the sake of their potential children. Nothing in the lives of the couple warrants a suspension of this rule. The sacrifice for the sake of children called for here gives just one indication of what the pope asks of both parents.

Gender Differences

However, both parents are not asked to sacrifice in quite the same way. John Paul II believes that mothers are simply better at sacrifice, in part because they learn sacrifice naturally through the experience of pregnancy.[6] Like Mary, who, when asked by God to carry the Christ-child to term, said, "Let it be with me according to your word" (Luke 1:38), women say "yes" to becoming vessels for the developing life of another human being. Pregnancy involves a great deal of sacrifice, which varies, of course, from woman to woman. When women speak of these sacrifices, they talk about the weight gain, the things they give up (alcohol, smoking, and caffeine), the sleepless nights, the pains, the swelling of hands and feet, the baby's movement, and the complications that entail still more sacrifice. That pregnancy entails sacrifice seems hard to contest. The pope, however, says more than this. He says that women, already naturally more able to sacrifice than men, learn to be even more sacrificing, giving persons through their pregnancy experience. Further, they become somehow better connected with the mysteries of life, and especially the specific life in their wombs.[7]

This means that when children are born, women are already "naturals" at caring for babies. They already know how to mother; they are already mothers. Fathers, on the other hand, because they are outside the gestation process, learn their fathering from women. They have to be shown how to take care of this new human being because they have no natural way into the experience. Of course, the pope speaks not so much about the details of daily care as the disposition of a nurturer. Obviously, anyone can learn how to change a diaper or cook a meal. However, the pope believes that women, through their experience of pregnancy, come into the role of the nurturing parent much more naturally than men.

Public Roles

The pope's ideas about men's and women's public roles follow from his ideas about what comes naturally to each sex. He seems ready to approve women's public work and to assure that women who seek public work suffer no discrimination but anxious about the negative effects women's absence could have on the home. He assumes that men are the providers and tells them that their role as workers is crucial, but he also reminds them of the importance of their role in the home.[8] While the pope argues that all public work should be open to women, he claims that their first priority is their maternal role, and he cautions that work and family responsibilities must be "harmoniously combined."[9] Clearly, this caution stems from a belief that harmonious integration of roles will be difficult. He argues further that women should never be forced to work outside the home for economic reasons and suggests that society should better support women's work in the home.[10] Finally, he cautions that women should be truly feminine rather than masculine, but he does not specify the content of these terms.[11] Because this caution ends the section on public roles in his letter on the family, it seems that he feels concerned that women who enter public life will become less feminine, and perhaps the home will lose some of the warmth that women who devote their lives to it provide. Like many thinkers from the rise of the Industrial Revolution to the present, the pope is worried that bringing women into public life will lead to the diminishment of both public and private realms.

Responses

The pope gives Catholic women a strong defense of women's work in the family. Many who have made great sacrifices to stay home with their children find his words uplifting. They have experienced the pull of home and family, often rejecting the work world they once found attractive for the joys of daily nurturing. They believe the pope correctly characterizes men and women as different but equal in dignity. The pope's theology confirms their experience of mothering and their moral choices, and they applaud his countercultural voice, seeing him as their advocate.[12]

Others simply see the pope as a reasonable voice in a world that has gone overboard in a quest to do away with gender differences. Mary Ann Glendon, a Harvard law professor and the Vatican's voice at the 1995 Beijing conference on women, praises what she calls the pope's "dynamic feminism," his promotion of "partnership and mutual respect between men and women," and his rejection of "rigid biological determinism as well as the notion that sexual identity is indefinitely malleable."[13] She sees him as a wise moderate who understands gender difference but does not absolutize it.[14]

Some of the pope's critics, on the other hand, support the value of harmoniously combined work and family life but want to argue that both women and men ought to strive for balance. Catholic teaching on parenting also seems to point in this direction, as seen in chapter 5. Others wonder why the pope does not consider women's public work as a vocation or good in itself. Still others want to know what the pope means by "masculine" and "feminine," in an age in which many social scientists believe that some or even most gender differences are socially constructed or shaped by our environments. Theologian Gregory Baum's comments are typical of the pope's critics:

> In my opinion, missing in the Letter [*On the Dignity and Vocation of Woman*] is a longer reflection on the sign of the times, i.e. the presence of women in public life. Today women continue to be good mothers, but they include in their self-definition the full

human vocation, including their role as thinkers, actors, and leaders. Does one want to read the Bible as if it urged modern women to withdraw from public life? It may be sounder to emphasize the multiplicity of charisms and vocations in Church and society, which God distributes among women and men in a manner that continues to surprise us.[15]

Baum questions the pope's insistence that motherhood defines women in such a profound way that it makes all other callings peripheral, and he implies that society might have something to gain from the involvement of women in public life. His suggestion that both women and men might have several different but equally important vocations departs from John Paul II's idea that women and men have equal but different and complementary roles. Baum's affirmation of women's public lives no doubt stems from his experience in working with women, and what he knows from his experience makes him question the pope's theology. He hears the pope talking about what women are, but believes the pope is really talking about what he thinks women should be, without encountering the rich diversity of women's real lives.

Still, especially in comparison with earlier papal teaching on women, John Paul II's teaching can be seen as progressive. While Pope Leo XIII argued in 1891 that women are simply not suited for most public work,[16] John Paul II claims that women should have equal access to most jobs. Pope Pius XI in 1931 spoke with disdain about "false teachers" who claim that men and women are equal, called equality in marriage "unnatural," argued that "inequality and due accommodation" are necessary parts of marriage, and saw women's public work not as emancipation, but as "a crime" against the family.[17] John Paul II speaks with respect about those who have sought greater dignity for women, advocates equality, and recommends mutual self-giving in marriage. Clearly, there has been some dialogue with the world on this issue, and the church has come to see women's role in the family in new ways.

This brief entry into the Catholic dialogue on the role of women makes it clear that the pope has great respect for women's unique and irreplaceable role in families, and that those who affirm significant differences between men and women defend his view, while those who see more overlap between the sexes and their roles question it. Supporters and critics tend to celebrate the respectful tone of the pope's letter and note his appropriation of feminist scholarship at crucial places.[18] However, the pope's writings are just the beginning of the conversation in the Catholic community. Many Catholic theologians have begun to explore different ways of talking about women and motherhood.

Theologians and Motherhood

In response to the second wave of the women's movement in the United States, and out of reflections on their own experiences as daughters, wives, and mothers, Christian feminist theologians have begun to think about women in new ways. They have explored many different aspects of women's lives, most significantly gender, parenting, and the challenge of combining work and family.

Questioning Gender

Lisa Sowle Cahill, mother of five, professor of Christian ethics at Boston College, and one of the best known Roman Catholic moral theologians today has argued that the pope's characterization of women in *On the Dignity and Vocation of Woman* is an idealization inconsistent with men's and women's experiences.[19] In addition, she looks at the creation texts in Genesis differently from the pope. She emphasizes that the God of Genesis 1 transcends gender, for both man and woman are created in God's image. She claims that the fact that man and woman are created for each other means that sexual difference and relationship are good, but she does not believe that the texts emphasize gender differences or define gender roles. Rather, they show that "woman is not to be defined primarily in terms of her procreative role."[20] Instead, the man and the woman share the responsibilities of being fruitful and multiplying and ruling over all of creation. As partners they together bring forth a family and care for the world God created.[21] Even in Genesis 2, the creation story in which Eve is created from Adam's rib, Eve is created as Adam's helper, and according to Cahill, the Hebrew word does not have the lesser connotations that the English word has today.[22] Cahill notes that only in the third chapter of Genesis, after the man and the woman (and the snake) have sinned, are gender roles specified. He will toil hard and rule over her, and she will experience the pain of childbirth and desire his rule (and the snake will crawl on its belly). This, according to Cahill, does not reflect God's will. Rather, it is a distortion of God's will that comes after the Fall.[23] It is not the Christian ideal. The original equality and partnership of Genesis 1 and 2 is the Paradise we ought to seek.

Cahill does not suggest that the authors of the Genesis texts advocated the kind of equal relationships that men and women today might desire; she acknowledges that the authors of these texts probably shared some common assumptions of their day with regard to men's and women's capacities and roles. Yet she finds here a strikingly refreshing understanding of the ways in which men and women relate to God and to each other, without much emphasis on how gender influences relationship or vocation. That there are two different sexes and that they are called into a relationship in which they complete one another is, Cahill believes, impossible to deny. However, the Genesis texts fail to specify masculine or feminine roles in even the most general way. They emphasize equality and partnership and leave the implications of gender difference for future readers to worry about.

Indeed many have worried about them since. In order to get a good sense of how social scientists think about this problem today, Cahill reviews the latest research into gender roles. She concludes that most of the empirical research says that social roles vary for both sexes (men perform different tasks in different cultures, and so do women).[24] While cross-cultural analysis shows that in most cultures, more men than women do some tasks and more women than men do others, one cannot make a universal list of tasks that men or women always and everywhere do. Cultural custom and constraint must have something to do with why men and women have certain roles. Cahill claims then that male and female traits are predispositions, not rigid constraints.[25] In the empirical research, as in the Genesis texts, difference is a reality, but the forms it takes are not clearly defined. Rather, human beings have the capability to do lots of different things in a variety of ways, and gender does not seem to have a huge influence on how they do them.

Given the relative, though perhaps surprising, agreement between the Genesis creation stories and the latest empirical research, Cahill looks to the New Testament for further guidance on gender issues. There she finds a great deal to celebrate. The community of the first

Christians differed radically from other religious communities in its openness to all who professed Jesus as Lord. The Roman and Jewish religions, on the other hand, were embraced or passed down by families. At this time, families were households headed by a male patriarch that included multiple generations of relatives and servants. This means that women were told what religion they had to practice. Christianity gave them the option to choose for themselves, and this represented a real liberation.[26]

Cahill also calls our attention to the scholarship of Elisabeth Schüssler Fiorenza, who has added a great deal to knowledge of New Testament times. Schüssler Fiorenza has shown that women played active roles in the early Christian movement, as benefactors (Lydia), missionaries (Junia and Prisca), apostles (Mary of Magdala), deacons (Phoebe), and possibly even ministers of the Eucharist.[27] The roles women played after Jesus' death were, according to Cahill, consistent with the inclusivity toward women practiced by Jesus himself. Jesus was remarkable for his times in that he spoke to women in public, included them in his ministry, and rejected societal norms that unfairly privileged men.[28]

None of these actions seem remarkable to us, but in Jesus' time, they were all quite radical. As discussed in chapter 3, Jesus' affirmation that Mary could listen to him teach, despite her sister Martha's protest that she should help with the housework, can be seen as a radical move to include women in the community of those called to listen to God's word and do it. This suggests that women are disciples first, just like men. Choosing to do the work of discipleship means choosing the better part. The hard thing, of course, entails figuring out just what that work is. Still, it seems clear from Jesus' interactions with women that he did not want to exclude women from public life. His actions point in exactly the opposite direction.

Cahill's analysis of empirical studies and recent scriptural scholarship shows, then, that gender, while not irrelevant, is not an all-encompassing category that wholly defines how a person will live out his or her Christian vocation.

Questioning Sacrifice

In the 1970s, the second wave of the feminist movement in the United States turned its attention to motherhood, and women began to speak for the first time about the difficulty of living up to the image of the perfect, all-giving mother. In the decades that followed, feminist thinking about motherhood increased, and eventually, theologically trained women who were also mothers began to write about motherhood from their perspective. Christine Gudorf stands out as one of the most important thinkers in this area. In her work she speaks about "parenting," so as to acknowledge that some of the same phenomena affect fathers. However, she also notes that women are particularly vulnerable to the excesses about which she speaks, and thus it seems appropriate here to discuss her work under the category of "motherhood." The most important question she raises concerns the moral propriety of parental sacrifice. Against most prevailing theological views, she argues that sacrifice without the expectation of return is not a good ethical framework for parenting. Instead, she claims that "complete agape as either intention or result is impossible. Love can never be disinterested. It can be patient, but never disinterested."[29]

Gudorf believes that if parents do not recognize the impossibility of perfect, selfless love, they set themselves up not only for failure in loving, but also for a failure to recognize the interrelatedness and interdependence of all human beings. This can result in the potentially harmful domination of parents over children.[30] "Most love," says Gudorf (the mother of three children, two of whom are adopted and mentally handicapped) "is mutual; all is directed at mutuality. It could not be any other way, for we find love rewarding."[31] She learned this, she says, by parenting children with special needs and realizing that she and her husband had an interest (as all parents do) in their children's success (for more success for kids means more freedom for parents). Only when we acknowledge this are we free to love without disguising our needs and turning them against others. In a long footnote, Gudorf says that women are particularly vulnerable to this kind of disguised love, for they are more likely, due to their socialization, to give of themselves and to deny their own needs. This results in distorted relationships in which women give too much in some ways and not enough in others.[32] Gudorf calls into question this "sacrificial" mothering, which is really controlling and ultimately unfruitful.

In a later article on in vitro fertilization, Gudorf asks why parents choose artificial means to have children. She acknowledges the validity of parents' desire for physical identification with their children, but argues that "without some parental ability to stand back from the child and encourage individuation in the child, full personhood becomes problematic for the child."[33] If parents cannot separate themselves from children and allow children to grow, they are not parenting properly. They have an inappropriate amount of power over the child whom they are attempting to shape. Women, according to Gudorf, sometimes claim this power and control over dependent children. They, more often than men, seek to live through them. However, "it is dangerous for adults to fill personal needs exclusively through parenting. We need to have other avenues for nurturing, for intimacy, for community involvement, for activity, outside of parenting, if we are to avoid using a child for our own ends."[34] Adults who are too invested in their children can damage their children instead of helping them.

Gudorf's reflections suggest, then, that women, who are more likely to overidentify with their kids, need to step back, give their kids room to grow, and focus on growing themselves for a change. Here, she warns mothers that trying to live only for their children is not a smart way to raise healthy children or to be healthy women. In a later essay, she goes so far as to say that "the romanticization of parenthood as sacrificial" supports patriarchal control of supposedly weaker women and children, masks parental abuse of children, and suggests that children owe parents gratitude for having them.[35] Ultimately, relationships of power on one side and gratitude and obedience on the other solidify, making mutuality impossible.

Gudorf's work on parenting suggests that parents, and especially mothers, often have real problems distancing themselves from their children, because their identities center on their parental role. In contrast to most Christian authors writing on parenting, this mother of vulnerable children declares that selfless love is not a possible or desirable goal for parents. In doing so, she calls into question that powerful cultural ideal of the all-giving mother that haunts so many women and fills them with feelings of inadequacy. This frees women to think about what else might fill their lives, for motherhood alone, clearly, is not enough for most. The hope is that when their lives are more full, women (and men) will be able to love their children more honestly and mutually.

Combining Work and Family

Bonnie J. Miller-McLemore's book *Also a Mother: Work and Family as Theological Dilemma* has on its cover a picture of a mother and child. The child is reaching up for the mother, and the mother is reaching one arm up to the tree above her. Miller-McLemore sees in the picture a child's need for her mother's love and the mother's desire both to give that love and to reach beyond herself for something more. The book explores the dilemma these seemingly conflicting desires present for contemporary Christian women. Miller-McLemore writes as a Methodist mother of three children and a theologian. She writes out of her experience as a woman who wanted to spend more time mothering her children than most academics do and more time working than most at-home mothers do. She wants an integrated life, in which work and family are both important priorities, but she has no "script" to follow. She knows no women who have done what she is attempting to do, and she is forced to become very clear about what she wants most, for she has time for little else.[36]

Miller-McLemore's struggle to live out mutuality in parenting with her husband, Mark, is ongoing. Her children pull her toward them, and her work pulls her toward it. She gives and receives both at home and at work and finds participation in both spheres mutually enhancing. Her experience with her children, for instance, brings the insight that "children themselves refuse to be something that one does on the side as an extra curricular activity when convenient. From a theological perspective, children are not products; children are gifts."[37] Her involvement with her children gives her perspective on children that most theologians lack, while the distance she gets from her children while she works allows her to process the experiential insights and make them part of a theological discussion on work and family.

Ultimately, Miller-McLemore seeks the balance of the woman in the picture of the cover of her book, who already knows that "only when she reaches for what is hers will the child, who has dropped her own doll to wet her lips on the delight of the apple, learn to reach for life herself. Only by loving herself can the mother fully love her child."[38]

Like Gudorf, Miller-McLemore affirms the necessity of self-love and rejects the model of the sacrificial mother who gives everything she has to her children. Like Cahill, she believes that gender need not determine the particular form of Christian vocation a person takes up. She offers readers what she herself wanted: a new model of a working mother whose role is not determined by cultural or traditional religious ideals but is based on the desires of individual persons for fulfillment and service in different areas of life. In her "pitch-in family," she and her husband decline the extra work that would cost them time with their children, but they also demand more of their children, asking them to play an active part in supporting the family home.[39] They seem to have found an enviable balance between work and family.

However, in a later essay, entitled "Family and Work: Can Anyone 'Have It All?'" Miller-McLemore wonders why the culture vilifies women for wanting such a balance while assuming that men can "have it all."[40] Going back to the Genesis creation story, she claims that Eve, too, is punished for wanting it all. She suggests that women reclaim Eve's healthy desire for wisdom (without forgetting that finitude is part of the human condition) and become "Daughters of Eve" by daring to hope that they can have lives that combine work and family. Still, she acknowledges that the tension between the two will remain a serious problem, even if societies become as family-friendly as feminists would like. This problem will not simply fade away.

Yet Miller-McLemore would not wish for that; working through it will, she thinks, yield more balanced lives for women and men. Her work speaks directly to what has become a central dilemma for contemporary Christian women, and it offers a road in between the early feminist ideal of a working woman who leaves her children behind, and the traditional ideal of a woman whose only vocation is motherhood. For Miller-McLemore only the murky middle ground of a woman who serves both at home and at work makes sense.

Reading the Pope into Dialogue with Theologians

If the pope were to speak with Miller-McLemore, he probably would find fault with her contention that men and women must fight instincts that seem natural but are probably more rooted in culture. He would most likely feel uncomfortable with her insistence that she loves her work as much as she loves her family. Miller-McLemore does not work because she must. On the other hand, in some sense, Miller-McLemore agrees with John Paul II that women's work and family commitments must harmoniously combine. She, too, is concerned about how work can encroach on a woman's identity as a mother. She differs because she thinks that men, too, must work to harmoniously combine work and family, and that women can be consumed by motherhood. She wants work and family for all, and in this desire, she is in harmony with the pope's concerns about family life, but not his theories about gender.

Similarly, while the pope might agree with Christine Gudorf that parents should not have undue power over children, he sees sacrifice as the appropriate model for mothers especially, but ultimately for all parents. He seems to put no limits on the level of sacrifice mothers can be expected to make. He knows that women do make incredible sacrifices for their children, and he praises and encourages this kind of mothering, rather than calling it into question.

Finally, while the pope would agree with Cahill's depiction of Jesus as someone who had great respect for women, he does not see in Jesus' treatment of women an affirmation and legitimization of their public roles. Rather, he sees women affirmed in their essence, and that, for him, means mothering. His strong sense of gender difference leads him to see distinctiveness where Cahill sees fluidity.

Thus each of the Christian feminist theologians discussed would share the pope's concerns about family, but differ with him about gender, sacrifice, and public roles. All of these women are mothers. Gudorf and Miller-McLemore each have three children; Cahill has five. None can be labeled "anti-motherhood" in any sweeping way. All celebrate motherhood as a good gift but mourn the overemphasis on it that has led so many women to forgo the search for public identity and public work that, they think, can be an important part of a Christian woman's vocation.

The Search for a Mother-God

As Christian feminist theologians have searched for ways to think through their rich identities as public and private persons, they have often thought about the language used to talk about God. Although at first glance these two discussions might seem unrelated, thinking in this area might be the key to ongoing dialogue about motherhood in today's church, for ideas about the gender of God have the power to reshape ideas about gender at home and at work.

Many theologians have argued that it makes no sense to speak of God only as male, for two reasons. First, God is infinite, beyond everything that we are. God cannot be identified with any one gender. God is not male because God is more than male and female and anything else we can imagine. Speaking about God as if "He" were male is, then, a form of idolatry, because we are worshiping something that is not God (i.e., a male God) as if it were God.[41] We embrace God's largeness by calling God not one name (Father) but many names. Second, it is wrong to call God only Father, because, in the famous words of theologian Mary Daly, "When God is male, male is God." That is, when we think of God as masculine, masculine attributes (and those who have them) tend to seem more godly, and those who do not tend to seem farther removed from the divine.[42]

The solution, according to many, requires breaking the habit of calling God "He." To do this, we need to begin to conceive of God as "She." Because we are so used to thinking of God as Father, it seems natural to begin by calling God "Mother." This solution has a great deal of biblical warrant, for the Scriptures image God as an angry mother whose cubs are taken away (Hos 13:8), a mother comforting her child (Isa 66:13), and a mother who does not forget her children (Hos 11:3–4).[43] The biblical writers also compare God to a woman kneading bread (Luke 13:18), a mother giving birth (Deut 32:18), and a woman groaning in labor (Isa 66:9).[44] Using mother-language has the virtue of retaining an analogy associated with the experiences of parenting and being parented, which seem as close as we get on this side of heaven to understanding divine love. In fact, it seems almost ludicrous to ignore an analogy that has so much power. As Sallie McFague says, "All of us, female and male, have the womb as our first home, all of us are born from the bodies of our mothers, all of us are fed by our mothers. What better imagery could there be for expressing the most basic reality of existence, that we live and move and have our being in God?"[45]

The problem with maternal God-language lies in the potential identification of God with the very kinds of mother-stereotypes that feminist theologians have identified as problematic. Mother-God is nurturing, nursing, birthing, sacrificing, and loving. While good and powerful images, they can be limiting. As Elizabeth Johnson claims, we want to avoid romanticizing, which, "while defining the role positively, actually limits and effectively subordinates women."[46] Johnson suggests that we keep in mind the analogical nature of all language about God. All images are somewhat like, but also unlike, God. However, it is also important to think through the implications of calling the one who mothers, God. Doing so means calling those who do the work of birthing and nurturing on earth God-like, recognizing women's likeness to God, reemphasizing their creation in God's image. In addition, we need to think about God as powerful, mighty, and mother all in one breath. Doing so helps us to rethink our understandings of mothers and of God.

Moreover, mother is not the only important female God-name. Elizabeth Johnson suggests calling God "Sophia-Spirit," because Sophia, the Greek word for Wisdom (a prominent name for God in the Hebrew Scriptures), is feminine.[47] Sallie McFague suggests friend and lover as well as mother.[48] In both cases, the combination of female images is fundamentally important. It forces the recognition that just as God is mother, sister, lover, wisdom, and friend, so too are women mothers, sisters, lovers, lovers of wisdom, and friends. Women are all of these things and all of these things are godly. Women, like God (and of course, like men) have many parts. Recognizing the many-ness in God is an important step toward recognizing the many-ness in women.

Perhaps this is precisely the recognition that can bridge the differences between the pope and women theologians, for interestingly enough, John Paul II also calls upon God as mother in his discourse on mothers.[49] This suggests that a reading of the pope's writing on motherhood that finds hope in affirmations of women's dignity, equality, and right to public work might just be correct, even if more dialogue with feminist theologians will have to occur before the official Catholic vision for women as mothers is fully conceived. In the meantime, Christian mothers who are struggling to balance their many roles might take comfort in the knowledge that many in the Christian tradition have looked at women like them and found an apt analogy for the God of all.

Can a Mother Have a Self?

The dialogue between John Paul II and three prominent Christian theologians presented here is an attempt to rethink the definition of a good mother. Much more dialogue will have to occur for men and women in the church to understand each other. Margaret Hebblethwaite writes in *Motherhood and God* that her project "is about finding God in motherhood, and finding motherhood in God. . . . I have tried to evoke a sense of what it feels like to be a mother, but I do not want to stop there. I want to show how God can bring meaning to the experience, and the experience can bring meaning to God."[50] Hebblethwaite's work speaks to the illumination that comes when theologians who are also mothers think out loud about their lives. As they do that, perhaps far fewer young Christian women will look with worry at mothers in the park, for they will be able to conceive of themselves as mothers in new ways. They will know that they can be mothers and also sisters, friends, and workers. They will know that they can be mothers without losing themselves.

When I think back over the last eight years with my sons, I am amazed at all that has happened. I became one of those mothers in the park that I had feared, and I realized the park was a wonderful place to be. I nursed all my boys for a year, submitting myself to their eating schedules, and enjoyed it. In the process of caring for my sons, I changed. My relationship with my son Thomas is perhaps the best example. With his birth, I realized I wanted to be home even more, so I decided to put off applying for full-time jobs for several years. As he has grown Thomas has come to have interests that are far from mine, and because he asks, I have read many books about airplanes, enacted many battles from Star Wars, and played many games of baseball in the park. My friends from graduate school would not recognize this person, this mom in the park, and yet they would. Even though to my son's friends, I am simply "Thomas's mom," to my students and colleagues I am also many other things. I did not lose myself as I feared I would. I have found that motherhood is a process of transformation, but it need not be an annihilation of the self, especially not of the Christian self called to serve both at home and in the world.

Discussion Questions

1. Have you ever experienced anxiety about becoming a mother or father? Does the ambivalence of mothers in this chapter seem selfish or understandable?

2. What key points are raised by respondents to the pope's teaching on motherhood? Would you respond similarly to one of the respondents?

3. Evaluate the validity of Cahill's claim that neither the Genesis creation stories nor modern social scientists treat gender as an all-encompassing category.

4. Is Gudorf correct to argue that parents should aim for mutuality, not sacrificial love?

5. What potential problems might there be with Miller-McLemore's vision of work and family for all? Does the pope's division of labor make more sense?

6. Is the search for a mother-god relevant to the contemporary discussion of motherhood?

– S E V E N –

Fathering in
Christian Families

Dominic's Doll

When our youngest son, Dominic, was two, my husband decided that Santa should bring him a doll. Dominic, who carried a blanket (his "That") with him everywhere and was often quite nurturing with his Star Wars action figures, seemed a perfect candidate for what would be the first doll in our three-boy household. We bought him a very plain boy baby doll with a bottle. When he opened it on Christmas morning, after seeing his brothers' light sabers and his own other, more masculine gifts, he tossed it aside without a second thought. "It's just Christmas," we thought. "He's overstimulated and can't deal with one more gift. He'll come around." But for weeks, Dominic expressed no interest in playing with his doll.

Then one night my husband, Martin, who is very talented in the art of voice imitation, gave the doll a squeaky voice, a manic personality, and a name, "Baby." Now sometimes in the evenings before we settle down to read stories, "Baby" will ask the boys to feed him or change his diaper, and he will beat up on them if they do not respond to his requests. "Baby," an aggressive, cartoon-like character, sometimes manages to get Dominic to hug and feed him, but unless Daddy is around to bring him to life, Dominic leaves him alone.

On those nights on which "Baby" has center stage, I sit back and watch my husband playing with a doll, surrounded by three laughing, adoring boys, and I wonder about fatherhood. Is Dominic's reaction to the doll an indication that nurturing does not come naturally to males? Does the very "masculine" way my husband and our sons play with the doll suggest that men and women care for children differently? What happens when my husband helps our sons play with a doll? Are patterns formed that will eventually allow our boys to embrace the nurturing of their own children? Will my husband's fathering, his interaction with them, shape them into men different than their friends, who are primarily raised by their mothers? Will our sons buy dolls for their sons, and if so, how will they play with them?

These days social scientists pay lots of attention to fatherhood. Experts ask some of the same questions that occur to me as I watch the males in my family interact. They ask about men's capacity for nurturing, whether men and women care for children differently, about the importance of fathers in children's lives, and how greater involvement of fathers might influence future generations of men. In short, they want to know what men can do, and how important it is that they do it.

All of these questions are important to Christian discussions of fatherhood because ethical discussions of what fathers ought to do depend in part on knowledge of men's capacities. The social science literature proves especially important here because the Christian tradition includes very little reflection on what it means to be a father. The few existing accounts of fathering are tied to discussions about the fatherhood of God. This chapter summarizes the recent social scientific findings on fathers and brings that information into dialogue with more specifically Christian reflection on the God Jesus called "Father." Both discourses point toward an ideal of fatherhood as a central vocation in men's lives, thereby furthering the argument that gender does not significantly affect the ethical norm of dual vocation for the Christian parent.

A Brief History of Fatherhood

Some historical perspective might help provide a context for the new social science data. It establishes that things were not always as they are now, and thus need not continue as they are. Robert Griswold surveys the history of fatherhood in his book *Fatherhood in America* and argues that fathers in America were once much more involved in their children's lives. Preindustrial work patterns on farms or in family-owned stores from the 1600s to the mid-1800s allowed men more time with their children. In addition, men took responsibility for the moral instruction of their children.[1] Child rearing manuals in these times were directed mostly to men, because they made decisions on how to rear children.[2] Children saw their fathers a lot more, because work and home were not as separate as they are now. Fathers thus had important roles in instructing children (especially sons) about their future work and had more time to engage in the kind of moral discussion that is commonly associated with mothers today.

During this time, fathers were not identified primarily with providing, in part because both men and women contributed to the task of providing for the home. In colonial times, the household "was a little factory that produced clothing, furniture, bedding, candles, and other accessories. . . . It was taken for granted that women provided for the family along with men."[3] Despite obvious differences in roles, women and men shared the tasks of providing for and instructing their children.

After the Industrial Revolution, most fathers' work moved out of the home and away from their children. Their role shifted from moral instruction to breadwinning.[4] The provider model of fatherhood became, according to Griswold, the most central, and it remains so today. It is not insignificant that in our culture "mothering" means nurturing, while "fathering" means supplying the sperm for one's offspring and perhaps financially supporting that offspring until it can support itself. The breadwinner role constitutes a primary way modern American men have understood their responsibilities as fathers.

The emergence of this role was not without its costs. Men concentrated on providing at the expense of relationships, for "when the division of labor removes the man from the family dwelling for most of the day, intimate relationships become less feasible."[5] In addition, the increasing pressure on men to provide more and more for their families diverted them from strengthening relationships with their wives and children. They were expected to be good providers first, and if they managed to also be loving or tender husbands and fathers, that was admirable, but not by any means required.[6]

In the 1920s and 1930s, with the rise of psychology and especially with the popularity of Freudian psychology, men came to be seen not only as breadwinners, but also as male sex-role models.[7] They were crucial to their sons' development as healthy, heterosexual men.

Their increased involvement with their sons in sports and other recreational activities seemed important. Their masculine but involved role included roughhousing, barbecuing, and advice-giving. Experts warned that if men were not around to train their sons in masculine ways, their sons would suffer.

In the 1960s and 1970s, as gender roles were questioned and many women left the home for the workplace, a new ideal began to emerge. While still a provider, the new father nurtures his children as his wife does, playing with sons and daughters, providing some of their physical care, and striving for strong, emotional relationships.[8] Dealing with these new demands for increased intimacy and nurturing and taking on more household responsibilities is a daunting task for many men, and an unwelcome one for some.[9] The new father has only partly emerged, most sociologists say, because earlier ideals remain dominant. So, although behavior has changed a little and ideals a little more, the new father has not yet fully arrived. This is a time of transition, in which a new ideal captures the imagination of some, while older ideals still influence the behavior of many. In this context we struggle with the question, "What does it mean to father today?"

What Modern Fathers Do

Although working mothers still put in more childcare hours than working fathers, fathers do more now than they did in the 1970s, when the women's movement took off.[10] Men in dual-career households now provide almost one-third of all childcare in the home, though most wives still "manage" the family.[11] Most writers agree that men's participation in child rearing has increased, though many caution it has not increased as much as many people assume. A revolution comparable to women's entry into the workplace has not yet brought men fully into their children's lives, but things are moving in that direction.[12]

Social scientists disagree about how to characterize men's interaction with children. Most agree that when men are involved, they tend to have greater involvement in the care and feeding of young children, probably because young children require so much care. Surprisingly, they have less involvement with older children, despite the cultural assumption that men are not as able to care for younger children but are quite capable of interacting with older children.[13] If men are in fact more involved, at least with younger children, social scientists wonder if they are involved in different ways than they used to be. Does more involvement mean different involvement?

According to some studies, men are changing in significant ways and becoming more like women, especially when they interact with older children. In one study men reported that they listened to children talk about their worries more often than their wives did, undermining stereotypical views of males as incapable of emotional interactions with their children.[14] Breakthroughs like this seem to come when men get involved in child rearing early on. When involved from the beginning, they tend to stay involved and break out of stereotypical patterns, so that sometimes their fathering begins to look like what we tend to think of as mothering.[15] According to this group of researchers, fathers make an impact not primarily as masculine role models but as warm and nurturing parents.[16]

Still, other researchers point out that many of the old patterns persist. Even in white middle-class families, men become more involved with sons than daughters, showing that the male sex role ideal has not completely faded away. Moreover, in dual-career families, men's work still takes precedence (no matter how much their wives earn) and keeps them away from their children more often.[17] These patterns of less male responsibility for children and traditional interactions with children are even more visible in working-class families, where traditional gender ideology may make it difficult for men to embrace the new ideal.[18]

In my classes and neighborhood, I find evidence both of new trends and traditional models. On the one hand, about two-thirds of my students are women, and women seem more likely to take my marriage class because they are thinking about marriage and concerned about how they will combine career and family. Most of these women assume that they, not their husbands, will have primary responsibility for their children. However, they do not share their mothers' assumption that mothering will be their only career. In addition, although I always have a few men in my class concerned about their future fathering, most of my male students simply do not think as much about balancing work and family responsibilities.

In my neighborhood, I see the results of those different emphases. Most women I know work, but they work part-time, sacrificing advancement in their chosen fields (psychology, teaching, nursing, law, etc.) because they want to limit the hours their children spend in day care and be there when their children come home from school. Most men I know are more active than their fathers were. They feed, bathe, and comfort children, and pick children up from school or day care when their wives cannot, but few are more involved in parenting than their wives. While they have changed their view of fathering, embracing some parts of the New Father ideal, they are still their family's primary breadwinners and they have not yet made the radical changes in their work lives that would enable them to become "new" fathers.

What Can Fathers Do?

Why haven't most fathers yet made radical changes in their lives? Are men not as capable as women of building nurturing relationships with children? Are they naturally less sensitive, expressive, or caring? Are they more suited for the more traditional breadwinner-by-day/father-knows-best-at-night role?

Some authors think so. David Blankenhorn, a leader in the influential Institute for American Values and author of the controversial book *Fatherless America,* argues that American families need fathers, but not "new" fathers. Blankenhorn traces most major social ills to the absence of fathers in families, but he argues not for more nurturing fathers, but for more committed traditional fathers. He proposes that Americans uphold the almost forgotten ideal of "The Good Family Man." What does it mean? Blankenhorn explains very clearly and simply, "Good: moral values. Family: purposes larger than the self. Man: a norm of masculinity.... Rough translation: He puts his family first."[19] Blankenhorn put flesh on his ideal by conducting interviews with 250 parents in eight states. He asked his subjects what it means to be a good father. He claims that people mainly talked about fathering in four different categories. Good fathers or good family men provide (act as the primary breadwinner), protect (keep the family safe from anyone who threatens it), nurture ("help their wives manage the household and assist their wives in providing the day-to-day affection and attention that children want and need from both of their parents"), and most importantly sponsor (encourage, advise, and prepare their children for adulthood).[20]

Blankenhorn's distinction between the third and fourth categories is telling. Sponsorship is crucially important. It comes out of masculine sensibilities and is therefore fundamental to fathering. According to Blankenhorn's subjects, nurturing, while important, is something men do to help out their wives, who act as the primary nurturers. Blankenhorn describes how fathers "supplement and complement the strength of mothers, who are the conductors, the emotional quarterbacks, the primary day-to-day overseers of the children's well-being."[21] He attributes this difference in roles to a difference in gender, saying that ordinary fathers see their fathering as a complement to their wives' mothering. Thus men do not nurture as much as women, but they sponsor more than women, and for this reason men as men are necessary to the family. They have distinct capabilities and they ought, according to Blankenhorn and many like him, to focus on those instead of trying to become their wives.[22]

Much of recent social science literature on fathering, however, calls these assumptions into question. One prominent sociologist reviewed recent research on paternal involvement and concluded that fathers and mothers influence children in similar, rather than distinctive, ways.[23] Another looked at child development studies and argued that men have just as much capacity as women to become attached to babies and that men's development of nurturing capabilities is crucial to successful parent-child relationships.[24]

One might argue that the emphasis on fathers' need to learn nurturing suggests that this behavior does not come naturally to men. Perhaps, then, Blankenhorn is right, and men would be better off concentrating on their natural strengths. However, women have much more cultural encouragement to nurture, and thus it makes sense that nurturing comes easily to many of them. Still, even mothers speak of the painful transition to parenting and the slow development of the capacity to sacrifice.[25] Moreover, new research by sociologist Scott Coltrane supports the view that all parents learn nurturing through their experience. His study of couples who share childcare tasks shows how fathers became more nurturing through their active participation in their children's lives.[26] Fathers in his study talk about "learning how to pay more attention to the details of his children's lives and to anticipate when they might get cranky or encounter difficulty with another child. This was best accomplished, according to many shared parenting couples, when fathers were left alone with children on a regular basis."[27] When given the opportunity to do the work, then, fathers succeeded.

But if these skills can be learned, why do many fathers seem to lack them? Coltrane noticed that men and women who did not share parenting tended to have the view that men were less capable of nurturing, and they used this to explain why their roles were more complementary than similar. Men and women who did a substantial amount of sharing, however, tended to "focus on the compatibility of their parenting skills and the similarities in their relationships with their children. For instance, they all reported that their children were emotionally 'close' to both parents." When asked whom his children went to when they were hurt or upset, one early and equal sharing father commented:

> They'll go to either of us, that is pretty indistinguishable. In fact it has long been the case that they'll address us and confuse us in addressing us. They'll say, "Dad, I mean Mom," or "Mom, I mean, Dad," and it has more to do with who they've been with for the last twenty-four hours. So they're hardly conscious of which one it is, in most cases.[28]

Coltrane found that the more parents shared childcare, the less distinguishable Mom and Dad became. Instead of mothering and fathering, he found parenting. Coltrane believes that as men and women continue to share the work of family life, their roles will continue to converge. The new father will truly emerge, and he will look an awful lot like the new mother, who will, in due course, have adjusted her parenting to reflect her new lifestyle.[29]

Effects of Fathers' Involvement on Children

If active, nurturing fathering is the future, it makes sense to ask if this is beneficial. The literature on fathers is vast and growing, making it difficult to say anything with certainty, but two major findings emerge.

First, a vast array of sociological literature indicates that families lacking a father are seriously disadvantaged. Though one might disagree with Blankenhorn's analysis of what fathers bring to the family, it is hard to discount his evidence linking social problems like crime committed by young males, teenage pregnancy, suicide, domestic violence, sexual abuse, and child poverty to the absence of fathers.[30] In a well-known article titled "Does Marriage Matter?" Linda Waite of the University of Chicago also establishes a link between single-parent households and children's drop-out rates and child poverty.[31] Waite relies to some extent on the research of Sara McLanahan and Gary Sandefur, who conclude that children living with just one parent are less likely to graduate from high school and college, more likely to become teen mothers, and somewhat more likely to lack direction as young adults.[32] To those who would argue that many of these negative effects have to do with income, not the loss of a father per se, McLanahan and Sandefur argue that a lot is at stake even for middle-class families.[33] While some social scientists believe that one cannot say for certain that the absence of a father is harmful because too many other factors contribute to a child's well-being,[34] the overwhelming majority assert that fathers matter and that their absence and lack of involvement harm families.

The flip side of the absent father problem is the involved father benefit. Many studies document the benefits of involvement for men, marriage, and children. While men complain of the drudgery and difficulty of child-rearing work (and sometimes report that more childcare means less happiness),[35] they also enjoy their interactions with their children and see themselves growing as persons as a result of those interactions.[36] While married couples experience increased conflict stemming from their mutual responsibility for their children,[37] they also experience increased empathy and solidarity.[38] While children do not benefit from just any father (and clearly lose when fathers are abusive or emotionally distant),[39] they clearly win when fathers become deeply and intimately involved in their lives.[40]

It seems then the sociological data on fathering justifies encouraging fathers to know and care for their children in more profound ways. How does the Christian tradition respond to this data? Does the

Christian tradition point in the same direction or focus on the models of earlier eras?

God the Father Reconsidered

The discussion of fatherhood in the Catholic tradition is very brief. John Paul II devotes only a few paragraphs to the subject in his letter *On the Family*. This short section assumes the father's breadwinner role but challenges fathers to move beyond "machismo," embracing their wives as equals. The pope's acceptance of equality in the relationships between husband and wives and his critique of machismo might be considered liberal. However, his assertion that people can be equal in dignity and still play different roles reveals his conservative side. He does not ask men to put fathering before work, as he asks women to put mothering before work. Rather, he assumes that men's work will never be "a cause of division in the family but [will] promote its unity and stability."[41] Moreover, when he describes men's fathering (which he upholds as crucial for the success of the family) he begins with men's love for their wives, implying that men in some sense parent through their wives.[42]

The pope suggests that fathers model themselves after God the Father, "revealing and reliving on earth the very fatherhood of God."[43] The choice of God the father as model is telling, for women are not told to model God for their children. Rather, like Mary, they should mother their children and teach them devotion to God. This fits nicely with the pope's idea that fathers are the leaders of the family who oversee the big picture, ensuring "the harmonious and united development of all members of the family,"[44] but stand somewhat outside the nurturing circle of women and children.[45]

How does all of this apply to the daily lives of Christian fathers striving to imitate God the Father? Again, the pope gives a general vision but leaves us to fill in the details. Surprisingly, despite all the attention social science has recently paid to fatherhood, theology has said very little. The lack of reflection on what it means to be a father is even more surprising given the fact that father is the central metaphor for God in the Christian tradition. Much energy has been spent in recent years criticizing the reliance on father-language for God and exploring new metaphors that may transform the way Christians think about God.[46] This is important and necessary work. However, there is still some value in reflecting on what it means for so many Christians to call God "Father."

When most Christians think about why they call God "Father," they reflect back to Jesus' own use of the word in prayer. There exists a great deal of scholarly debate over Jesus' use of the term. Theologian Robert Hammerton-Kelly, following Joachim Jeremias, makes the classic case that Jesus called God "Abba," or "Father," in prayer. This was, he claims, something new — something Jesus' Jewish tradition did not give him. The significance of the name, he argues, comes from what it reveals about Jesus' intimacy with God (the name "Abba," which Hammerton-Kelly claims was originally a babble-word best translated "Daddy," gives evidence of this). Jesus calls God "Father" and invites his followers to share in this way of naming God and in the intimacy this practice suggests.[47] Christians, according to this argument, have an obligation to take this central component of their tradition seriously and call God "Father."

Many contemporary biblical scholars have challenged this idea. They claim that although "Father" was common in early Christian usage, it was also common in Jewish piety at the time of Jesus, so we cannot know for certain that Jesus himself used the term.[48] Even if he did, these scholars argue, "Abba" does not mean "Daddy." It is, rather, the term an adult son or daughter would use for a father. Further, since it was used during the Roman occupation of Palestine when the emperor was called father, it may have political implications.[49] Thus, according to one scholar, "'father' as an address to God cannot be shown to originate with Jesus, to be particularly important to his teaching, or even to have been used by him. If indeed 'father' was used by Jesus, the context is less likely to be familial intimacy than resistance to the Roman imperial order."[50]

Not all biblical scholars subscribe to this minimalist reading of the New Testament evidence. For instance, feminist biblical scholar Elisabeth Schüssler Fiorenza accepts Hammerton-Kelly's claims about Jesus' use of father language and argues that this usage, along with Jesus' warning to "call no one your father on earth, for you have one Father —

the one in heaven" (Matt 23:9), comprises a piece of his larger message of resistance to the patriarchal structures of his time.[51] Thus Jesus
called God "Father" because he wanted to make the point that God has
ultimate power, not human beings or institutions. Calling God "Father"
is then a subversive act, because it displaces the authority of the family. This claim is not contradicted by the assertion that father-language
challenges the political authority of the times; calling God "Father"
when the emperor is addressed this way displaces political authority but
it also calls into question men's roles in families. Such an attempt to
question familial and political authority appears consistent with Jesus'
message of the coming of the kingdom of God, which is open to all
without respect to gender or class. Thus it is possible to see both Jesus'
use of "Abba" and his questioning of the use of "father" as a title for men
on earth as evidence that the Christian tradition challenges traditional
ideas about male authority inside and outside the family.

Despite the continuing scholarly debate about the claim that the
historical Jesus used the term "Father" in a unique way, there is no
doubt that father-language, with all its intimacy and patriarchal challenge, eventually became central in the Christian tradition. The early
Christians thought it important to name God this way, which suggests something of their intimate relationship with God. Generations
of Christians have, for the most part, followed their lead in liturgy and
prayer. What is the significance of this emphasis? What do Christians
mean when they call God "Father?"

For some theologians, the significance of father-language lies in
God's masculinity. John Miller, author of *Calling God "Father,"* maintains that in the Hebrew Bible, "the strongest, most benevolent power
at work in the universe...is neither son, daughter, nor mother, but
a unique father-God who is compassionately and effectively involved
and concerned with the welfare of his children."[52] According to Miller,
this understanding of a masculine father-God transformed fatherhood
in the biblical community by allowing males to place their energy and
desire for power at the service of women and children whom they supported and protected.[53] Fathers also became "the spiritual guardians
of their families," taking leading roles in family religious rituals and
directing the moral formation of their children.[54] For Miller, God is
clearly named "Father" in the Bible and provides for men the only

viable model for fathering, for "only God can cause males to fall upon their knees in voluntary submission. Or, put differently, only God can teach adult males to act as his obedient sons, and therefore good husbands to their wives and good fathers to their sons."[55] According to Miller, the Father God of the Bible shows men how to be strong while avoiding destructive or oppressive tendencies.

However, other theologians view the Bible differently. In a small personal tract, historical theologian Kenneth Parker challenges the traditional idea that the God of the Old Testament is an all-powerful, fear-inspiring, controlling God. He notes that the God of Genesis 2

> doesn't seem very organized and appears confused about his goals. Think about it: he makes the heavens and the earth, created man from dust, and then decides that he needs to provide a place for man to live.... This is when the Garden of Eden got started with plants for food and a river running through it. Like a muddled papa, he sees that man is lonely and creates birds and animals only to realize at the end of the process that he has forgotten the most important companion for man: woman.

At first, God "doesn't control man's reactions to the world being discovered, but takes delight in observing man's response." Yet this God tried to protect and control his creations by forbidding them to eat from the tree of knowledge, forbidding them to know all he knew. Parker affirms that he, too, has struggled to control his children. However, like the God of Genesis 2, Parker eventually comes to realize that he must grant his children their freedom,

> even though it leads to divine sorrow. That was the price of being a Creator fashioning creatures that create. Perhaps this is the most important lesson my sons have taught me. I am not, as their father, molding clay. I am forming lives — lives that will take direction independent of *my* choices, despite *my* deepest desires for them. I cannot direct, I can only lead.[56]

Parker is intimately involved in the rearing of his sons, trying to model the caring, committed God he knows as Father. He understands God the Father not so much as a strong, servant leader but as a loving, noncontrolling, involved parent.

Some process theologians go even further, viewing the biblical God as a "motherly father," a father who gives birth to a son,[57] and dies on the cross for his people, suffering with and for them.[58] This God is not far removed from the motherly image of the "Pietà." Pope John Paul I once said that "God is a father, but he is even more a mother."[59] If this is the Christian image of father, it is a radical image of a nurturing and sacrificing father, not a cold and distant one. This God, is, at least according to some scholars, a God transformed by his experience of being a father. These authors believe that God is not static or unmoving, but is rather involved with human beings and constantly changing or evolving, just like human fathers who are sometimes transformed by their care for children.[60] God who is called "Father" tells the Israelites in the Old Testament that he will be their God and they will be his people only if they keep his commands. Yet he forgives them again and again, despite the fact that they do not live up to the demands of the covenant. He never stops being their God, no matter what they do. Once intimately involved with them, he finds he cannot abandon them. Eventually, he finds that he loves them so much he would rather offer his own life than be separated from them. Some theologians find in the Bible a God who loves his people and suffers along with them even unto death.

Jesus himself provides the ultimate example of a self-giving man who teaches men about fathering simply by being someone who gives himself away.[61] Jesus illustrates the importance of self-giving love with the parable of the Prodigal Son (Luke 15:11–32), which centers on the father whose love is so powerful that he welcomes his lost son home with no questions asked. Even before he knows that his son has repented of his sinful ways, the father runs to meet his son and gathers him in his arms. This story offers a powerful model of a father who forgives beyond justice, embracing when others would shun.[62]

This image of father, the ultimate Father — who delights in his children and offers them their freedom, who never abandons his children, whose covenant commitment to Israel knows no bounds, who gives himself for his children, who welcomes wayward children home, and who is always there — offers a powerful challenge to the many fathers in our day who are not there for their children. Some theologians believe that abandoning this language would mean losing a great resource for calling fathers back to the family. Diane Tennis, a theologian who was abandoned by both her father and her husband, speaks eloquently to this point.[63] When women like Tennis and the male theologians discussed above affirm the need to call God "Father," it is difficult to ignore their pleas.

It seems we have much to gain from retaining fatherhood language for God if we remain conscious of the fullness of God's fatherhood. A father who suffers with his son and by extension all of his children is a father worth upholding. In recent discussions of God-language, many feminists have stated that they cannot embrace a symbol that does not speak to them. How can they call God "Father" when their own fathers were so uncaring? Perhaps emphasizing that God is the kind of father children *should* have and men *should* strive to become would answer some of these concerns.

Still, it is difficult to deny the problems that the image of God as father presents. The God of the Hebrew Scriptures especially can seem to some contemporary readers a controlling, overbearing, and violent tyrant. One needs to read the tradition as a whole, however, retrieving those parts of the tradition that offer men a nurturing father image after which to model their own fathering and contextualizing those passages in which God seems more aptly described as king, warrior, and judge. Even the most conservative advocates of calling God father typically defend God the father as a model for fathers who strive for "a lordship of service and of sacrifice" and speak movingly about the sacrificial love of their own fathers.[64] It is possible to retrieve the biblical image of God the Father without advocating the patriarchal models of earlier times.

Bringing God the Father Home

Of course, men themselves must then work out in their own terms what it means to be a father in a postmodern world. Looking to God the Father as a challenging model will help, as will thinking through the implications of Jesus' sacrifice and the willingness to forgive of the father of the prodigal son. Yet these images are quite general. They have more to do with "fathering" in general than with the specific tasks of feeding, playing with, talking to, diapering, coaching, and counseling children.

Thus, like women seeking to understand their Christian vocation as mothers, men will need to pay attention to the experience of those living through the nitty-gritty of parenting. When they do that, they will no doubt affirm that today fathering means much more than siring, providing, protecting, sponsoring, and nurturing on the side. Fathers who do the work of fathering find that they can become full parents to their children, not just assistants dependent on their wives' organizational and emotional impulses. Their love is deep, abiding, passionate, and grounded in everyday acts of loving-kindness. That is what the love of "Abba" God the Father is like, and that, more than any gender roles created by cultures, is what will count for Christian fathers who want to be central in their children's lives.

One might object that advocacy of an ethical ideal of active, nurturing fathers is not a new or controversial position. However, when one realizes that, on average, fathers interact with their children for fewer than thirty minutes a day, it is difficult to argue that contemporary families value fatherhood.[65] When few in the Christian community question the idea that men must work long hours to support middle-class families they rarely see, it becomes hard to maintain that fatherhood matters to Christians. This proposal is radical because active fathers — those who spent significant time interacting with children — are not the norm.[66] While some men can and do nurture, many more do not. Christian men are challenged to do better by the sociological data that shows the importance of fathers, by an embracing father-God who will not abandon his children, by the son of God who empties himself to save them.

In Christian terms, men are called simply to discipleship, to following the example of Jesus in public and in private. Jesus did not ask different things of his male and female followers. God does not ask different things of mothers and fathers, beyond pregnancy and nursing. Rather, the dual vocation of parenthood belongs to everyone. Christian mothers must ask themselves if they are fulfilling the public side of their vocation, while Christian fathers ought to challenge themselves to participate more fully in the private lives of those they love most.

Discussion Questions

1. What does the "Dominic's Doll" incident suggest about gender?

2. Have fathers changed significantly, or do the old patterns persist?

3. Is Coltrane right to suggest that nurturing is learned, or is Blankenhorn more correct to argue that a father should concentrate on being a "Good Family Man"?

4. Is it important to call God "Father"?

5. Is Rubio going too far when she writes that "active fathers are not the norm"?

– EIGHT –

Welcoming the Children

Stephen's Theological Dilemmas

When our son Stephen was four, he got into one of those classic four-year-old theological conversations with his preschool teacher. The teacher said something about Mother Nature, and Stephen informed her that Mother Nature was not real. "I believe in her," said the teacher. "You mean, you don't believe in Jesus?" "No," the teacher replied. "Are you a Jew?" Stephen pressed. "No," she said. "You're not a Jew, and you don't believe in Jesus?" Stephen replied in confusion. "No," the teacher said, "but it's okay if you do. We can believe in different things and still be friends." Stephen seemed satisfied with this answer, but he continued to try to work through the problem his teacher presented him with. That night he told his dad that since his teacher did not believe in Jesus, he didn't like her anymore. He told me that since his teacher did not believe in Jesus, he didn't either. "Besides," he said, "How can there be two Gods?"

The next day in my American Religious Diversity class, we were talking about how to live in a pluralistic world where so many people believe in so many different things. I told my students the story about Stephen and suggested that when he was confronted with religious pluralism for the first time, he came up with two possible solutions: he was wrong or "the other" was wrong. Unhappy with both positions, he tried them out by speaking about them to his dad and me. I guessed that many of my students would find his dilemma familiar and offered to present some alternative theological solutions to replace my son's first tries at figuring out how to deal with religious diversity.

This story suggests several themes relating to children explored in this chapter. First, what kind of care and guidance do children deserve? Would it be better if children did not have to face dilemmas of pluralism at early ages? Would they fare better in their own homes? Second, the theological insights of children surprise many parents. What can be learned from children? What would it mean to honor children as models of discipleship, as Jesus seems to have asked Christians to do? Third, what role should adults other than parents play in the rearing of children? Do they have a legitimate role as shapers of children's values and character? Fourth, what can adults ask of children? What would it mean to take them seriously as disciples in their own right?

Not very many Christian thinkers have asked these questions. This attempt at a theology of and for children is a relatively new enterprise in which theologians apply their knowledge about Scripture and tradition to the complex issues of how to raise a child.[1]

What Do Children Need?

Before asking what children need, we need to know what Christians think about where children fit in the family and how Christians understand children in relationship to their parents. John Paul II describes children as a gift from God and claims that a couple's relationship with their children deepens the one-flesh unity between a husband and wife.[2] His valuing of children is not unusual for a modern Christian, but his incorporation of children into a theological understanding of marriage is. When the Bible speaks about marriage in theological terms, the images used (two in one flesh, the union of Christ and the church, etc.) do not include children. Rather, the relationship between husband and wife is upheld as holy, and even this, as seen in chapter 3, does not constitute the dominant strain of the scriptural witness on marriage. Children, like lusty women, were often seen as a distraction from the single-mindedness required of those desiring holiness. Still, early in the Christian tradition, children begin to occupy a place of great importance in the family. They were seen as a justification for sexual relations in a time that prized celibacy and virginity and as an extension of the small Christian community begun by the parents.[3] Thus early Christian writings in support of marriage put children at the center of the family.

Contemporary Christian theologians look back to that tradition to justify a concern for the care of children today. They argue that children in our society are victimized by poverty and by divorce. Some even call for a liberation theology for children.[4] Others simply review the details of child suffering and ask for compassion. The U.S. bishops, for instance, begin a pastoral letter on children by asking readers to consider the following facts: every year in the United States 1.6 million children are aborted; one out of five children in the United States lives in poverty; the infant mortality rate in the United States is higher than in most Western nations; the United States has the highest divorce rate, the highest teen pregnancy rate, the highest child poverty rate, and the highest abortion rate in the Western world; teenage suicide has tripled in the last thirty years; more than 2.5 million children are abused every year; gunshot wounds are the leading cause of death for teenage boys; more than 25 percent of teenagers drop out of school; more than 8 million children lack health insurance; divorce has quadrupled in thirty years; almost one-fourth of children grow up in single-parent families; more middle-class families find it difficult to afford housing, healthcare, and education; all families face huge social pressures from a culture that is not family-centered.[5]

They conclude that "the tragic fate of too many children is not simply an economic problem, but a sign of moral failure and a religious test."[6] In the rest of their letter, they look to the Christian tradition for resources that speak to the important commitment to children's needs. They, and other theologians, assert that since the church has had a special concern for the care of children throughout its history, Christians ought to be the first ones protesting the current situation.

Many Christian writers claim a general commitment to children, especially the most vulnerable ones. Some emphasize that parents' responsibility to rear the children they bear is rooted in the natural connection between parent and child. Others, like historian Ted Peters, believe that attempts to locate Christian responsibility for children in biology say too little. According to Peters,

> Jesus stressed beyond-kin altruism. When he enjoined us to love our neighbor, he frequently illustrated that teaching with stories of foreigners such as the Good Samaritan. He told us to love our enemies. He gave no priority to one's biological kin, family, tribe, or nation. Applied internally to families, this translates into love

of social kin even when they are not biological kin. Sociobiology may be illuminating but, in my judgment, it certainly is insufficient for such an ethical foundation a Christian could embrace.[7]

Peters, who has several adopted children and is a passionate advocate of adoption, argues that natural bonds are not the foundation of Christian love for children. Against those who would emphasize the bodily connection between mothers and children in pregnancy and the genetic connection between parents and their offspring, Peters makes the powerful claim that Christians love children not because children belong to them, but because children belong to God. Their commitment to their children is rooted primarily in love, not biology.

What, then, does that commitment entail? For some, it is total. Diane Jacobs-Malina, writing out of concern for abused and neglected children, asserts that parents exist to meet children's needs.[8] Others, like theologian Christine Gudorf, assert that while parents must avoid using children as a means, parental love, like all love, should find its ultimate end in mutuality.[9] Parents and children exist for each other, and while parents are necessarily the primary givers in the beginning, they also receive, from the very beginning. Popular writers like Dr. Laura Schlessinger angrily remind parents that "children's very existence needs to be the central focus of family."[10] For her, this means that one parent must care for children at all times, for no "institution or other person [can] ever re-create that consistent, loving, and personal parental presence."[11] Children need, and have the right, to be cared for by their parents. Others argue that while parents have important responsibilities to get involved in their children's lives, the key is not full-time influence, but approaching family life as one would approach any other aspect of Christian life. That means figuring out what a disciple of Christ ought to do.

Because the second approach seems better grounded in Christian Scripture and tradition, this chapter focuses on parenting as discipleship. While chapter 5 argued for discipleship as a predominantly public ministry, it allowed that some family ministry can be viewed in this light, that is, caring for children may be seen as a part of Christian discipleship. Rodney Clapp's book *Families at the Crossroads* is particularly helpful for fleshing out a fuller understanding of this concept. Clapp says children are to be welcomed into the lives of parents because Jesus told his followers, who would have kept the children away from him, "Let the little children come unto me" (Matt 19:12–15) and because he asked them to do the same with strangers. Unlike most commentators, Clapp sees children as strangers. Children, he says, "come to us as aliens and have to learn to live in our world." They reveal to their parents parts of themselves that they do not know well and ask painful questions that force parents to clarify their core values. They show parents with their surprising wisdom that they are not theirs, but God's. In their expression of need, they remind parents of their connection to others.[12] In all of these ways, Clapp argues, children are strangers. When Christian parents welcome and care for children, they learn how to welcome strangers. In this sense, caring for children is not caring for one's own, but caring for God's own.

While Clapp might underestimate the natural pulls that connect most parents to their children, and thus the many ways in which children are not strangers, he illuminates something important here. Caring for children is sacred and fundamentally important work precisely because of the ways in which children are not our own. They are gifts that can never be fully trained or conformed to our expectations. I never expected our four-year-old to ask questions about the divinity of Christ. I was nearly speechless when he did. After all, his questions force me to explain my faith, to consider what sort of faith I want to pass down to him, and to think about what role other adults will have in answering his questions. Even though I thought I had all of that settled, our child led me to think again about questions of faith and child rearing.

What does he deserve from us, his parents? In general, a commitment to care for and shape him the best way we know how, along with a profound respect for who he is and will become. We do not own him, and nowhere in the Christian Scripture or tradition do I find a command that says we must give him everything, but we certainly must rear him and try to protect him from harm, even as we ready him for a life apart from us. Even as we try to fulfill his needs, we will receive the gift of his presence, which, the Christian tradition tells us, will illuminate the meaning of discipleship.

The Child as Model of Discipleship

One of the most startling things that Jesus says in the Gospel has to do with children, for in his teaching, "the child becomes the criterion of discipleship," "the actual envoy of the kingdom."[13] In Mark 10:15, Jesus tells his disciples, "Whoever does not receive the Kingdom of God like a little child will never enter it." His society regarded children as small adults in training and obligated parents to practice strict discipline. Children were understood to be simple or nonrational creatures who stood in need of training.[14] Given this culture, Jesus' advocacy of the child as a model follower becomes all the more striking. To those who thought of children as objects requiring care and formation, Jesus suggests quite plainly that children have qualities adults ought to develop.

What does it mean to become like a child? For theologian James Francis, the child's low status in society makes her a role model. When Jesus asks his adult followers to look more closely at children, he is telling them again that "the greatest among you must become like the youngest, and the leader like the one who serves" (Luke 22:26).[15] Central to Jesus' ministry was a reversal of social order, a refusal to honor status, an insistence that those on the bottom of society had something that those on the top lacked. Children are a part of "the least of these," and this means that they ought to be heard. Children's ability to receive, their innocence, their humility, and their dependence on others — all of these qualities force adults to consider who they are in relation to God and other people. According to Francis, Jesus' attention to children:

> contains a radical message in the reversal of the usual relationship of adult to child and represents a sharp reevaluation of the pivotal social value of honor. It is not merely the learning of a lesson from the child but a turning around to adopt the way of the child both in ready trust and dependency as the only way into the Kingdom, and in identifying with the weak and the dispossessed as itself the way of the Kingdom.[16]

When I think of what our own children have taught me in this regard, I feel overwhelmed. I can remember many conversations when I have listened to a child of ours talking about God and life, aware that I was hearing real insight that did not have as its source anything my husband, Martin, or I had said. One day at church our son Stephen asked me if women could be priests. "No," I told him gently, bending down so that I could look into his eyes "not now, but I hope that will change someday." "Well, I'm starting the Maritist religion," he told me. "For Mary, get it? And in my church, women can be priests, but anyone who doesn't think they should be can't be in it." He had insights into the significance of Mary that I had never considered. Another day Stephen came home from school distressed that his new friend would not allow the African American kids at school to play a game with him. "I told him the story of Jackie Robinson, twice, and he still didn't let them!" I marveled at his swift action, his refusal to stand back and not do the right thing, and his insight that telling a story was the best way to make his point without losing his friend. Another night I sat beside him as he tried to understand divorce (or "diverse" as he first called it), which had become an issue when we moved to a street on which two families consisted of moms with kids who came to stay every other week. Stephen talked to me with his hands, telling me that people who loved each other were "like this" (fists interlocking, pretending to hug and kiss, even fighting), while people who were getting divorced were "like this" (fists slowly moving apart).

In each situation I felt Stephen's vulnerability as someone learning for the first time about some very sad realities. I struggled with my reluctance to reveal what I thought was imperfect and with his ability to grasp the imperfection and respond ahead of me. In each case, I was ministering, but even more, being ministered to. My own vulnerability was revealed to me because I did not have the answers for him, because he acted or imagined himself acting on his own. I envied his ability to grasp the essence of things, feel sadness and anger, and imagine solutions. I hope that I can embrace some of his "way."

Contemporary society seems reluctant to turn to children and do as Jesus did and asked us to do. Jesus took the children in his arms, and he told his followers that when they embraced a child, they embraced him — "Whoever welcomes one such child in my name welcomes me, and whoever welcomes me welcomes not me but the one who sent me" (Mark 9:36–37). Our culture, however, shows a subtle, and sometimes not so subtle, indifference to children. One author posits that our inability to accept children comes from a reluctance to accept weakness in ourselves.[17] Others mourn the lack of respect for children's voices, movement, and schedules in an adult-focused world. They suggest that despite changing rhetoric, adults really do not want to see or hear children if they disrupt adult ways.[18] The new trend of putting children on drugs to control them provides just one example of this phenomenon. Another is the increasing tendency to organize so much of children's time (with day care, school, before and after school care, extracurricular activities) that adults do not have to deal with the energy and unpredictability of children's play. The insistence of popular religious and political voices on parental discipline and power is yet another. Into this atmosphere come Christian voices insisting that their tradition says something different about children. They ask:

> Is the state of our society such that children can really feel accepted and well in it? Don't they often feel more or less vividly that there is basically no place for them, or, if there is one, that it is at best on the periphery? And at the latest when they leave the niches and reserves arranged for them by education, they are regarded as a burdensome disruption of the peace.... Aren't special demands made here on a church which has received and has to hand on the good news of the unconditional acceptance of children?[19]

If so, according to theologian Janet Pais, then despite their fear of chaos, Christians should agree that "good parenting, in fact, must include the ability to accept a little chaos in one's life. We like to think that we can control everything, but we can't. We aren't meant to. And children make this abundantly clear." Pais reminds us that Jesus, God the Child, brings chaos, too: How we receive them both proves key.[20]

The voices of theologians who speak on behalf of abused children are particularly strong on this issue. From these advocates, many of whom have survived child abuse, come warnings about limiting parents' power and paying attention to the good in children. One theologian warns that when adults try to control children, they ignore the fact that Christ took the flesh of a child. She suggests they try to focus on the image of the child Jesus and on the divine child incarnate in each person.[21] The infant Jesus, she claims, brings Christians face to face with a God-child. Many Catholic theologians argue that God becoming human means everything human is honored. Those who speak for abused children recall that God first came as a baby, signifying that "vulnerability reveals God."[22] Instead of violating that vulnerability, feminist theologian Rita Brock suggests we ought to hold it in sacred trust.[23] Moreover, others have asserted, honoring the vulnerable child means enabling children to say no to adults, even their own parents, when necessary.[24] As abuse survivor Janet Pais reminds us, "The child, every child, is Christ for you. There is no need to be afraid."[25] In listening to their sons and daughters, then, parents are sometimes in the presence of Christ, and this belief should shape their response.

Caring for Children: Godparents and Other-Mothers

If the Christian Scriptures offer a model of care, concern, and respect for children, they do not particularly emphasize the relationship between parents and children. In the Christian tradition, however, clearly children quickly assumed a central place in thinking about the family. Still, the tradition holds on to the idea that parents do not own children, nor do they have full responsibility for them or power over them. Rather, children ultimately belong to God and are formed not just by parents but by a church community. Godparents are a primary example of the respect the Christian tradition has for the role adults other than parents play in the rearing of children.

The early church baptized adults after a lengthy process of catechesis and preparation that their sponsors shepherded them through. Sponsors guaranteed the faith and integrity of new Christians and helped them make changes in their lives that would allow them entrance into the church. In about the fifth century, in response to St. Augustine's idea that original sin is passed down to all persons and must be washed away, infant baptism became universally practiced, and the adult catechumenate all but disappeared. Godparents arose in response to the problem that baptism requires a statement of faith. Godparents supply the needed faith for the infants being baptized and promise that the child will be raised in the church and educated in the faith.[26]

Today godparents support the parents in their primary role as religious educators of their children. The revised baptism liturgy, which dates only from 1969, for the first time requires parents to attend. Earlier generations of Catholic parents often stayed home while the godparents took children to the church for baptism. The new rite has "an increased emphasis on the role of parents as their child's first teachers"; it gives to parents liturgical roles that godparents previously held, and in most parishes parents, not godparents, are required to attend the orientation.[27] Some argue that our increasingly mobile society makes godparents obsolete.[28] Others believe that strong godparents "who are willing to work with parents to teach children the basics of their faith" are needed now more than ever. They see alternative models in African American Catholic churches and Hispanic Catholic communities in which godparents and other adults in the community do take an active role in making sure that children are raised in the faith.[29]

The Catholic tradition of godparents recognizes that parents are not always the best guarantors of their children's faith or faith formation. Rather, other adults in the community sometimes serve as important sponsors of children.[30] This tradition ought not to be forgotten. A religious rite that asks godparents to bring children to church while parents stay home says a great deal about Catholic thinking on faith and family. Perhaps the new rite has moved too quickly to a parent-centered model more in line with the parent-centered formation model of contemporary culture but less in line with the profound traditional insight that parents need help forming children. The fact that despite the difficulties godparents face in having an influence on their godchildren most Catholics do not think that godparents are obsolete and have hope for the practice says much about the continuing validity of this insight.[31]

In our son Stephen's life, theological questions and insights have come not only from conversations with and about godparents,[32] but also in conversations with teachers and other adults. A believer in Mother Nature raised questions in his head about his beliefs, caused him to think about the significance of his faith, and forced him into relationship with "the other" in a very personal way. In his teacher's gentle insistence that whatever their different beliefs they could be friends, he found a model that goes beyond tolerance to genuine encounter. His teacher did not deny their differences or even try to smooth them over. She showed a deep respect for his faith and evidenced a faith of her own. A godmother of sorts, she taught him something that day, and while I hope that his Catholic godparents will one day teach him more about the faith of his baptism, I pray that he will not forget her witness, a witness that I, a fellow Christian, could never have given him.

Many would argue, though, that this is precisely the problem with exposing children to other adult teachers. Parents want influence over their children. They do not want other adults doing the moral formation they claim is their own. This desire should not be discounted. It is natural for parents to have a desire to form their children and John Paul II certainly affirms parents' place as primary educators of their children.[33] Still, it seems possible and perhaps more traditional to allow for parents' primary interest in combination with the influence of other adults.

This is precisely what African American women talk about when they tell stories of "other-mothers" who are significant in the lives of their children. In many African American communities, children are mothered by more than one woman. Because of their strong sense of connectedness, other adults are given more influence over and assume more responsibility for children's lives. For instance, in these communities it is much more common for adults to correct or discipline children who are not their own. Children are seen not as private property, but as vulnerable human beings who need the care not only of blood-mothers, but of grandmothers, sisters, aunts, cousins, and neighbors, their other-mothers who share in the project of child raising.[34] The other-mother model gives a positive valuation of the role of other caring adults in the lives of children. Miller-McLemore notes, in contrast, that at most white American gatherings, most parents see themselves as responsible for their children only. "Few would discipline another child, even if they found the behavior wrong or inappropriate.... To do otherwise oversteps certain customary bounds. Many an Asian, African, or African American mother would see these boundaries as rather reckless and absurd. In many ways they are."[35] The alternative vision she presents upholds more of a "village" ideal in which parents and children step out of their nuclear family boundaries into the larger Christian and human families.[36]

Christian theologians like Stanley Hauerwas argue, based on the New Testament tradition, that for Christians the first family is not the nuclear family, but the church. He claims that just as marriage is a vocation, so is parenting. That means that parenting is an office of the whole community, and not just of those who happen to have children. Both the single as well as the married exercise parental responsibility for the community; they just exercise different forms of that responsibility. Therefore those who teach, those who take care of the sick, those who stand as moral examples, all perform a parental role.[37]

Hauerwas believes that adults in the community can and must parent each other's children, and he has real confidence that Christian communities so constituted can form the characters of Christian people. For Hauerwas, it is not the family that forms us, but the church. He asserts that "if we have not first learned what it means to be faithful to self and other in the church, then we have precious little chance of learning it at home."[38] Character, according to Hauerwas, is formed in Christian community and by the Christian tradition. He ridicules the popular phrase "the family that prays together stays together," which suggests to him that the good of religion lies in its benefits for family unity. Instead, he suggests that the church provides the glue for the lesser but still important community of the family.[39] Hauerwas's insights about the significance of the church affirm in yet another way the positive influence of adults outside the family on young Christians within.

With godparents, other-mothers, and the ideal of the church as first family, Christians challenge the dominant idea of families as havens unto themselves. They open themselves to the influence and shaping of others who also care for their children.

Children as Disciples

When our son Stephen was wrestling with profound theological questions, he caused me to think about how he deserves to be cared for, how open children are to receive and question their faith, how much influence nonparental teachers and role models should have in his life, and what I can expect of him. Obviously I cannot expect him, even at this very young age, to believe everything I do or accept without question the demands I may place upon his life. Already we have bat-tled over going to church. He has run away in protest, though only down the street, and has made his body go limp so that I have to carry him into his Sunday school room. Once there, according to his teach-ers, he is helpful, happy, and brimming with (mostly very orthodox!) theological insights. He continues to practice his own style of devotion whenever he is near a statue of Mary, to talk to me about the greatness of God, and to profess occasional unbelief. What are we to do with this young, becoming and yet not-becoming Christian who is ours but not ours? What are his responsibilities to siblings, parents, and church?

Many writers acknowledge that parents are simply not able to shape children according to their wishes. The view of child as blank slate on which parents write is outdated. Professor of religious education Anton A. Bucher writes that children are not just empty vessels into which we pour things; "they also form themselves."[40] He cites studies of infant development showing that even from the earliest weeks of life, children develop a sense of themselves and get annoyed when they cannot do things in their own way. He cites education experts who say that children interpret everything they take in, so education only works if children interpret what is said in the intended way and accept it.[41] He calls attention to the original ways in which children think about theology and philosophy and asserts that they do not simply mimic adults. Their insights are their own. The child is a subject who "perceives things in its own way and reconstructs an independent view of the world."[42]

All of this should indicate that parents do not fully control children and are not fully responsible for them. Not simply objects of parental modeling and training, children are subjects, creating themselves by filtering through all the various "teaching" that comes to them and deciding what to accept. They are not simply shaped by others; they also shape themselves.

The Christian tradition contains many stories of young adults who reject their upbringing to join the church. Francis of Assisi ranks among the most famous.[43] Francis grew up in a wealthy family that expected him to take over the family business, but he chose a life of poverty and service instead. Like many other religious, he felt called to leave behind the world of his birth and embrace a new community. The stories of the saints offer a profound recognition that individuals, even children, can choose or not choose Christian life. Thus when discussing children, it is not enough to talk about those who aim to shape them. We must also talk about children themselves as moral actors in their own right.

Contemporary Christian thinkers assume this model when they speak about what children contribute to families. John Paul II claims that children "offer their own precious contribution to building up the family community and even to the sanctification of parents."[44] The implication here is that children are not only served *by* families, but also serve them, even unknowingly. The pope highlights one particularly powerful example of this when he points out that children are signs of the reality of their parents' love.[45] As I always tell my students, you are proof that your parents had sex at least once! Your very existence gives evidence of your parents' passion and union. This sign value becomes even more powerful in interethnic or interracial marriages in which children clearly look like both parents. Each day parents encounter the gift of their children's physical reality, proof of their connection. Their children's bodies reveal their one-flesh unity. When divorce breaks families apart, children stand as reminders that relationships that seem broken never quite disappear. In their very presence, then, children are gifts to parents.

Beyond this, children offer gifts of their own making. The U.S. bishops speak of children "acting as God's instruments" and of parents "being formed by God through [their] children."[46] Children act as God's instruments simply by showing up and being recognized as new creations of abundant goodness, but they also form their parents in more active ways. Children often make their parents stop, look, and appreciate the goodness in the world. They notice the purple flowers in the grass, the airplane flying overhead, the hill that begs to be climbed and run down, the dog that must be petted, and the worm that is sizzling on the summer sidewalk. They notice and refuse to ignore what they see, no matter how pressing another obligation. They appreciate the grandeur of the world like no one else. They also appreciate those who love them. Our sons have showered me with more love than I could possibly give them. They try to outdo each other in describing their love for me, telling me that they love me first "two hundred," then, "twenty-seventeen-a million," or finally, "infinity." Even, or maybe especially, on the days on which I feel I have been less than adequate as a parent, they tell me how beautiful I am, run up and give me knock-down hugs, and insist that I am the best mom they have ever had. I can only respond to all of this with deep love for them and their Creator. In their love for me, my sons are divine instruments, calling forth wonder and awe.

Many Christian parents have written of experiences of love, but children can also act as God's instruments by inspiring anger and professing hate. Less frequent than feelings of love, but every bit as intense, are feelings of anger that most parents admit to. After hours of relentless crying or whining, a long day of sibling rivalry, or a long period of parental testing, it is a rare parent who has not sometimes thought, "I want to throw him out the window!" We can read this anger as evidence (for those who need it) that human beings are not in control of every aspect of their lives, including their very selves. Intense anger is revelatory because it is a reminder of the weakness of human persons, of how much parents need something bigger than themselves to rely on. In moments when my children express their own hatred, I am similarly humbled by the realization that I cannot control my children's feelings toward me.

I am also sure that my greatest and most challenging task is to tell them of my persistent love for them despite what they do or say, and, what is more, to mean it. My children challenge me to love without limit every day, no matter what, and reveal my inadequacy as a "good enough" but imperfect parent who keeps on trying, knowing she will keep on failing. More than graduate school, marriage, or anything else I have ever tried, my children have taught me that I am finite (limited by my human-ness) but God is not.

Bonnie Miller-McLemore has also suggested that children teach parents during pregnancy and during lactation. As we saw in chapter 5, she believes that in pregnancy, unity and interdependence with another are learned, for "in the pregnant body, the self and the other coexist. The other is both myself and not myself, hourly, daily becoming more separate, until that which was mine becomes irrevocably another. In the pregnant moment I am one, but two."[47] In lactation, writes Miller-McLemore, "I know by knowing physically the feelings of the other, because they are paradoxically both mine and not mine."[48] Nursing mothers know that they are connected to others, that meeting the needs of others within and outside their families is natural and necessary. For Miller-McLemore, both experiences result in "maternal knowing," an experiential knowledge having to do with empathy and connection. This special knowledge shapes women and can, if shared, shape fathers and others as well. Once again, the child leads the way.

Children lead, too, because they force their parents to think about who they are and how they really want to live. If parents are responsive, children's questions ("Why do you have to go to work?" "Why can't we go outside and play after dinner instead of doing the dishes?" "Why aren't there any black kids on our street?" etc.) can be provocative and rightly so.[49]

Moreover, as Miller-McLemore writes, "working out a life with or without children demands that people consider their limits of life, letting some aspirations go while claiming others instead. These may be among the hardest decisions of rightful living."[50] Children take so much time, and parents have to make difficult choices in order to have enough time for themselves as individuals, their marriage, their children, their work, and their other interests or passions. Limits must be set and recognized, for children refuse to fit neatly into one's previous life.

Finally, children force clarification of values because they represent the future.[51] Faced with those who will outlive them and carry on their name, parents must decide what stories to tell, what traditions to teach, what values to make central. They have to become tradition-bearers, not just tradition-receivers, and that means they have to know what is important and what is not.

Many of the ways children form parents discussed above are based on who children are and what they do instinctively, rather than actions they perform because they know they ought to. It would be strange and unnecessary to command a child to ask probing questions or take time to smell flowers. Yet when they do these things, they are, in fact, acting as disciples of Christ who inspire and challenge those around them. What more might we ask of children? If one accepts the arguments made thus far in this chapter (that children have a right to be cared for, that other adults may play a role in that care, that they are — according to Jesus — models of discipleship, that they are subjects in their own right, and that they form their parents by their presence and natural actions) and the last two chapters (that Christian mothers and fathers can and should care for their own children and the children of others), what implications does this have for questions about what children ought to do in families?

Perhaps the most important insight gained from this discussion is that children as subjects, as beings capable of religious understanding, as dependents of parents who do not exist solely to serve children's needs, do have family duties and responsibilities. Their relationship with their parents begins at an extremely lopsided point (parents give and infants mostly take) but moves gradually toward mutuality.[52] For instance, chores comprise a crucial part of family life. Children ought to take responsibility for chores in families not just because they will learn discipline by doing so, but because through this work they will understand that no one in the home exists just to serve them; rather all members of the family help each other so that life inside the home runs smoothly and life outside the home is possible. By sharing in the work of the home, they come to understand that they are connected to others, because if they do not do their part, everyone else will suffer.

Children taught from an early age to think of their family as a community of disciples where all are responsible for all (according to the abilities of each) will be more likely to do their share. In what Miller-McLemore calls a "pitch-in family," everyone knows that his or her role is crucial. In contrast to the "milk and cookies family," in which (whether Mom works or not), Mom is ultimately responsible for meeting people's needs and making sure things run smoothly, the pitch-in family asks more of children.[53]

Does this mean that children lose? Not necessarily. If they lose a few hours of free time with friends each week, they stand to gain a few hours more of a parent's time for talk or play. If they lose some of the blissful freedom of childhood, they gain experience in loving others through their actions. Miller-McLemore asks whether

the narrative of the "pitch-in" family [is] more wholesome than the cookies-and-milk narrative. . . . Embodied in this pithy phrase is the idea that given love, children also need daily exercise at the practice of loving others as they love themselves, and this means a family system in which their pitching in is also essential to the family's functioning.[54]

The argument here is not "milk and cookies would be nice if we could afford it but since we need the money, we all have to help Mom out." Rather, it is "we are all disciples of Christ with public vocations, family responsibilities public and private, and personal needs and wants." For children, school is the training for future work and an arena in which to practice Christian virtue; for adults, work — paid or not — fulfills a commitment to church and/or society. The success of family life depends on family members' capacities to respond to each other and others in love, and this requires a just and reasonable distribution of duties.[55] Pitch-in families can claim "we are all in this together, for our sake and the sake of others."

In my own family, because our children are still young, my husband and I find ourselves very much at the stage in which we give more than they. Still, we try to tell our children that we work because we feel called to, not because we need the money, that they have to help because we are a team, not because we cannot do it alone, that we expect a lot of them because they have an obligation to engage in loving service, not because it will teach them to be tough.

Putting the emphasis on their abilities and obligations as Christians, we risk underestimating their needs and overestimating our own. The voices of children who feel neglected and lonely continue to echo in my head. However, a strong sense of children's intrinsic value and of their right to be cared for can mitigate this tendency and allow for a different kind of family space in which children receive the love they need and the respect they deserve.

Discussion Questions

1. Where are the obligations of parents to children rooted — in love or biology?

2. Evaluate Rodney Clapp's claim that children are strangers and should be treated as such.

3. Should Christians look to children as models of discipleship? Does this claim assume a simplistic notion of faith?

4. What key insights do victims of abuse offer to Christian parents?

5. What evidence does Rubio provide for the claim that the Christian tradition allows other-parents to care for children? Do you find this evidence convincing?

6. Does the pitch-in family model ask too much of children?

Divorce and Remarriage in Christian Families

Tensions in an Age of Divorce

According to most sources, about half of all marriages contracted today (45 percent of all first marriages and 60 percent of all second marriages) will eventually end in divorce.[1] The culture is becoming more and more accepting of divorce. Teachers know to tell children to get permission from Mom *or* Dad, to ask before assuming that a mother or father shares a child's last name, to expect that some of their students will be suffering through a separation or divorce. Greeting card companies have cards to celebrate divorce and second marriages. Some Christian denominations have even created rituals to mark divorce as a turning point in the lives of believers. Divorce no longer sets one apart; it affects almost everyone in some way.

Even though the divorce rate has increased exponentially since the 1950s, it is important to put this increase in perspective. Divorce rates have steadily risen since the turn of the twentieth century, though the increase leveled off in the 1950s. The 1960s counterculture did not initiate the trend toward seeing divorce as a viable option, though it certainly pushed the trend further, as did the no-fault divorce laws that became popular in the 1970s. However, recent studies reveal a decline in the divorce rate after a peak in the early 1980s, perhaps because of a greater awareness of the effects of divorce on children.[2]

For Christians, the issue proves particularly complex. Several New Testament texts specifically address divorce, and while most commentators agree that these texts include the authentic words of Jesus, discerning their meaning is difficult. In some texts, Jesus seems to rule out divorce and remarriage altogether, but in other places he seems to allow for exceptions. In addition, while the Roman Catholic Church has traditionally not allowed for divorce or remarriage, most Protestant and Orthodox churches make exceptions for both. Heated discussions of divorce among theologians have centered on interpretations of Scripture, explorations of traditional teaching, and pastoral problems such as whether remarried persons should receive the Eucharist or serve in positions of authority in local parishes. Such issues need addressing, but others are more pressing in a culture and church in which divorce and remarriage often happen: What are the effects — positive and negative — of divorce? What are the ethical obligations of parents and children in broken and reconstructed families? How can broken and reconstructed families live out the vision of domestic church that is given as a gift and challenge to all families in the church? With these questions, the discussion moves beyond the moral legitimacy of divorce and remarriage to a Christian family ethic for all kinds of families.

What Did Jesus Say and How Much Does It Matter?

While few in number, the biblical texts on divorce are overwhelmingly negative. The scriptural witness of divorce is found in six New Testament texts: 1 Corinthians 7:10–11; 1 Corinthians 7:12–13, 15; Mark 10:2–12; Matthew 19:3–9; Matthew 5:32; and Luke 16:18. In two of the three synoptic Gospels (Mark 10:2–12 and Luke 16:18) Jesus states that divorce is not allowable for any reason and claims that remarriage following divorce amounts to adultery. These words are significant, for they represent a rare instance in which Jesus directly responds to a concrete moral issue. The Jesus of the Gospels typically speaks more indirectly in parables and exhortations, but in this narrative Jesus gives his opinion on a current, specific moral dilemma. Asked about divorce, Jesus says that although the Mosaic law allowed for it, God's original plan as set forth in the book of Genesis was lifelong marriage.[3] He explains, " 'For this reason a man shall leave his father and mother and be joined to his wife, and the two shall become one flesh.' So they are no longer two, but one flesh. Therefore what God has joined together, let no one separate" (Mark 10:7–9; parallel in Matt 19:5–6). When the disciples question him again, he asserts that the man who divorces his wife and remarries commits adultery, as does the wife who divorces a husband and remarries. The prohibition on divorce and remarriage applies to both men and women and seems absolute.[4]

Most commentators agree that though the circumstances of the dialogues may be frames used by Luke and Mark, the saying attributed to Jesus is, in fact, his.[5] Two possible alternatives are laid before him, but he rejects these and offers his own more conservative view. In Matthew and Mark, his response is placed in the context of a debate between different groups of Jews. The Hillel school thought that divorce should be granted for even trivial reasons if men were dissatisfied with their wives, while the Shammai school believed that divorce was justifiable only for serious reasons.[6] Jesus' view differs from those of both schools. His absolute position and his grounding of that position in one-flesh unity seem clear.

Matthew 19:3–9, however, complicates the picture, because Matthew's Jesus adds an exception clause — "whoever divorces his wife, except for *porneia*, and marries another commits adultery." A vigorous debate over the clause's authenticity is ongoing. Did Jesus add this exception or did Matthew, and does it matter?[7] Interestingly, many liberal Protestant and Catholic scholars who believe it is Matthew's addition still take it to be authoritative because it is part of the New Testament tradition. Joseph Fitzmyer, for instance, agrees that "judged form-critically, the New Testament divorce texts yield as the most primitive form of the prohibition one that is absolute or unqualified," but claims that to make this absolute prohibition normative would be to give into fundamentalism.[8] Similarly, Richard Hays argues that it does not matter who added it: "The point is that some early Christians — whether Matthew or his predecessors — found it necessary to supplement the received tradition with a qualification."[9] Fitzmyer and Hays agree that the New Testament accepts diversity and reflects adaptation, and they believe contemporary Christians should as well.

More conservative Catholic scholars tend to accept the exception clause as authentic, but interpret it differently. The argument centers on the meaning of *porneia*. The traditional scholars argue that the word in this context means incest, as it does in related passages (most notably Acts 15:20, 29, Acts 21:25, and 1 Cor 5:1), and not adultery, because Matthew would have used the Greek word *moicheia* if he wanted to speak specifically about adultery, as he does in 19:9.[10] They note that this difficult command fits with other hard sayings; Jesus was not known for making exceptions.[11] They also call attention to the trajectory of the story that begins with two opposing views and ends when Jesus offers a different, more shocking opinion. If *porneia* simply means adultery, as many scholars believe, then the amazement of the disciples is hard to understand. If *porneia* means incest, then, these scholars believe, Jesus taught that unlawful marriages are not valid and divorce (defined as separation from an erring spouse) is possible, but remarriage is not.[12]

Conservative evangelical scholars tend to take the more common view that *porneia* means adultery, but they too argue that the clause is meant to apply to separation, not remarriage. In a groundbreaking article, William Heth argues that Jesus must be referring to separation. He notes that the church fathers clearly interpret it this way from 100 C.E. or so onward; thus "if Jesus did not introduce the idea of separation without remarriage, someone else must have done so."[13] Jesus' understanding of divorce derives from his view of marriage as one-flesh union. Divorce does not dissolve a previously existing marriage (it still exists, despite the separation), and thus remarriage is adultery. Under the exception clause, then, a man may dismiss his wife (and separate from her) only if she is guilty of adultery, but remarriage after divorce is adultery regardless.[14]

As the preceding analysis indicates, if scholars could agree on the authenticity of the exception clause, they might still disagree on its meaning because of the controversy over the interpretation of *porneia*. Scholars commonly translate it as adultery, incest, or sexual immodesty. Richard Hays makes a strong claim that we should view *porneia* as "a summary term for all the sexual offenses proscribed in the Holiness code of Leviticus 18–20."[15] This would mean that the term includes both adultery and incest as well as bestiality, homosexuality, and intercourse during menstruation. Hays believes the author intends to soften Jesus' absolute teaching by adding a broad exception for various kinds of sexual immorality. Even if we accept this definition, however, the problem of how to interpret it in a contemporary context remains.

Paul's commentary on divorce, in 1 Corinthians 7:10–11 and 12–14, does not make things any easier. He assumes Jesus' absolute prohibition of divorce and remarriage but adds his own exception: if a believer is married to an unbeliever who wants a divorce, the believer is free to divorce. The "Pauline privilege" gives believing Christians an out. How are contemporary Christians to interpret Paul's exception? Does he make it in the spirit of Christ's teaching, recognizing that Jesus set up not an absolute law but an ideal to which exceptions would inevitably be made? Or does Paul's exception acknowledge that Jesus was talking about Christian marriage but not secular marriage? Or is Paul departing from the law of Christ?

The Jesus tradition on divorce seems most clear in the Markan and Lukan texts, which allow for no exceptions and call followers of Jesus to a higher standard. Paul admits that his exception is his own, and while Matthew does not, few scholars dispute that it is. It seems doubtful that sexual offenses like adultery justify divorce for Christians. The biblical tradition includes many examples of spouses who remain loyal to straying partners, the most prominent being Hosea (who stays with the prostitute Gomer) and, metaphorically speaking, Yaweh (who maintains his loyalty to Israel despite her constant affairs with other gods). These examples articulate a powerful biblical theme that good people keep their commitments even when others do not. Jesus, who preached a morality untouched by legal casuistry, would not seem to encourage exceptions to marriage vows on this basis alone.

Further, the argument that the New Testament canon includes exceptions is vulnerable to the criticism that not everything in the New Testament is of God. Perhaps the early Christian communities adapted Jesus' teaching on divorce. They also adapted his teaching on the equality of men and women in order to better fit into their society and left future generations of Christians a legacy of "love-patriarchalism" that mutes the radical equality preached by Jesus. Later Christians adapted Jesus' harsh sayings on violence and money to mixed ends. Are these authentic adaptations or have Christian people looked for ways to soften Jesus' teaching because they felt unable to live it out? While adaptation of Paul's teaching may prove legitimate and even necessary, the same cannot be said of Jesus'. The words and example of Jesus of Nazareth demand the highest fidelity. However, a review of the crucial questions contemporary Christian theologians have raised with respect to Catholic teaching on divorce shows the uniqueness of this view.

Indeed, many Catholics question the church's absolute prohibition of divorce.

Catholic Teaching on Divorce and Its Critics

When John Paul II talks about divorce today, he uses the personalist language that has become his trademark. He speaks not so much about breaking a promise, but about the impossibility of taking yourself back after you have given yourself away. He claims "an unbreakable oneness" between a man and woman who have been united in a sacramental marriage; their marriage is indissoluble.[16] The pope uses language that seems descriptive ("couples are not only able to overcome 'hardness of heart,' but also, and above all, they are able to share the full and definitive love of Christ") but is really illustrative of the ideal he holds.[17] He believes that couples ought to be able to overcome their problems and knows that Christ has promised to be there for them, so he claims that if they truly give everything to their marriage, they will be able to remain one. Their task or vocation is to stay together and work at their marriage so that they will continue to be a sign for others of the enduring love of God.[18] Through the sacrament of marriage, God gifts them with the strength to endure. Thus marriage both *is* indissoluble (of its nature, because God wills it so) and *must be* indissoluble (it requires a lifelong commitment).

In recent years, many Catholic theologians have begun to question this insistence that what *should* be the case (lifelong oneness in marriage) *is* in fact the case. Bernard Cooke has made perhaps the most persuasive argument that the church ought to recognize the solubility of real-life marriages. Cooke claims that marriage is not intrinsically indissoluble as a covenant, for if one person breaks the covenant and leaves, the remaining person cannot be expected to keep the covenant alone. Neither is marriage unbreakable as a sacrament, for the sacrament is in the relationship; if the relationship is over, the sacrament no longer exists. Christian marriage, according to Cooke, should symbolize God's fidelity and it cannot do this if the relationship is broken. Husband and wife together "are the sacrament, not simply because they are recognizable in the community as two who publicly bound themselves by marital contract, but because and to the extent that they can be recognized as translating Christian faith into their married and family life."[19] If not truly one in relationship, they cannot be described as one in any meaningful way. Furthermore, it does not make sense, according to Cooke, to view the marriage ceremony or moment of consummation as the point of no return, because marriage is a process, not an act.[20] As time goes on couples become more married or not very married. Some who become married at first later become less married as they fall out of love.

Many find Cooke's arguments persuasive at a very basic level because so many have personal experience with marriages that seem broken. We see marriage progress (or fail to progress). We see couples who cannot move beyond their anger and we wonder what, if anything, remains of these marriages.

However, Cooke's argument is problematic because it assumes a view of marriage as relationship. If one assumes instead, as John Paul II does, that marriage is a communion of persons committed to love, life, the betterment of society, and the mission of the church, the marriage relationship as such becomes much less central. The sacramental understanding of marriage is rooted in much more than the relationship. In this perspective, relationships may progress forward, slip, recover, and slip again, but they do not lose their sacramental significance. Contrary to Cooke, one could argue that the couple whose romantic love has begun to fade may still have sacramental sign value in the Christian community *if* they continue to show compassion for each other and their children and a zeal for the good of society and the church. The ongoing commitment to stay together despite continuing troubles serves as a witness in itself. God may be present in these marriages, even when a man and woman are not fully present themselves. In short, even though some marriages may appear dead and incapable of communicating anything, when viewed from a broader perspective, they may have enduring value. However, the value may not necessarily lie in the relationship, but rather in the shared commitment to discipleship. The efforts of couples who struggle to hold their marriage together for their children, sacrificing the joys of intimate relationship for an unwavering commitment to family and community, are a witness to the truth that even if relationships fail, sacrament may remain.[21]

The Christian valuing of discipleship over relationship leads to a different perspective on the boundaries of commitment as well. In a widely read book called Personal Commitments, Catholic theologian Margaret Farley develops the idea that human commitments are of their very nature provisional because their existence implies the possibility of failure.[22] In a more recent article on divorce, she suggests that marriage, like any serious commitment, cannot be binding if it is impossible to sustain, no longer serves its intended purpose, or conflicts with another obligation.[23] For Farley, marriage is a promise that, like other promises, can be broken in certain circumstances.

Farley's experiential argument, like Cooke's, proves convincing at a gut level because it is rooted in a deep sense of what goes wrong in human marriage. We all know couples who seem so far from their promise to love and honor each other that continuing their marriage seems pointless. However, like Cooke's, Farley's argument cannot withstand the criticism that marriage is a commitment to more than a relationship. It is also a commitment to children and to co-discipleship in church and society. Partners promise that it will be lifelong because of their sense of vulnerability. That does not mean the commitment itself is malleable, but that they will call upon the strength of others during difficult times and remember the well-being of others when all attempts to revitalize the relationship seem exhausted. Marriage in the Christian tradition is not just about the couple, and it would be a lot more vulnerable if it were. Christian marriage commits spouses to a broader community of persons, and thus arguments that center on the death of personal relationships can only go so far. The distinctiveness of Christian marriage lies in the idea that its meaning transcends the love of one man and one woman. Christian couples who commit themselves to lifelong covenanted marriage bear an obligation to honor that commitment beyond the brokenness of relationships.[24]

Effects of Divorce on Children

A full consideration of the ethics of divorce requires an understanding of what divorce does to children. In the 1970s and 1980s many researchers believed that if divorce made parents happier, it would also help children. However, it has become increasingly clear that in most cases divorce is harmful to children. In 1991, sociologists Paul Amato and Bruce Keith published an article entitled "Parental Divorce and the Well-Being of Children: A Meta-Analysis" in which they reviewed ninety-two studies from the 1980s that compared children in intact families to children in divorced single-parent families. The authors conclude that though children of divorce "experience a lower level of well-being than do children living in continuously intact families," family conflict is sometimes a better predictor of negative outcomes than family structure.[25] However, many 1990s studies contradict these findings. Why? The conclusion of the study hints at the problem. The authors assert that

> the long-term consequences of parental divorce for adult attainment and quality of life may prove to be more serious than the short-term emotional and social problems in children that are more frequently studied. Further research on adult children of divorce — in particular, longitudinal studies, of children as they enter adulthood — would be of great value in understanding this phenomenon.[26]

In the 1990s, researchers started completing those long-term studies and their research now shows that divorce, more often than not, has serious negative consequences for children. Judith Wallerstein's long-term study of sixty middle-class families has received a great deal of attention because Wallerstein has published several popular books documenting her findings. The latest, *The Unexpected Legacy of Divorce,* reports on her subjects twenty-five years after she first interviewed them. Wallerstein's earlier studies introduced concepts like the "sleeper effect" (when girls seem to recover from divorce but experience problems entering into serious relationships later in life) and the "overburdened child" (who finds he must hold the family together because of a mother or father's diminished capacity to parent).[27] Wallerstein reported that though she and fellow researchers expected that most children would rebound from divorce fairly quickly, instead they found that only 34 percent of children were doing well after five years, only 45 percent of children were doing well after ten years.[28] At the twenty-five-year follow-up, Wallerstein discovered that a majority of adult children of divorce still suffered from the effects of the divorce.[29] Challenging the myths that happier parents make for happier children and divorce is a temporary crisis, adult children of divorce claim the years they spent growing up in postdivorce families left them with unresolvable anxiety about love, relationships, and families.

I have presented these findings in class for several years now, with varying responses. Sometimes children of divorce insist they are better off. However, others say things like, "I don't know if I'll ever get married," "How can I believe in love if it didn't last for my parents?" attesting to the reality of Wallerstein's findings. Before the new study came out, I remember a male student talking about how divorce affected him. He spoke of always feeling nervous, uncertain about his future, and worried that something bad would happen. I did not understand his comment at the time, but after reading Wallerstein's new study, it makes sense. My student simply described the feeling that Wallerstein calls, "waiting for the other shoe to drop" — an anxiety about life that makes children of divorce some of divorce's harshest critics. In a telling paragraph, Wallerstein writes:

> Not one of the men or women from divorced families whose lives I report on in this book wanted their children to repeat their childhood experiences. Not one ever said, "I want my children to live in two nests — or even two villas." They envied friends who grew up in intact families. Their entire life stories belie the myths we've embraced.[30]

While Wallerstein carefully notes that she does not oppose all divorce and does not believe that divorce is universally harmful to children, her research clearly shows that compared to children in intact families (even conflicted intact families), children of divorce are usually disadvantaged. They suffer as children dealing with the upheaval of the divorce and often get little support. In postdivorce families, they continue to deal with transitions, new relationships to lovers, stepparents, and stepsiblings. Those with good support systems and those who naturally need little parenting land on their feet, while the less supported and more vulnerable suffer. Adolescence includes earlier sexual experiences for girls, more social instability for boys, and gender-transcending worry about following in their parents' footsteps. However, Wallerstein sees the most devastating effects in adult children of divorce. While they search for love and commitment, they are haunted by bad memories and hampered by the lack of a template for intimacy. Unlike children from intact families, they expect to fail at marriage, and they do so more frequently. Although Wallerstein certainly saw children of divorce who succeeded against the odds, most of her subjects were not able to do it.[31] Her twenty-five-year study provides solid evidence that most of the time divorce has negative effects on children.

Many recent studies from the 1990s confirm Wallerstein's findings. Sara McLanahan and Gary Sandefur studied children growing up in single-parent families and found that "children who grow up in a household with only one biological parent are worse off, on average, than children who grow up in a household with both of their biological parents, regardless of the parents' race or educational background, regardless of whether the resident parent remarries."[32] Their research shows that children from single-parent families are twice as likely to drop out of school, twice as likely to have a child before age twenty, and one and a half times as likely to be out of work and school in their late teens and early twenties.[33] These three factors are important, they say, because they are keys to economic success, which is closely linked to personal and social well-being.[34]

Why is the contrast so stark? Children in single-parent families simply have less support than those in two-parent families. First, economically it is more difficult to support two households than one, especially when fathers tend to keep more than half of their income. The average nonpoor family experiences a 50 percent decline in income after divorce. Second, fathers who live apart from their children usually have a weaker commitment to them, which undermines the children's trust in both parents, increases uncertainty about the future, and reduces social capital (community resources). All of this makes raising children more difficult. Third, single mothers experience high levels of stress and depression and are more likely to be inconsistent parents.[35] Less invested noncustodial parents and highly stressed single custodial parents do not make a strong combination. So far, the research shows little evidence that joint custody alleviates these problems.[36]

What of remarriage? Are two parents better than one, even when they are not biologically related to the child? Most recent research does not seem to indicate that. According to Barbara Dafoe Whitehead, author of the well-known article "Dan Quayle Was Right," "remarriage neither reproduces nor restores the intact family structure, even when it brings more income and a second adult into the household."[37] She attributes this to weaker attachments, lower investment, and more destabilizing change. In a related article, Whitehead argues that low parental investment is the problem in most divorce cases; parents try to substitute love for stability and find it is not enough. She laments the reality that talk about caring for children is replacing "daily donations of parental time, attention, and supervision that are the currency of parental love."[38] Like many authors, she finds the data on divorce effects overwhelmingly negative.[39]

Despite the negative findings of most divorce studies from the 1990s, some newer studies emphasize children's resiliency and their ability to adopt effective coping strategies. In a comprehensive review of the literature on the effects of divorce on children, David Gately and Andrew I. Schwebel found that children of divorce are more mature, empathetic, and androgynous than their peers and have higher self-esteem.[40] These children were able to deal with the challenge divorce presented for them and grow as people. Because their parents had less time and energy to invest in them, they matured faster and became independent earlier. In single-parent families, they and their parents took on dual roles, so they became more androgynous. As they coped with the challenges of divorce, their self-esteem improved. Because they saw human failure and suffering up close, their capacity for empathy increased. Stronger children turned the crisis of divorce into an opportunity for growth.

Many newer studies attempt to extend these positive effects by offering strategies whereby parents and others can teach children more effective coping skills so that divorce is more of a challenge than a crisis. One such study ends hopefully with the idea that "factors that lead to positive outcomes of divorce need to be accentuated in order to prevent negative stigmas, self-fulfilling prophecies including the intergenerational transmission of marital dissolution, as well as dysfunctional families."[41]

Perhaps it is possible, then, to have more "good divorces," where children bounce back and become stronger and more compassionate people. If so, we certainly ought to try. However, it seems important to acknowledge the sad reality that the positive qualities celebrated in children of divorce are the hard-earned fruits of their suffering the emotional and/or physical loss (short or long-term) of one or both parents. Children are more mature because they have known crisis. They are more independent because they have been left alone more. They are more compassionate because they have endured suffering. These character strengths may indeed serve them well in later life, but the process that engendered them is not one anyone would wish on a child.

Perhaps John Chrysostom of the East, who wrote that a married couple with a child becomes not just two, but three in one flesh, said it best.[42] Divorce wrenches apart people who ought to be together. Flesh is torn, and children, especially, often feel lonely, unloved, abandoned, and fearful of the future.[43] This is what the studies on divorce reveal. If the future is to hold something better for children, Christians must think seriously about their obligations to children, which sometimes means parents taking on suffering so that children can avoid it. Recent sociological research has established that children can survive and thrive in unhappy marriages within which conflict is minimized and parents make clear to children their lifelong commitment to the family.[44] Simply based on a reading of the divorce effects literature, it seems clear that if parents can stay together without forcing ongoing conflict onto their children, they ought to do so. When conflict seems impossible to overcome, the issue becomes more difficult from a sociological perspective. Many of the negative outcomes of divorce are associated with conflict, and recent studies suggest that high-conflict intact marriages prove just as harmful for children as divorce. However, from a theological perspective that takes into account the scriptural witness, the best of the Catholic tradition, and the experience of children, it seems that Christians have an obligation to find a way not only to minimize conflict but to renew the marriage communion. Sometimes, however, couples will not be able to carry out this obligation; they will fall short of the Catholic ideal. Nonetheless, as part of the Christian community, they deserve the community's support and ethical reflection.

Pastoral Issues: Remarriage and Communion

What happens to divorced Catholics within the church community? According to official Catholic teaching, divorced Catholics can participate fully in parish life, including the Eucharist, but divorced and remarried Catholics cannot because they are living in a state of sin that objectively contradicts Catholic teaching. Thus while individuals who commit other sins may confess and return to full participation in the community of faith (promising to sin no more), remarried persons who continue in sinful ways cannot. An exception is made for those remarried couples who stay together for the sake of their children but do not have sexual relations. Otherwise, the church asks remarried Catholics to forgo communion, reconciliation, and public roles in the church, though they may attend mass and participate in parish activities. The official teaching sets remarried Catholics apart.

Most Catholic theologians, however, now believe that remarried Catholics should be able to receive communion, arguing that many who do not have annulments are subjectively certain that they would get one if they applied, or that denying spiritual nourishment to those in pain is wrong.[45] One might also claim that the Eucharist is an extension of Jesus' ministry, and Jesus did not exclude anyone from his table. If fact, others criticized him for eating with sinners. If contemporary Christians cleave to that vision, they will open the Eucharist to all of church sinners, that is, to all of us.

Christian churches also ought to support their divorced and remarried members by extending help to them in the form of counseling, support groups, and healing rituals. None of this need undermine the teaching about divorce. The church simply offers its comfort to those members who particularly need it. Pastoral compassion in the case of divorce is entirely consistent with an uncompromising stance regarding its morality. The church has extended its mercy and compassion to murderers on death row, among other sinners. Surely there is no reason not to do the same in the case of divorce.

Obligations during and after Divorce

What, then, are the ethical obligations of divorced Christians? In a paper on divorce a student of mine tells the story of how her divorced parents put their differences aside for her wedding day. Although both had remarried, they even posed for a family picture that included just my student, her husband, and her parents. My student said that she treasures this picture because it shows her family together again — if only for a brief, but important, moment. This picture symbolizes divorced parents' primary obligations: remaining as one flesh (to the fullest extent possible) and putting children's needs first.

Although parents who divorce agree to separate and break the bond between them, the children they bore together symbolize the reality that what God has joined, no human being may separate. The parts of the parents that have come together in their children cannot be torn apart. So, too, the parents must in some important sense remain together. Their relationship as a couple is important to the children. They cannot fulfill their obligations simply by being present to children individually. Instead, they must continue as one in important ways. For instance, they ought to tell their children about the divorce together, and prepare their children for what will come.[46] Although they will not live together after the divorce, they ought to show their children that they care for one another, respect one another, and do not feel uncomfortable in one another's presence. Their relationship should continue in a different form. They should not deny their unity simply because they are no longer in love. They have shared a part of their lives with each other. Of course, divorce involves great pain and, often, betrayal, and thus this sort of continuing unity may seem impossible. Perhaps in some cases it will be. Nevertheless, if the marriage cannot continue, the ongoing unity of the couple seems a second-best alternative that still respects the marriage vow and the biblical understanding that in marriage the two become one flesh.

The duty to put children first furthers this obligation of unity. The sociological literature on divorce identifies one of the crucial problems of divorce as parents who get so wrapped up in their own crises that they cannot meet their children's needs. This is where parents have to sacrifice in order to "do divorce" better. Much recent research on divorce helps parents do just this, underscoring the idea that there can be a "good divorce" if parents work at it. Putting children's needs first means being prepared to delay transitions (e.g., the onset of new relationships, the sale of a house, or a change in care arrangements) until children adjust to the initial shock. After that first difficult period, it remains important to maintain household structures and routines and make extra time to spend with children who will need comfort.[47] To avoid the typical problems of divorce, parents need to be physically and emotionally available for their children, despite their own difficulties. According to the best long-term studies, this additional availability will need to continue throughout adolescence and young adulthood, so that young adults from broken families are able to enter lifetime commitments with more confidence and better chances of success. Overall, the sociological data on divorce suggests that if parents minimize conflict and better care for their vulnerable children, the wounds of divorce may run less deep.

To return to the Christian one-flesh analogy, parents who remain unified and put their children's needs first, remaining in some spiritual sense a one-flesh family, can help lessen the damage done by the physical tears in the flesh of the family. Would it be better if the parents could manage to stay together? In most cases, probably, but given the limits of human capacities and the reality of human frailty not everyone will be able to make this choice.[48] Yet they too have obligations. If total unity and total sacrifice of adult needs prove impossible, perhaps partial unity and partial sacrifice are achievable. Parents who divorce can still strive to honor their commitments to each other and to their children.

Domestic Church Reconsidered

How do these broken but committed families fit in the life of the church? Is church teaching on families addressed to them? Can they be considered holy? Can they carry out the mission of the family? Catholic teaching is unequivocal on these questions: Although never viewing divorce as the answer to a failing marriage, the church does not exclude divorced families from its teachings. The U.S. bishops make this particularly clear in their letter "Follow the Way of Love." Here they call all families "holy," for in their view "a family is holy not because it is perfect, but because God's grace is at work in it, helping it to set out anew every day on the way of love." More explicitly, the bishops claim that a change in family structure does not diminish the holiness of a family. "Wherever a family exists and love still moves through its members, grace is present. Nothing — not even divorce or death — can place limits upon God's gracious love."[49] The bishops do not believe that

God puts structural limits on love. Despite the ideal of an intact family, God is present and at work even in (perhaps especially in) the most broken families. Because of God's presence, these families are holy.

According to the bishops, broken families fall under the heading of domestic church. Catholic family teaching uses this term more and more to express the idea that families comprise the most basic Christian communities.[50] Many Christians know this by experience, and they often express it when they talk about the ways their family instilled faith in them. For many, family is the primary experience of Christian community, the one where they feel the most comfortable, the one they feel is most real. Domestic church imagery finds its roots in biblical references to the first Christian churches, which were, in fact, in homes, and in the writings of the early church fathers like John Chrysostom, who spoke of the family as a church in miniature. Contemporary theologians who write about domestic church tend to focus on the idea that "families can embody Christ in the day-to-day experiences of their lives and are connected precisely as foundational churches to the whole people of God. In principle, domestic churches ... incarnate ideals of reconciliation, justice, peace, hospitality, and prayer."[51] The practices of the family, not its structure, are central to its identity as domestic church. Similarly, when the U.S. bishops speak about families as domestic churches, they follow their general discussion with a long list of things that families do. They include: believing in God, loving without giving up on others, practicing intimacy, professing and witnessing to the faith of the Gospel, educating children in the faith and being educated by them, praying together, serving one another, forgiving and seeking reconciliation, celebrating life, welcoming strangers in need, acting justly and working for justice in the community, affirming life as a precious gift from God, and raising up vocations.[52] The bishops tell families who may not believe they are holy that they are, indeed, doing God's work. Ordinary moments and extraordinary challenges of every family's life present, the bishops insist, opportunities to live out one's Christian vocation; divorce does not change that.

It is possible that divorce, because it represents a short-term crisis as well as a long-term problem for families, provides additional opportunities for discipleship. It presents more opportunities to move beyond the limits of traditional relationships, to become open to the loving compassion of another. Broken families must be welcoming churches for their members, and the research showing children of divorce have more compassion than children of intact families reveals that sometimes broken families can do what intact families cannot. While obviously not a reason to get divorced, this may be a way to think about how the most broken of families have something to teach the rest. Whether a family represents "the family," or one of the many differently structured "families" discussed in the first chapter of this book, God is present inasmuch and insofar as that family makes Christ present within and outside the home. Finally, a family's structure proves much less central to its Christian identity than does its mission.

Discussion Questions

1. How would you characterize the New Testament message on divorce?

2. Can marriages end?

3. Is a good divorce possible?

4. Is it unrealistic to ask divorced parents to remain two in one flesh?

5. Can the church oppose divorce, on the one hand, and use domestic church imagery to describe broken families, on the other?

– T E N –

What Is Family For?

Justice and Passion

In the family in which I grew up, family and community were connected. As a family, we actively participated in a small church community; we sometimes picketed at a local grocery store in support of the United Farm Workers; and when we came together for dinner, we often discussed social and political issues connected to my father's work as a lawyer for people who could not afford to pay. We brought our individual experiences in community activities (including scouting, soccer, ballet, church committees, and the board of a halfway house for ex-convicts) back to the family when we were together. This enriched our conversations. Because we had experiences (both as a family and as individuals) that went beyond our family, we had more to talk about when we were together. Our commitments outside the family strengthened our common identity.

In this model of family life, justice and love are connected. The love among parents and children flows outward into social, communal, and political commitments. Those same commitments contribute to a richer culture of the family within the home. A sense of family mission energizes its internal and external life. If one accepts the arguments made thus far in this book, some sort of mission like this seems necessary for all Christian families. This concluding chapter suggests that Catholic social teaching provides direction for families seeking to embrace a social mission.

However, some may fear that the movement toward a more socially concerned family means a movement away from a family that values passionate relationships between husbands and wives, and parents and children. Others claim that in an unloving society, the family first and most importantly has a mission to love. The late social critic Christopher Lasch, for instance, mourned the loss of the family's status as a "haven in a heartless world."[1] After hearing criticism of Lasch's privatized notion of the family, some might argue that a haven in a heartless world is often the best parents can offer their children, especially during the difficult teenage years. This view certainly has value as a partial strategy; sometimes holding things together on the inside will be all a family can manage. However, in the long run, the Catholic ideal of the family as domestic church with a definite social mission has greater merit than the "haven" ideal, for if all families decided to abandon the evil world for their small places of refuge, the world would be less graced with their presence. Eventually, the world would intrude upon families, in spite of their efforts to secure themselves against it, and it would hamper their efforts to be good to one another. In contrast, the Catholic ideal can help families embrace the challenge of building loving relationships among members and humanizing the world.

A family with a strong social commitment need not inevitably be void of strong commitments among its members. Historian Jean Elshtain sees in many attempts to make the family more public a certain totalitarianism that "require[s] that individuals never allow their commitments to specific others — family, friends, comrades — to weaken their commitment to the state."[2] However, Elshtain presents a false dichotomy. To ask of the family a serious public commitment is not to demand that all private commitments end. Sometimes a family's values and actions will serve as a protest against the values or actions of the state or community, but if the family witnesses to its values in public ways and strives to change the society to which it belongs, then it serves *both* private and public commitments, strengthening its identity and cohesiveness through its efforts to transform the world.

Could a family achieve its full potential without involving itself intensely in larger communities? This proves a difficult question to answer. However, there would seem to be a certain emptiness in a family that chooses to value itself. This emptiness resembles that which eventually overtakes a conversation focusing only on personal concerns or a relationship about only two human beings. In the short run, these conversations and relationship may be satisfying, even intensely so.

Eventually, however, unless the two go outside of themselves, they will have little left to say or do. Ultimately, there should be something more to relationships than "just the two of us."

Many philosophers who have written on friendship have made precisely this point. Robert Bellah, for instance, recalls Aristotle's view that a "shared commitment to the good" constitutes the most important component of friendship.[3] Friends should help each other be good citizens, "for friendship and its virtues are not merely private, they are also public, even political, for a civic order, a 'city,' is above all a network of friends."[4] According to Aristotle, true friends take pleasure in one another's company and in their shared commitment to the polis. For him, a friendship without that crucial public dimension is not a true friendship at all.

If husbands and wives have true friendship, their relationship should be about more than themselves. A marriage based solely on love and sacrifice of one to the other lacks the fullness of a marital friendship in which both spouses see their love for each other as the beginning of love for others. Spouses who are friends can attest to the richness of married love that goes beyond itself. Of course, in most cases marital love goes beyond spouses in the love for children. Many theologies of marriage see children as the necessary larger component of marital love, and children do in fact provide a broader sense of purpose for most married couples. However, this does not seem quite what Aristotle alluded to. Friends are called upon to care for a wider community, for the common good or the good of the polis. This understanding of friendship is also part of the Catholic tradition that asks families to look beyond themselves and thereby find their own commitments strengthened by love for others.

By questioning the dichotomy between family and community, the Catholic tradition encourages families to ask, "What, ultimately, are we about?" It offers for reflection a model of the family that has room for both the intimate passion that exists among parents and children and the social passion that animates the struggle for justice in the world. In the areas of work, time, and money, it gives families a way to attach greater consideration to important social values, such as solidarity and the common good.

Catholic Social Teaching and the Family

During his visit to the United States in 1999, John Paul II challenged Americans to renew their commitment to their most vulnerable citizens and neighbors. He asked them, as he asked them many times before, to choose life, which "involves rejecting every form of violence: the violence of poverty and hunger, which oppresses so many human beings; the violence of armed conflict, which does not resolve but only increases divisions and tensions"; as well as violence against the unborn.[5] In his speeches, the pope drew upon a long and rich tradition of Catholic social teaching that emphasizes solidarity and the common good.[6] This body of teaching sees human persons as essentially social beings who are unable to be fully human alone.

Recall that John Paul II sees the mythical story of Adam and Eve in the book of Genesis as a story about the necessity of human relationship. He emphasizes that Adam looks at all the creatures God had created up until that point and finds them unsuitable mates. Only when God puts Adam to sleep and creates Eve from his rib does Adam, overcome with joy, exclaim, "This at last is bone of my bones and flesh of my flesh" (Gen 2:23). This is the first biblical story Christians read, and in it they come to know that they are called to mutual and self-giving relationships.

What begins with Adam and Eve in the most intense fashion gets extended by analogy to all human beings. Human beings are not meant to live alone. Rather, they are called to live in relationship — in community — with one another. Thus they are bound to look beyond their own personal good in order to seek the good of the larger community of persons to which they belong. In the words of the pope, human beings have the duty to "situate particular interests within a coherent vision of the common good."[7] This means that individuals, and even individual families, cannot just take care of their own. Catholic social teaching requires them to value the good of others as well. Furthermore, Christians have a responsibility to practice the value of solidarity, which resembles the common good in that it refers to a commitment beyond oneself and one's family, but differs in that it calls for a specific obligation to serve and empower the poor. Valuing solidarity inevitably leads to embracing the struggle for justice with and on behalf of the poor and marginalized.[8]

Catholic social teaching centering on these themes addresses primarily individuals, not families. However, the tradition holds that the family is a domestic church with both a personal and a social vocation. Families, as small church communities, foster loving relationships, teach about the faith, ritualize important occasions, and serve the needs of the larger church and the world. "Domestic church" language does not simply suggest a similarity between families and churches; it insists that families *are* small churches with a responsibility for fostering love within and living Christian social values outside its boundaries. Families are communities of love with a social mission. John Paul II has made this point more strongly than any recent pope, saying that the family is "called to offer everyone a witness of generous and disinterested dedication to social matters through a 'preferential option' for the poor and disadvantaged."[9]

This social mandate of the family stands as perhaps the greatest strength of Catholic social teaching on the family. In contrast to those who argue that being a good family is primarily a private task, Catholic teaching emphasizes that moral thinking about the family makes sense only when done in a communal context.

The idea that families should incorporate the values of solidarity and the common good into their lives is complemented by other aspects of Catholic teaching on the family. For instance, as chapter 3 explained, recent reforms in the Catholic wedding liturgy signal a renewed attention to ways a couple's relationship exists in the context of the larger community. The church asks couples who seek marriage to make the participation of those who gather for the wedding ceremony a priority in order to underscore the idea that all who attend the wedding witness to it and are involved in the sealing of the couple's bond. No longer can couples view their marriage as simply a union of two. In the new wedding ceremony, as a couple opens itself to the community, the community promises to support the couple in good times and bad. The new liturgy guidelines suggest that marriage, a relationship that opens itself to all, must entail a commitment to the good of others.

Similarly, as noted in chapter 5, when Pope John Paul II speaks directly to the family as opposed to married couples, he asserts that families have four tasks: loving each other, serving life, serving the church, and taking appropriate social-political action on behalf of vulnerable people in their society. Clearly, family members are called to do more than simply love each other; their work begins but does not end there. According to the best of the Catholic tradition, the family cannot concern itself solely with the welfare of its own members; it has an obligation to take seriously the welfare of local, national, and even international communities. The family is, for John Paul II, a communion of disciples of Christ that must situate its own good in the context of the common good and make a commitment to serve the poor in some way.

Catholic social teaching provides a helpful starting point for thinking through the relationship between family and society, for it calls Christian families to uphold values of solidarity and the common good as they make the most crucial moral decisions of their lives: decisions about work, time, and money.

Work

What role should work play in contemporary families? Most historians of the family agree that families in the postindustrial world differ in fundamental ways from families in earlier times because they do not normally find their group identity in their work.[10] Because most families do not run farms or shops together, the work they do no longer defines them. Rather, families stand apart from the jobs individual parents do to support them. No longer centered around a common mission, the family's function is uncertain. In the age of the welfare state, when many families receive from the government services they cannot provide for themselves (like elder care, food stamps, and health care), the function of the family grows more questionable. In recent decades, when more and more middle-class families have begun buying services they used to perform (like meal preparation, house cleaning, and day care), family goals have become even more uncertain. Thus today it is necessary to ask, "What does the family do? What would it mean for the family to be itself, as John Paul II asks it to be?"[11]

Many would argue that the contemporary family exists primarily to nurture and support its members. This view assumes a romantic ideal of the family and asserts the necessity of a commitment to care for family members above all else. However, since the Catholic tradition calls families both to nurture and to service, the family should be seen not as a haven of love but as a community of disciples. Its members have a mission to serve one another and the world. Each family must work out its specific mission in its own terms, but the work of adult family members will be crucial in defining that mission. Work does not have to cease being central to a family's mission in the postindustrial age. Rather, the work that mothers and fathers choose to do can be fundamental to a contemporary family's public identity.

In my own family, my father's work as an attorney for the government-funded Legal Services defined us in many ways. The relatively low pay meant that we did not enjoy some of the luxuries many of our friends did. The political nature of the work meant that our conversations frequently centered on politics. The public nature of the work meant that we often had to defend our values to neighbors and friends. My father's work did not account for all that our family stood for, but it did play a major role in forming our ideas about our identity as a small Christian community. My example is undoubtedly somewhat elitist; few have the privilege my father enjoys of doing this kind of intellectually challenging and morally invigorating work. Still, many people see work as something more than individualistic pursuit of self-fulfillment or monetary gain. Teachers, health-care workers, social workers, business people, day-care providers, government workers, and many others choose their work at least in part because of their social commitments. Surely their work defines them in significant ways and influences their families in ways no less important.

Perhaps many people in our society do not see their work as constitutive of both themselves and their families because they see the public and private dimensions of their selves as two different things. Robert Bellah and his colleagues argue that the lives of Americans are diminished because they have separated themselves too much from their work and have come to see work only as a way to secure income.[12] These authors wish to provide people with a renewed sense of work as a calling. Their views echo those of John Paul II in his letter on work. Recall that the pope argues that the human person is oriented toward self-realization through work and states that a person should work out of a desire to "realize his humanity."[13] If work is so closely connected with the self-realization of Christians, then parental work cannot help but be a fundamental aspect of a family's self-realization as a community of disciples.

Contemporary culture resists the notion of work as an ethically important dimension of family life. Many would agree with a well-known social commentator who argues that "parents who have satisfied their elementary economic needs [should] invest themselves in their children by spending less time on their careers and consumeristic pursuits and more time with their youngsters."[14] Certainly the first five years of a child's life are a particularly important time during which it would, in most cases, prove beneficial for parents to have greater flexibility in their work hours. However, as chapters 5 and 6 show, the notion that *only* elementary economic needs can compete with the needs of children for full-time parental nurturing is disputed by those who argue that full-time care for young children, mostly on the part of the mother, is not necessary or even desirable. Some of these writers are concerned about the role of women in society; they point to the possible destructive consequences of the isolated mother and child and speak to the need of women to participate in the larger public world. Others denigrate this need for public work as selfish. However, the desire to contribute to one's community is what Catholic teaching calls a commitment to the common good.

Putting the "self-less" attempts of parents to meet the needs of their families in radical opposition to the "selfish" pursuits of parents in the public sphere misunderstands something very basic. When parents decide how to balance the demands of the workplace with the demands of family members (especially children), they often struggle with the problem of balancing their family's needs with the needs of students, patients, clients, or causes they serve. According to Catholic teaching, parents have a duty to care for their children, but they also have a duty to contribute to the community through work. They cannot abandon their obligations to the common good simply because they have children. They should be encouraged to consider how they might best serve members of the community through their work. While raising children necessitates some downscaling of public commitments, parents need not feel that they must sacrifice all social concern for the sake of their children.

The work vs. family dilemma is not simply a question of individualism vs. self-sacrifice for a greater good. In reality, many goods are at
stake when parents make decisions about work: the benefits of parents'
spending time with their children, the benefits of children's exposure
to different adult role models, the gifts parents have to offer to communities. Questions regarding the ethics of work, when viewed in the
larger context of solidarity and the common good, become more difficult, but more properly situated for a Christian discussion of what the
family is about.

Time

Questions about work are intimately related to questions about time,
for most families feel that they lack the time to be the kind of families they want to be. Even if families commit to work for the common
good, they also need time for themselves. An often-cited 1989 survey of American families reported that most Americans see lack of
time as the crucial problem facing families today.[15] Lack of family time
affects not only parents who work more and consequently see their children less. Children today also see their grandparents, aunts, and uncles
less because of increased mobility. Parents see their teenage sons and
daughters less because more of them work part-time. Husbands and
wives find it harder to take time for each other. Most agree that more
time would help them and others to be better families. Anyone who has
experienced the pressures of contemporary family life would doubtless
agree. Time poses a serious problem for many families. If society values
families, it certainly should make it possible for families to spend more
time together.

Some changes are already occurring. The government has finally
made twelve weeks of unpaid family leave a given for large businesses,
and more employers offer flextime, job sharing, or reduced hours for
reduced pay. Many people are forced to work part-time; others choose
to work part-time or downsize into less demanding jobs because they
want more time with those they love most.

What, then, can be done with this time? Why do families want time?
There is a danger that more family time will simply encourage greater
privatization in American culture. If families simply spend more time

together at the mall or in front of the TV set, they will have gained little. Yet many families may find it hard to think of time any differently. As sociologist Robert Bellah notes, Americans have developed a very private ideal of leisure. Especially since the rise of the middle class after World War II, private leisure came to be seen as the most important element of the good life, for "here intimacy, solidarity, and voluntary accomplishments in sport, art, or craft flourished, crowned life, and made it whole."[16] The family gathered around the TV set or the backyard barbecue became the symbol of success.

Catholic social teaching calls this idealization of private leisure into question and asks families to think not only of their own interests, but also the interests of those in their communities most in need of help. To be valuable, the time families spend together need not be private. In fact, Bellah claims that most people derive little satisfaction from the most typical of leisure activities, TV-watching. He argues that when we engage in leisure that is "mildly demanding but inherently meaningful — reading a good book, repairing the car, talking to someone we love, or even cooking the family meal — we are more apt to find that we are 'relaxed.'"[17] Would not leisure spent in activities that help others have a similar effect?

Significantly, Catholic social teaching calls families to spend some time serving the common good and practicing solidarity. Families might serve the common good in a variety of ways, including volunteering at the school their children attend, participating in civic or religious organizations, and becoming active in their own neighborhood. All of this contributes to the common good. However, if middle-class families serve only other middle-class families, then the common good is only partly realized and solidarity with the poor and marginalized remains a distant ideal.

The Parenting for Peace and Justice Network, based in St. Louis, gives an example of an alternative model. Families who belong to the network engage in service activities together, share ideas about how to live more simply, and believe it is possible to parent well without abandoning a strong commitment to those in need.[18] The growing Voluntary Simplicity movement, which involves people all over the country who attempt to live on less money, scale back work commitments, and spend time doing what they really want to do, also emphasizes community service.[19]

Families can use more time to build their own small community of disciples by serving the common good. Each family must decide on its own specific mission. What is important is that they use the time they gain not to isolate themselves from society but to gain the freedom and space they need to think about what they can do together for others.

Money

How do commitments to solidarity and the common good affect families' choices about how to spend money? Is this an important ethical question? Some might argue that spending is a private issue because each family is different and spends relatively little in comparison to businesses or governments. Contemporary culture tends to trivialize this aspect of the moral life, ignoring the reality that the way families choose to spend their money significantly affects their lives and the lives of others. However, if one takes Catholic social teaching seriously, financial decisions have ethical import.

In contrast, a 1995 story from the Business Section of the *Los Angeles Times* provides readers with a map showing how an average college-educated couple can buy a house, send their kids to college, and live comfortably while saving enough to become millionaires by the time they retire.[20] It suggests that most families can get out of debt and achieve the same goal by following the prudent example of this ideal couple. What is presented as a simple article on personal finances is in fact a statement of important values. This couple has one major goal in life: wealth. They succeed because, after more than forty years of frugality, they end up as millionaires who can spend their time traveling around the world. To achieve their goal, the couple relies upon two steady, uninterrupted incomes. The map does not allow for exploring different career options, volunteering, or easing workloads when children arrive. It does not consider the social import of the couple's work or the fact that they will miss out on time alone, time with children, and time spent in nonlucrative community activities. The money the couple earns goes directly into necessary expenditures and long-term investments. The ethical values controlling their decisions about work, time, and money are personal security in the present and personal wealth in the future. There is no room for consideration of solidarity or the common good. The family is treated as a private community that does well when it meets its own needs. The article assumes readers will consider this family a good role model. Yet, considering what values this family denies in order to gain material success, their priorities should not be accepted too quickly.

Pope John Paul II calls that model into question when he asks families to consider seriously the ethical import of their way of life:

> I wish to appeal with simplicity and humility to everyone, to all men and women without exception. I wish to ask them to be convinced of the seriousness of the present moment and of each one's individual responsibility, and to implement — by the way they live as individuals and as families, by the use of their resources, by their civic activity, by contributing to economic and political decisions and by personal commitment to national and international undertakings — the measures inspired by solidarity and love of preference for the poor.[21]

John Paul II finds lifestyles and expenditures extremely important. Christian families cannot claim to uphold values of solidarity and the common good simply by voting for the right candidates or supporting the right causes. They must scrutinize their daily lives and their use of resources, asking whether their use of resources is consistent with the values they uphold in the public sphere. They do not live in isolation, because everyone is connected to everyone else by seemingly mundane choices that have social import. According to Catholic social teaching, "we are all really responsible for all."[22]

Most families, not accustomed to hearing this emphasis in Catholic thought, think of their economic decisions primarily in terms of making ends meet and giving what is left over to charity. However, if values like solidarity and the common good are family values, then this is inadequate. The Catholic moral vision speaks to the broader ethical responsibilities of families with regard to money.

American Catholic families hear this message but often feel stretched to their limit. They work hard and yet seem to have less than their parents did. As continuing debates over tax breaks for the rich suggest, even those who earn $100,000 or more do not see themselves as wealthy. The deep dissatisfaction of the middle class means that most families feel that they do not have the luxury of sharing more of what they have.

Families at the bottom of the income distribution really are limited by their lack of ability to fill basic needs. Still, the American ideology of consumerism makes most families' lives much emptier than they might be. This ideology constrains their choices, eats up their time, denies them happiness, and constricts their ability to act on commitments to the common good. Even those who recognize their own excesses find it difficult to break free of something so pervasive. Families of all income levels consider themselves needy. The process by which desires have become needs is not clear.

Where does this dissatisfaction come from? Catholic ethicist John Kavanaugh's book *Following Christ in a Consumer Society* gives a particularly vivid account of the destructive force of an ideology fed by dissatisfaction.[23] Kavanaugh attempts to illustrate this phenomenon by comparing a family content with a relatively simple lifestyle to a family dissatisfied with internal relationships and simple pleasures, one that turns to consumer culture for pleasure. Of the first family he writes, "If you just like talking to people, visiting them, spending time in conversation with them, if you enjoy living simply, if you sense no need to compete with your friends or neighbors — what good are you economically in terms of our system? You haven't spent a nickel yet."[24] The second family is, of course, very good for the American system, because it wants so much. Kavanaugh points out that capitalism as an economic system needs dissatisfaction in order to survive. It encourages people to feel unhappy with what they have and urges them to seek fulfillment in consumption.

At the same time, consumerism discourages intimacy, relationships, and respect for persons as they are. It makes families feel they must keep up with everyone else. They end up working longer hours, spending ever more time shopping, and buying things they cannot afford on credit cards that keep them tied to working too much in jobs they do not like.[25] Families fill the emptiness the culture creates in them with things, and persons necessarily become secondary. There is no time or space for valuing relationships with family and friends, let alone making room in their lives for the poor.

Kavanaugh rightly contends that consumerism functions as a kind of armor isolating people from their friends and family and allows them to refuse to hear the cries of the poor. When so many American families, who are so much better off than most other families in the world, feel unable to commit themselves in solidarity to the world's least fortunate, something is wrong. Social analysis exposes the power of the ideology that significantly impacts family economic decisions and may allow families to think seriously about how they can better value solidarity and the common good in their lives.

Consider the case of the Murphys, a family of six in Washington, D.C. Bill and Sharon Murphy have run a shelter for homeless families for over twenty years. They live in the main building of the shelter with their four children and two homeless families. Over the years, they have financed and renovated several other buildings, so that they now help many more families make the transition from the streets to their own homes. They receive only small stipends for their work and have lived simply for all of their married life. The Murphys' simple lifestyle, hospitality, refusal to work merely for money, and general valuing of persons over things challenges all families who seek to fulfill a commitment to the common good. The Murphys have found an extraordinary way of making economic decisions that value family and community. Few families will be called to this kind of life, but it is important to hear stories that illustrate so well the social values families are called to embrace. Other families make smaller sacrifices — sharing a home so that they can do the work they love, living and working in the inner city, or opening their home to women or children in need of temporary refuge. These models challenge middle-class lifestyles and provide inspiration for families seeking to move beyond the popular but unnecessary dichotomy between family and community.[26]

The Family Meal

Many contemporary commentators on the family speak of the demise of the family meal as a symbol of the decline of the family. They argue that the restoration of this daily ritual is crucial to the health of family life. Robert Bellah even goes so far as to call the family dinner hour a missing sacrament, and he worries about what happens to families when no one has time to prepare or sit down for a common meal. Bellah identifies several fundamental aspects of the sacramental meal: time together, a commitment to limit work so that time is available, a corresponding willingness to forgo the extra money that work would bring in, and a shared responsibility for the meal that assumes both husband and wife have public commitments outside the home.[27] A Catholic understanding of a sacramental family meal would presume all of this and something more. Sacraments in the Catholic tradition are about unity and action. Sacraments concern what the church is in itself and what the church does for society in order to become itself. A Catholic sacramental understanding of the family meal reveals in a profound way that the family is a community that, like the church, has duties both to itself and to society.

What would a Catholic understanding of a sacramental family meal look like? Catholic theologian David Hollenbach claims that sacramental celebrations provide important insights into the church's social role, and he uses the Eucharist to illustrate his point.[28] Since in the Eucharist sharing food symbolizes the unity of all persons in Christ, he believes that it makes sense to think of feeding the hungry as a central part of the Christian mission. Hollenbach sees in the sacramental meal a moral imperative. In the sharing of food, Christians celebrate who they are. If sharing food was Jesus' way of symbolizing his commitment to the earliest Christian community and, ultimately, to all people, Christians must also share food in and with their communities.

Significantly, many New Testament texts identify Jesus as someone who eats with sinners. Many times when eating with friends he also welcomed the marginalized in his own society.[29] This included those considered unclean, tax collectors, and prostitutes. Jesus refused to turn anyone away from a table at which he was eating. This was a powerful witness in his times, and many of his contemporaries criticized him for it. Jesus made inclusivity an important ethical norm in his ministry. The Jesus who preached that the last would be first, told the story of Lazarus and the rich man, and announced that those who fed the hungry and clothed the naked would be on the right side on Judgment Day, also made sure that the meals to which he was invited were celebrations of all God's people. Thus when Jesus finally gathered the disciples for the last supper the night before he died and, as John has it, washed their feet, he told them once again who he was and who they must be — and he told them with a meal, a meal that became the model for the church's Eucharist. Meals that the church celebrates, then, ought to reflect some of this concern for social justice.

If one can think of a Christian family as a "domestic church," one can consider their meal, in some sense, eucharistic. In a traditional Catholic sense, it can be thought of as a sacramental (a vehicle of God's grace) like holy water or the rosary. The family meal, like the Eucharist, is important, not because it is the high point of the family's life, but because it symbolizes what the family is and what it does. If the family meal is neglected, not only do the relationships among family members suffer, but so does the sense of what the family is about. The meal brings the family together and provides an opportunity for shared talk, celebration, and mission.

In my own family, dinner conversations about my father's work as a lawyer became fundamental to the identity of all three children. They influenced our career choices, shaped our politics, and gave us a strong sense of civic responsibility. Similarly, my parents took up into their own lives and identities their children's challenges in journalism, theater, debate, and youth groups. Both kinds of conversations led into discussions of larger social issues. Both brought our family closer together. As we shared stories about our work and argued about our values, we became more a part of each other's lives. We grew as a family because we took the time to talk, and because we had something bigger than ourselves to talk about.

Now, with my husband of ten years and my three young sons, I am trying to create my own version of this family ritual. As my children are all under the age of nine, just getting them to sit down with us for ten minutes without spilling anything is an accomplishment. Still, we pray, thanking God for everything from rain to *Star Wars*, we invite friends and family over as much as possible, and we try to maintain an inclusive table where all who wish to join us are welcome. Little by little, we are beginning to talk about serving the poor and the larger social issues everywhere around us. In the ritual of the family meal, I hope that my children will discover, as I did, much about what it means to be a Christian.

If family meals are to be sacramental, they must be about more than just family members, just as the Eucharist is about more than just the church. Families are public as well as private, concerned with both love and justice. Families should share meals together not only so that their members may enjoy each other's company and solidify bonds that will be crucial to all members, but also because families are small communities with social missions. If families do not gather as communities of love in their homes, they cannot then be communities of love for the world, but if they gather only to love themselves, they do less than the Christian tradition requires of them. Families are called to and capable of much more.

Discussion Questions

1. Does Rubio adequately address the concerns of those who worry that a socially concerned family will neglect its own good? Can concern for justice conflict with passion for loved ones?

2. How do you understand solidarity and the common good? In what ways are families you know committed to these values?

3. Does it seem unrealistic to claim that all parents' work must contribute to the common good? Are responsibilities to provide and care for one's family more important?

4. Is time a significant problem for contemporary families? If so, is Rubio correct to argue that more time should be used to serve the community?

5. Is consumerism a destructive force for most families?

6. Does Rubio correctly describe family meals as sacramental?

Notes

1. Family or Families?

1. "MassMutual American Family Values Study," cited in Michael Lawler, *Family: American and Christian* (Chicago: Loyola Press, 1998), 30.

2. Alasdair MacIntyre, *After Virtue: A Study in Moral Theory* (Notre Dame, Ind.: University of Notre Dame Press, 1981), 263.

3. Bill Clinton campaigned on this issue and offered concrete support in the form of the Family and Medical Leave Act, which he signed soon after taking office in 1992 and extended in 1996. This act allows working parents to take twelve weeks of leave to care for new babies or elderly parents and then return to work.

4. Katherine Dowling, *Los Angeles Times*, March 15, 1998, B5.

5. Arlie Hochschild, *The Time Bind: When Work Becomes Home and Home Becomes Work* (New York: Henry Holt, 1997), 3, 8–9.

6. Barrie Thorne, with Marilyn Yalom, eds., *Rethinking the Family: Some Feminist Questions* (Boston: Northeastern University Press, 1992), 6–11.

7. Jane Collier, Michelle Z. Rosaldo, and Sylvia Yanagisako, "Is There a Family? New Anthropological Views," in Thorne, *Rethinking the Family*, 34–35.

8. Thorne, *Rethinking the Family*, 9.

9. Ibid., 24.

10. Judith Stacey, "Backward toward the Postmodern Family: Reflections on Gender, Kinship, and Class in the Silicon Valley" in ibid., 95–96.

11. Ibid., 96–102.

12. Ibid., 109.

13. Ibid., 14–22.

14. Hochschild, *The Time Bind*, 3, 8–9.

15. According to Hochschild, men's lives suffer when the second shift is not shared too. Tensions build between husbands and wives who are not in agreement about how to divide household labor. The happiest couples, Hochschild says, are those who share the second shift (ibid., 211).

16. Michael Lawler, *Family: American and Christian* (Chicago: Loyola Press, 1998), 22.

17. Ibid., 30–34.

18. Ibid., 41.

19. Lawler does eventually argue against most divorces but he bases his argument on the effects of divorce, not loyalty to the ideal (ibid., 76).

20. Lisa Sowle Cahill, *Between the Sexes: Foundations for a Christian Ethics of Sexuality* (Philadelphia: Fortress, 1985), 96.

21. See for instance, the essays in Lisa Sowle Cahill and Dietmar Mieth, eds., *The Family* (Maryknoll, N.Y.: Orbis, 1995).

22. One might argue that conservative Christians are traditional or premodern, but I believe that most contemporary conservatives are more properly defined as those who believe in a more monolithic truth.

23. James Dobson, *Dare to Discipline* (Wheaton, Ill.: Tyndale, 1973).

24. For instance, one chapter is entitled "A Moment for Mom" and addresses the subject of how stay-at-home moms can take care of themselves.

25. Ibid., 221.

26. Stephen J. Post, *Spheres of Love: Toward a New Ethics of the Family* (Dallas: Southern Methodist University, 1994), 2.

27. Ibid., 3.

28. Ibid., 4.

29. Interestingly enough, Stackhouse's book, *Covenant and Commitments: Faith, Family, and Economic Life* (Louisville: Westminster John Knox, 1997), carries a back cover recommendation from Stephen Post.

30. Ibid., 13.

31. Ibid., 19.

32. Ibid.

33. Ibid., 30.

34. Cahill, *Between the Sexes,* 38.

35. Pope John Paul II, *On the Family* (Washington, D.C.: United States Catholic Conference, 1981), no. 3.

36. Elsewhere the pope gives a more extensive reflection on the Genesis texts in which he notes that these texts are fundamental because Jesus refers back to them in his own affirmation of the importance of marriage in Matthew 19:4. He also finds that the whole structure of gendered human relationships is revealed here for all times. See Pope John Paul II, *On the Original Unity of Man and Woman* (Boston: Daughters of St. Paul, 1981).

37. *On the Family* nos. 11–15. The pope sees virginity or celibacy as a parallel vocation to marriage, a more excellent way of living in communion with God, but a way to which far fewer people are called (no. 16).

38. Ibid., no. 17.

39. Ibid., no. 4.

40. Ibid., no. 8.

41. National Conference of Catholic Bishops, "Follow the Way of Love," *Origins* 23, no. 25 (December 2, 1993): 435.

42. Ibid.

43. Ibid., 436.

44. Ibid., 436–37.

45. Ibid., 440.

2. The Catholic Marriage Liturgy

1. Chuck Gallagher, *The Marriage Encounter: As I Have Loved You* (Garden City, N.Y.: Doubleday, 1975), 109.

2. Ibid., 154.

3. Joseph Martos, *Doors to the Sacred* (Garden City, N.Y.: Doubleday, 1981), 409.

4. Ibid., 420

5. Paul Covino, ed., *Celebrating Marriage: Preparing the Wedding Liturgy: A Workbook for Engaged Couples* (Washington, D.C.: Pastoral Press, 1994), 3.

6. Martos, *Doors to the Sacred*, 425.

7. Ibid.

8. Ibid., 438. All marriages before the council were considered valid as long as both husband and wife had given their consent.

9. Ibid., 446. The guidelines also allowed for more flexibility in the ceremony.

10. Vatican II was a series of meetings in Rome from 1962 to 1965 attended by bishops from all over the world. The goal was a renewal of the church. Some of the most significant changes were liturgical. For example, the priest now faced the congregation, the language of the mass was the vernacular, and there was a new emphasis on participation of the congregation in spoken responses and singing. See Austin Flannery, ed., *Vatican Council II: The Conciliar and Post Conciliar Documents*, rev. ed. (Northport, N.Y.: Costello Publishing Co., 1988).

11. Covino, *Celebrating Marriage*, 27.

12. Ibid., 14–15.

13. Jo McGowan, "Marriage versus Living Together," in *Perspectives on Marriage: A Reader*, ed. Kieran Scott and Michael Warren (New York: Oxford University Press, 1993), 129.

14. "Marriage," in Francis Schüssler Fiorenza and John P. Galvin, eds., *Systematic Theology: Roman Catholic Perspectives* (Minneapolis: Fortress, 1991), 2:307–46.

15. Ibid., 332.

16. Austin Fleming, *Prayerbook for Engaged Couples* (Chicago: Liturgy Training Publications, 1990), 37.

17. Fiorenza, "Marriage," 334.

18. Cited in Michael G. Lawler, *Family: American and Christian* (Chicago: Loyola Press, 1998), 49.

19. Lisa Cahill, "Marriage: Institution, Relationship, Sacrament," in *One Hundred Years of Catholic Social Thought: Celebration and Challenge*, ed. John A. Coleman (Maryknoll, N.Y.: Orbis, 1991), 115.

20. Ibid., 117.

21. Fiorenza, "Marriage," 335.

22. Ibid.

23. *The Church in the Modern World* in *Vatican Council II: The Conciliar and Post Conciliar Documents*, rev. ed., ed. Austin Flannery (Northport, N.Y.: Costello Publishing Co., 1988), no. 48.

24. Karl Rahner, S.J., *Theological Investigations,* vol. 10 (New York: Herder and Herder, 1973), 207.

25. National Conference of Catholic Bishops, *Marriage in Christ* (Collegeville, Minn.: Liturgical Press, 1991), 24.

26. Geoffrey Robinson, *Marriage, Divorce, and Nullity: A Guide to the Annulment Process in the Catholic Church* (Collegeville, Minn.: Liturgical Press, 1984).

27. Mark Chmiel, "Seven Sacraments of Everyday Life," *Praying: Spirituality for Everyday Living* (September 1998): 5.

28. Mark Chmiel and Mev Puleo, "The Holy Contour of Life," unpublished manuscript, 2001.

3. New Testament Vision

1. A recent *Los Angeles Times* poll, for instance, found that 67 percent of all parents surveyed said that they would prefer to stay home with their children rather than work. Cathleen Decker, "Parents Tell of Decisions, Struggles in Child-Rearing," *Los Angeles Times,* June 13, 1999, A1, A32.

2. Arlie Hochschild, *The Time Bind: When Work Becomes Home and Home Becomes Work* (New York: Henry Holt, 1997).

3. It is difficult for me, an ethicist with no training in Greek or Hebrew, to approach these texts. I hope, however, that my analysis of New Testament scholarship will be useful.

4. See Lisa Sowle Cahill, *Sex, Gender, and Christian Ethics* (Cambridge: Cambridge University Press, 1996), 124.

5. The Catholic Church has traditionally understood this passage to refer to close relations of Jesus, not siblings. Other churches, along with many contemporary biblical scholars, believe Jesus may well have had siblings.

6. C. S. Mann, *Mark,* Anchor Bible (Garden City, N.Y.: Doubleday, 1986), 259. See also relevant commentary on parallel passages (Luke 8:19–21, Matt 12:46–50).

7. Ezra P. Gould, *Mark,* International Critical Commentary (New York: Charles Scribner's Sons, 1961), 68.

8. See the controversial film *The Last Temptation of Christ* for more on possibilities that were, by all accounts, eventually rejected.

9. Joseph Fitzmyer, *Luke,* Anchor Bible (Garden City, N.Y.: Doubleday, 1986), 834.

10. Gerd Theissen, who wrote the influential *Sociology of the Early Palestinian Christianity* (Philadelphia: Fortress, 1989), makes this claim about the makeup of the early church.

11. Richard Horsley, *Sociology of the Jesus Movement* (New York: Crossroad, 1989), 117.

12. Elisabeth Schüssler Fiorenza, *In Memory of Her: A Feminist Theological Reconstruction of Christian Origins* (New York: Crossroad, 1989), 146.

13. Ibid., 147.

14. Ibid., 150.

15. See Cahill, *Sex, Gender, and Christian Ethics,* 141–50.

16. Schüssler Fiorenza makes the convincing claim that the anti-family ethos was applied to females as well as males, despite the Lukan redaction that might suggest the contrary. See *In Memory of Her,* 145–46.

17. Peter Brown, *The Body and Society: Men, Women, and Sexual Renunciation in Early Christianity* (New York: Columbia University Press, 1988), 5–7.

18. Ibid.

19. David Hunter, ed., *Marriage in the Early Church* (Minneapolis: Fortress, 1992), 6.

20. Ibid., 7. Hunter notes, however, that around the time Christianity was developing, there was in Roman thought a move toward seeing marriage more as a friendship. This trend influenced early Christian writers. See ibid., 7–8.

21. Brown, *The Body and Society,* 6.

22. Ibid., 5.

23. Andrew Jacobs, "A Family Affair: Marriage, Class, and Ethics in the Apocryphal Acts of the Apostles," *Journal of Early Christian Studies* 7, no. 1 (1999): 106.

24. Ibid., 107.

25. Brown, *The Body and Society,* 62.

26. See Horsley, *Sociology of the Jesus Movement,* 113.

27. Cahill, *Sex, Gender, and Christian Ethics,* 142.

28. The exceptions here are radical groups like the Essenes and Therapeutae who did live in celibate communities before the advent of Jesus' ministry. However, though these groups were well respected, they do not represent mainstream Jewish or Greek thought or practice. See Stephen C. Barton, "The Relativisation of Family Ties" in *Constructing Early Christian Families: Family as Social Reality and Metaphor,* ed. Halvor Moxnes (New York: Routledge, 1997). Barton claims that the evidence of alternatives and the praise of these groups indicate that Jesus is continuing a tradition rather than breaking it. I would argue that his evidence centers largely on elite groups, while the early Jesus movement is a broad-based family-questioning movement. Thus, in my view, Jesus does begin something quite new, though it does have some roots in radical strains of his tradition.

29. This is not to say that Judaism placed family ties over God, but it is to claim that Jesus saw a conflict between God and family that many in his time did not.

30. Horsley, *Sociology of the Jesus Movement,* 123.

31. Stephen Post, "Adoption Theologically Considered," *Journal of Religious Ethics* (Spring 1997): 149–68.

32. Ibid., 163.

33. Horsley, *Sociology of the Jesus Movement,* 107.

34. Post, "Adoption Theologically Considered," 73–74.

35. See Mann, *Mark,* 396. Even if children are given more dignity here, the particulars of how they are to be cared for are not specified.

36. Schüssler Fiorenza, *In Memory of Her,* 149.

37. See Cahill, *Sex, Gender, and Christian Ethics,* 151.

38. This interpretation is put forth by Don Browning et al., in *From Culture Wars to Common Ground: Religion and the American Family Debate* (Louisville: Westminster John Knox, 1997), 141–47.

39. *Passio Andreae*, 12 (MacDonald, 338–40), quoted in Jacobs, "A Family Affair," 129.

40. Ibid., 132.

41. A good example is Thecla, whose story is told in the Acts of Paul and Thecla, quoted in Jacobs, "A Family Affair," 133. Also relevant is the example of a couple that abandons earthly marriage for spiritual marriage in the Acts of Thomas (135).

42. See Schüssler Fiorenza, *In Memory of Her*, 208–18. See also Lisa Sowle Cahill's description of early Christian "families" that challenged cultural hierarchies in *Sex, Gender, and Christian Ethics*, 128.

43. Eva Marie Lassen notes that Christians used family metaphors to express equality, while Romans used family metaphors to express authority, and surmises that this must have been shocking to the Romans. See Lassen, "The Roman Family: Ideal and Metaphor," in *Constructing Early Christian Families: Family as Social Reality and Metaphor*, ed. Halvor Moxnes (New York: Routledge, 1997), 115.

44. Cahill, *Sex, Gender, and Christian Ethics*, 154.

45. Osiek, "The New Testament and the Family," in *The Family*, ed. Lisa Sowle Cahill and Dietmar Mieth (Maryknoll, N.Y.: Orbis, 1995), 8.

46. Brown, *The Body and Society*, 53.

47. Ibid., 36.

48. John M. G. Barclay, "The Family as the Bearer of Religion in Judaism and Early Christianity," in *Constructing Early Christian Families: Family as Social Reality and Metaphor*, ed. Halvor Moxnes (New York: Routledge, 1997), 75.

49. Cahill, *Sex, Gender, and Christian Ethics*, 153.

50. For an explanation and critique of this view, see John Howard Yoder, *The Politics of Jesus: Vicit Agnus Noster* (Grand Rapids, Mich.: Eerdmans, 1972), 108–9.

51. Schüssler Fiorenza, "Patriarchal Structures and the Discipleship of Equals," in *Discipleship of Equals: A Critical Feminist Ecclesiology of Liberation* (New York: Crossroad, 1993), 223.

52. Brown, *The Body and Society*, 53.

4. Traditional Ways of Speaking about Marriage

1. See Robert Orsi, *The Madonna of 115th Street: Faith and Community in Italian Harlem, 1880–1950* (New Haven: Yale University Press, 1985).

2. Peter Brown, *The Body and Society: Men, Women, and Sexual Renunciation in Early Christianity* (New York: Columbia University Press, 1988) 39.

3. Ibid., 39–40.

4. Ibid., 44.

5. Lisa Sowle Cahill, *Sex, Gender, and Christian Ethics* (Cambridge: Cambridge University Press, 1996), 152, commenting on Brown's work.

6. Carol P. Harrison, "The Silent Majority: The Family in Patristic Thought," in *The Family in Theological Perspective*, ed. Stephen C. Barton (Edinburgh: T. & T. Clark, 1996), 87.

7. Brown, *The Body and Society*, 58–59.

8. David Hunter, ed., *Marriage in the Early Church* (Minneapolis: Fortress, 1992), 14–15.

9. Harrison, "The Silent Majority," 102, discussing Clement's *Miscellanies*, III, 7, 8.

10. Ibid., 97.

11. "To His Wife," translated in Hunter, *Marriage in the Early Church*, 34.

12. Ibid., 35.

13. Ibid., 38.

14. Jean LaPorte points out that neither children nor sexual intercourse appear to be part of this vision. See her *The Role of Women in Early Christianity* (Lewiston, N.Y.: Edwin Mellen Press, 1982), 27.

15. Translated in Hunter, *Marriage in the Early Church*, 61.

16. Harrison, "The Silent Majority," 93, commenting on the trials of marriage as a literary topos in the early church fathers' writings on virginity.

17. Hunter, *Marriage in the Early Church*, 17.

18. "Against Jovinian," translated in Elizabeth Clark and Herbert Richardson, eds., *Women and Religion: A Feminist Sourcebook of Christian Thought* (San Francisco: HarperCollins, 1977), 67.

19. Harrison, "The Silent Majority," 99.

20. Ibid., 100.

21. St. John Chrysostom, "An Address," in *Christianity and Pagan Culture in the Later Roman Empire*, trans. M. L. W. Laistner (Ithaca, N.Y.: Cornell University Press, 1951), 93–94.

22. Ibid., 94.

23. Ibid., 95.

24. Augustine, *The Good of Marriage*, in Hunter, *Marriage in the Early Church*, 121.

25. Harrison, "The Silent Majority," 104.

26. See John Mahoney, *The Making of Moral Theology: A Study of the Roman Catholic Tradition* (Oxford: Clarendon, 1987), 44–68; Rosemary Radford Ruether, "Mother-earth and the Megamachine," in *Womanspirit Rising: A Feminist Reader in Religion*, ed. Carol P. Christ and Judith Plaskow (San Francisco: HarperSanFrancisco, 1992), 43–52.

27. Joseph Martos, "Marriage," in *Perspectives on Marriage: A Reader*, ed. Kieran Scott and Michael Warren (New York: Oxford University Press, 1993), 37.

28. Ibid., 43.

29. John Witte, *From Sacrament to Contract: Marriage, Religion, and Law in the Western Tradition* (Louisville: Westminster John Knox, 1997), 22.

30. Martos, "Marriage," 49.

31. Ibid., 51.

32. Witte, *From Sacrament to Contract*, 54.

33. Ibid., 58.

34. Ibid., 70–73.

208

35. Martin Luther, *Lectures on Genesis,* excerpted in *Woman and Religion: A Feminist Sourcebook of Christian Thought,* ed. Elizabeth Clarke and Herbert Richardson (San Francisco: HarperCollins, 1977), 145.

36. Ibid., 110.

37. Max L. Stackhouse *Covenant and Commitments: Faith, Family, and Economic Life* (Louisville: Westminster John Knox, 1997).

38. James Nelson, "Varied Meanings of Marriage and Fidelity," in *Perspectives on Marriage: A Reader,* ed. Kieran Scott and Michael Warren (New York: Oxford University Press, 1993), 109.

39. Michael Lawler, *Marriage and Sacrament: A Theology of Christian Marriage* (Collegeville, Minn.: Liturgical Press, 1993), 66.

40. See Margaret Farley, *Personal Commitments: Beginning, Keeping, Changing* (San Francisco: Harper & Row, 1986).

41. Christine Gudorf, *Body, Sex, and Pleasure: Reconstructing Christian Sexual Ethics* (Cleveland: Pilgrim, 1994).

42. Lawler, *Marriage and Sacrament,* 63.

43. Ibid., 18–19.

44. Ibid.

45. Ibid., 19.

46. Bernard Cooke, "Christian Marriage: Basic Sacrament," in *Perspectives on Marriage: A Reader,* 2d ed., ed. Kieran Scott and Michael Warren (New York: Oxford University Press, 2001), 48–49.

47. John Paul II, *On the Original Unity of Man and Woman* (Boston: Daughters of St. Paul, 1981), 132–33. The pope grounds his theology in an interpretation of the second creation story in Genesis. He sees Adam searching for a being with whom he can relate and rejoicing when he finally is presented with Eve, his helpmate and second self, 66.

48. Ibid., 80.

49. John Paul II, *The Theology of Marriage and Celibacy* (Boston: Daughters of St. Paul, 1986), 282–84.

50. Ronald Modras, "Pope John Paul II's Theology of the Body," in *The Vatican and Homosexuality: Reactions to the "Letter to the Bishops of the Catholic Church on the Pastoral Care of Homosexual Persons,"* ed. Jeannine Gramick and Pat Furey (New York: Crossroad, 1988), 120–24.

51. Ibid., 125.

52. John Paul II, *On the Family* (Washington, D.C.: United States Catholic Conference, 1981), no. 11.

53. Ibid., nos. 12–13.

54. Ibid., no. 13.

55. Ibid., no. 14.

56. Ibid., no. 15.

57. Ibid., no. 16.

5. The Dual Vocation of Christian Parents

1. Flannery O'Connor, "The Lame Shall Enter First," in Flannery O'Connor, *The Complete Stories* (New York: Noonday Press, 1946), 447.

2. Ibid., 480–81.

3. In the story Rufus is physically lame, but it is Sheppard, who lacks faith and compassion, who is truly lame. The story's title refers to the biblical idea that the last shall be first.

4. Ellen Galinsky, *Ask the Children: What America's Children Really Think about Working Parents* (New York: William Morrow, 1999), 251.

5. Ibid., xviii.

6. Ibid., 251.

7. Linda Woodhead, "Faith, Feminism, and the Family," in *The Family*, Concilium, ed. Lisa Sowle Cahill and Dietmar Mieth (Maryknoll, N.Y.: Orbis, 1995), 45.

8. Theologian Stephen Post affirms this insight in his book *Spheres of Love: Toward a New Ethics of the Family* (Dallas: Southern Methodist University Press, 1994). He argues that "the first sphere of love is the one where our natural sympathies lie." (146) This claim runs counter to those writers on agape who prioritize universal love over special relations.

9. Adrienne Rich, *Of Woman Born: Motherhood as Experience and Institution*, 10th anniversary edition (New York: W. W. Norton, 1986), 26.

10. Ibid., 24.

11. Sally Purvis, "Mothers, Neighbors and Strangers," *Journal of Feminist Studies in Religion* 7 (Spring 1991): 19.

12. Ibid., 21. Purvis, like Post, questions the agape tradition of Kierkegaard, Gene Outka, and others.

13. Ibid., 26–27.

14. Ibid., 30.

15. Ibid., 25–26.

16. See, for instance, Mitch Finley's *Your Family in Focus* (Notre Dame, Ind.: Ave Maria, 1993).

17. Carrie J. Heiman, *The Nine-Month Miracle* (Liguori, Mo.: Liguori Publications, 1986), Week 24.

18. Bonnie J. Miller-McLemore, *Also a Mother* (Nashville: Abingdon, 1994), 143.

19. Ibid., 149.

20. Ibid.

21. See John Paul II. *On the Family* (Washington, D.C.: United States Catholic Conference, 1981), no. 17. See also Stephen G. Post, *A Theory of Agape: On the Meaning of Christian Love* (Lewisburg, Pa.: Bucknell University Press, 1990), *Spheres of Love: Toward a New Ethics of the Family* (Dallas: Southern Methodist University Press, 1994), and *More Lasting Unions: Christianity, the Family, and Society* (Grand Rapids, Mich.: Eerdmans, 2000). Post relies on philosophical and sociological arguments for special relations.

22. John Paul II, *On the Family*, no. 16. The pope argues that uplifting celibacy confirms the goodness of marriage because it assumes that celibacy requires the sacrifice of something very good. I would argue that the celibacy tradition paradoxically affirms and questions the goodness of marriage.

23. William Spohn, *Go and Do Likewise: Jesus and Ethics* (New York: Continuum, 1999), 10–13.

24. Richard Hays, *The Moral Vision of the New Testament* (San Francisco: Harper-Collins, 1996), 85.

25. John Howard Yoder fits in here as well, since he claims that discipleship is political. See *The Politics of Jesus: Vicit Agnus Noster* (Grand Rapids, Mich.: Eerdmans, 1972).

26. See ibid.

27. John Paul II, *On Human Labor* (Washington, D.C.: United States Catholic Conference, 1981), no. 4.

28. John Paul II, *On Human Labor*, no. 6.

29. Ibid.

30. Ibid., no. 16.

31. Ibid., no. 25.

32. *The Church in the Modern World* in Austin Flannery, O.P., ed., *Vatican Council II*, rev. ed. (Northport, N.Y.: Costello Publishing Co., 1988), no. 43

33. *On Human Labor*, no. 6.

34. Dorothy Day (1897–1980) was the founder of the Catholic Worker movement. CW houses all over the country still offer shelter and food to the homeless, and publish politically oriented newspapers as well.

35. Dorothy Day, *Loaves and Fishes* (Maryknoll, N.Y.: Orbis, 1997), 221.

36. Dorothy Day, *The Long Loneliness: An Autobiography* (San Francisco: Harper & Row, 1952), 166.

37. John Paul II, *On the Dignity and Vocation of Woman* (Washington, D.C.: United States Catholic Conference, 1988), no. 19.

38. When Catholic thought addresses the worker or the parent generally, this is true. This insight gets lost when women or men are specifically addressed. See *On the Family*, nos. 22–25.

39. Post, *Spheres of Love*, 59.

40. Betty Friedan, *The Feminine Mystique* (New York: Dell, 1963), 15–17

41. Rich, *Of Woman Born*, 15.

42. Ibid., 29.

43. Ibid., 31.

44. Ibid., 32.

45. Carolyn Pape Cowan and Philip A. Cowan, *When Partners Become Parents: The Big Life Change for Couples* (New York: Basic Books, 1992), 81.

46. Ibid., 99.

47. Mitch and Susan Golant, *Finding Time for Fathering* (New York: Ballantine, 1993), 28–29.

48. Ibid., 61–62.

49. Robert Griswold, *Fatherhood in America: A History* (New York: Basic Books, 1993), 220.

50. Ibid., 2.

51. Ibid., 269.

52. Galinsky, *Ask the Children*, 49, 54. She notes that the mother's feelings about what she is doing, whether it is working or staying home, make the difference.

53. *On the Family*, no. 17.

54. Ibid., no. 28.

55. Ibid., no. 37.

56. Ibid., no. 39.

57. Ibid., no. 41.

58. Ibid., no. 42

59. Ibid., no. 44

60. Ibid., no. 44, 47.

61. Ibid., no. 47.

62. Ibid., no. 21.

63. Ibid., nos. 49–64.

64. *Parenting for Peace and Justice* (Maryknoll, N.Y.: Orbis, 1990).

65. Jack Nelson-Pallmeyer, *Families Valued: Parenting and Politics for the Good of All Children* (New York: Friendship Press, 1996), 40.

66. One could argue that if families have public missions, work is unnecessary to discipleship. This seems a valid claim for those parents who are deeply involved in their communities.

67. Galinsky, *Ask the Children*, 343–44.

68. Flannery O'Connor, *The Habit of Being*, ed. and with an introduction by Sally Fitzgerald (New York: Noonday Press, 1979), 90. The original phrase is from W. B. Yeats's poem, "The Second Coming."

6. *Mothering in Christian Families*

1. See Adrienne Rich's seminal book *Of Woman Born: Motherhood as Experience and Institution*, 10th anniversary ed. (New York: W. W. Norton, 1986), or Betty Friedan's more popular *The Feminine Mystique* (New York: Dell, 1963).

2. John Paul II, *On the Dignity and Vocation of Woman* (Washington, D.C.: United States Catholic Conference, 1988), no. 18, *and On the Original Unity of Man and Woman* (Boston: Daughter of St. Paul, 1981), nos. 132–33.

3. John Paul II, *On the Family* (Washington, D.C.: United States Catholic Conference, 1981), no. 22.

4. Ibid., no. 32.

5. See, for instance, Lisa Cahill, "Can We Get Real about Sex?" *Commonweal* 117, no. 15 (September 14, 1990): 497–503.

6. See John Paul II, *On the Dignity and Vocation of Woman*, nos. 18–19, where the pope links childbirth to the self-emptying sacrifice of the cross.

7. Ibid.

8. John Paul II, *On the Family* (Washington, D.C.: United States Catholic Conference, 1988), no. 21.

9. Ibid. no. 32.

10. Ibid.

11. Ibid.

12. See, for instance, Giles Dimock, "Women, the Woman, and the Church," *Social Justice Review* (July–August 1992): 113–15.

13. Mary Ann Glendon, "What Happened at Beijing," *First Things* (January 1996): 30–36.

14. See also Dimock, "Women, the Woman, and the Church," 113–15.

15. Gregory Baum, "Bulletin: The Apostolic Letter *Mulieris dignitatem*," in *Motherhood: Experience, Institution, Theology*, ed. Elisabeth Schüssler Fiorenza and Anne Carr (Edinburgh: T. & T. Clark, 1989), 149.

16. Leo XIII, *On the Condition of the Working Classes* (1891), no. 60 (Boston: Daughters of St. Paul, 1942). Pope Leo claims that women "are intended by nature for work of the home — work indeed which especially protects modesty in women and accords by nature with the education of children and the well-being of the family."

17. Pius XI, *Christian Marriage* (1930) (New York: Paulist, 1939), nos. 74–76.

18. Some conservatives were angered by the pope's agreement with feminists, especially his interpretation of Ephesians 5 as mutual subjection and his embrace of female names for God. Nancy Cross concludes an article lamenting the pope's feminism with a promise to be a faithful subject of the pope, despite her disappointment in him. See Cross, "A Traditionalist's Dilemma: What to Do When the Pope Goes Feminist," *Crisis* (January 1990): 32.

19. Lisa Sowle Cahill, *Between the Sexes* (Minneapolis: Fortress, 1985), 54. Elsewhere she claims that Motherhood is an overwhelming category in the document, despite the emphasis on equality. See *Women and Sexuality* (New York: Paulist, 1992), 54.

20. Cahill, *Between the Sexes*, 52.

21. Cahill, *Women and Sexuality*, 27.

22. Ibid.

23. Ibid., 29.

24. Cahill, *Between the Sexes*, 96.

25. Ibid.

26. Cahill, *Women and Sexuality*, 31. Their choices were often not well-received, because they disrupted the household. See Andrew Jacobs, "A Family Affair: Marriage, Class, and Ethics in the Apocryphal Acts of the Apostles," *Journal of Early Christian Studies* 7, no. 1 (1999): 105–38.

27. See Elisabeth Schüssler Fiorenza, "Women in the Early Christian Movement," in *Womanspirit Rising: A Feminist Reader in Religion*, ed. Carol Christ and Judith Plaskow (San Francisco: HarperSanFrancisco, 1992), or her book *In Memory of Her: A Feminist Theological Reconstruction of Christian Origins* (New York: Crossroad, 1989).

28. Cahill, *Women and Sexuality*, 33–34.

29. Christine Gudorf, "Parenting, Mutual Love, and Sacrifice," in *Women's Consciousness, Women's Conscience: A Reader in Feminist Ethics*, ed. Barbara Hilkert Andolsen, Christine E. Gudorf, and Mary D. Pellauer (Minneapolis: Winston Press, 1985), 182.

30. Ibid., 183.

31. Ibid., 185.

32. Ibid., 191.

33. Christine Gudorf, "Dissecting Parenthood," *Conscience* (Autumn 1994): 17.

34. Ibid., 22.

35. "Sacrifice and Parenting Spiritualities," in *Religion, Feminism, and the Family*, ed. Anne Carr and Mary Stewart Van Leeuwen (Louisville: Westminster John Knox, 1996), 300–302.

36. Bonnie J. Miller-McLemore, *Also a Mother* (Nashville: Abingdon, 1994), 220.

37. Bonnie J. Miller-McLemore, "Let the Children Come," *Second Opinion* 17, no. 1 (July 1991): 21.

38. Miller-McLemore, *Also a Mother*, 123.

39. Ibid., 126.

40. Bonnie J. Miller-McLemore, "Family and Work: Can Anyone 'Have It All?' " in *Religion, Feminism, and the Family*, ed. Anne Carr and Mary Stewart Von Leeuwen (Louisville: Westminster, 1996), 275–93.

41. See Rita Gross, "Female God Language in a Jewish Context," in *Womanspirit Rising: A Feminist Reader in Religion*, ed. Carol Christ and Judith Plaskow (San Francisco: HarperSanFrancisco, 1992).

42. Mary Daly, *Beyond God the Father: Toward a Philosophy of Women's Liberation* (Boston: Beacon, 1973).

43. See Elizabeth Johnson, *She Who Is* (New York: Crossroad, 1997), 180.

44. Johanna Kohn-Roelin, "Mother-Daughter-God," in *Motherhood: Experience, Institution, Theology*, ed. Anne Carr and Elisabeth Schüssler-Fiorenza (Edinburgh: T. & T. Clark, 1989).

45. Sallie McFague, "God as Mother," in *Motherhood: Experience, Institution, Theology*, ed. Anne Carr and Elisabeth Schüssler-Fiorenza (Edinburgh: T. & T. Clark, 1989), 106.

46. Johnson, *She Who Is*, 176.

47. Ibid., 87.

48. See Sallie McFague, *Models of God: Theology for an Ecological, Nuclear Age* (Philadelphia: Fortress, 1987).

49. *On the Dignity and Vocation of Woman*, no. 8

50. Margaret Hebblethwaite, *Motherhood and God* (London: Geoffrey Chapman, 1984), 1.

7. Fathering in Christian Families

1. Robert Griswold, *Fatherhood in America: A History* (New York: Basic Books, 1993), 12.

2. Ibid.

3. Jesse Bernard, "The Good-Provider Role," in *Perspectives on Marriage,* ed. Kieran Scott and Michael Warren (New York: Oxford University Press, 1993), 298.

4. Griswold, *Fatherhood in America,* 14.

5. Bernard, "The Good-Provider Role," 301.

6. Ibid.

7. Griswold *Fatherhood in America,* 207.

8. Ibid., 245.

9. Bernard, "The Good-Provider Role," 311.

10. Joan Aldous, Gail M. Mulligan, and Thoroddur Bjarnason, "Fathering over Time: What Makes the Difference?" *Journal of Marriage and Family* 60 (November 1998): 815.

11. Scott Coltrane, "The Future of Fatherhood," in *Fatherhood: Contemporary Theory, Research, and Social Policy,* ed. William Marsiglio (Thousand Oaks, Calif.: Sage Publications, 1995), 261. However, fathers' involvement has not, according to this study, increased significantly since the 1980s.

12. See Scott Coltrane, *Family Man: Fatherhood, Housework, and Gender Equity* (New York: Oxford, 1996), and Griswold, *Fatherhood in America,* for instance.

13. See Mary De Luccie, "Predictors of Paternal Involvement and Satisfaction," *Psychological Reports* 79 (1996): 1357.

14. Aldous et al., "Fathering over Time," 819.

15. Ibid.

16. See, for instance, Michael Lamb, "Introduction: The Emergent American Father," in *The Father's Role: Cross Cultural Perspectives,* ed. Michael Lamb (Hillsdale, N.J.: LEA Publishers, 1987), 13. Lamb notes that children with highly motivated fathers do better on measures of cognitive ability and emotional maturity, have less stereotyped ideas about gender, and have a firmer internal locus of control, 15–16.

17. Ibid.

18. See chapter 2 of Anna Dienhart, *Reshaping Fatherhood: The Social Construction of Shared Parenting* (Thousand Oaks, Calif.: Sage Publications, 1998).

19. David Blankenhorn, *Fatherless America: Confronting Our Most Urgent Social Problem* (New York: Basic Books, 1995), 202.

20. Ibid.

21. Ibid., 217.

22. Much popular fathering literature focuses on the unique contribution fathers make and uses this as a springboard for arguing that it is important for fathers to be around. It is seemingly more difficult to make the argument for active fatherhood without this notion of a distinctive role. See Mitch Golant and Susan Golant, *Finding Time for Fathering* (New York: Ballantine, 1992).

23. See Lamb, *The Father's Role.*

24. Henry B. Biller, *Fathers and Families: Paternal Factors in Child Development* (Westport, Conn.: Auburn House, 1993); see especially chapter 2 and 3.

25. See Sarah Ruddick, "Maternal Thinking," in *Rethinking the Family,* rev. ed., ed. Barrie Thorne, with Marilyn Yalom (Boston: Northeastern University Press, 1992), 176–90.

26. Coltrane, *Family Man*, 76–80.

27. Ibid. See also Diane Ehrensaft, *Parenting Together: Men and Women Sharing the Care of Their Children* (Chicago: University of Illinois Press, 1987).

28. Coltrane, *Family Man*, 81. Most parents in his survey said that men could nurture just as well as women, and those who thought so were most likely to be those who shared childcare already (81–82).

29. Specifically, Ehrensaft notes that traditional mothers are more likely to take over certain central household tasks and organize the lives of children. As they work more and adjust their priorities, they may become less engaged with the details of their children's lives, as their husbands become more engaged (Ehrensaft, *Parenting Together*, 116–17).

30. Blankenhorn, *Fatherless America*, 25–48.

31. Linda Waite, "Does Marriage Matter?" *Demography* 32, no. 4 (November 1995).

32. Sara McLanahan and Gary Sandefur, *Growing Up with a Single Parent* (Cambridge: Harvard University Press, 1994), 60–61. See also W. Brad Johnson, "Father Uninvolvement: Impact, Etiology, and Potential Solutions," *Journal of Psychology and Christianity* 12, no. 4 (1993).

33. McLanahan and Sandefur, *Growing Up with a Single Parent*.

34. See, for instance, William Marsiglio, "Fatherhood Scholarship: an Overview and Agenda for the Future," in Marsiglio, *Fatherhood*.

35. William Bailey claims that in his study of white middle-class families, "fathers who were most involved with their 3-mo. olds were the least responsive to their infants." Bailey surmises that this might be because fathers were drained by or resentful of the time they had to spend with their infants and suggests that father-child involvement may not be beneficial for all. His results are not surprising because infant care is draining for anyone. I would guess that involved fathers are no less responsive and pleased than involved mothers. The long-term results of the care, however, are something else entirely. See Bailey, "Fathers' Involvement and Responding to Infants: 'More' May Not Be 'Better,'" *Psychological Reports* 74 (1994): 92–94.

36. Coltrane, *Family Man*, 79.

37. Ehrensaft, *Parenting Together*, 165.

38. See Arlie Hochschild, *The Second Shift* (New York: Avon, 1987), 270; Lamb, *The Father's Role*, 16; Ehrensaft, *Parenting Together*, 168–69.

39. Marsiglio, *Fatherhood*, 10.

40. Lamb, *The Father's Role*, 15–16. Their cognitive skills are stronger, they are more empathetic, they hold fewer sexual stereotypes, and they are more internally motivated and controlled.

41. Ibid.

42. Ibid.

43. Ibid.

44. John Paul II, *On the Family* (Washington, D.C.: United States Catholic Conference, 1981), no. 25.

45. Theologian Marvin L. Krier Mich takes offense at the pope's portrayal of fathers, claiming, "There is no need to continue such limited and sexist thinking about

the role of the father. As a father who participated in both of our children's births, I disagree with his unbalanced focusing on the mother and child — leaving men outside. That has been the problem with too many pregnancies and births. The father has not taken up his responsibility and as a result, impoverishes himself, the child, and the mother." Mich, *Catholic Social Teaching and Movements* (Mystic, Conn.: Twenty-Third Publications, 1998).

46. See for instance Elizabeth Johnson's *She Who Is* (New York: Crossroad, 1993).

47. Robert Hammerton-Kelly, *God the Father: Theology and Patriarchy in the Teaching of Jesus* (Philadelphia: Fortress, 1979).

48. Mary Rose D'Angelo, "Abba and Father: Imperial Theology and the Jesus Traditions," *Journal of Biblical Literature* 111, no. 4 (1992): 614–16.

49. Ibid., 616.

50. Ibid., 630.

51. Elisabeth Schüssler Fiorenza, *In Memory of Her: A Feminist Theological Reconstruction of Christian Origins* (New York: Crossroad, 1989), 149–51.

52. John W. Miller, *Calling God "Father": Essays on the Bible, Fatherhood, and Culture* (New York: Paulist, 1999), 92.

53. Ibid.

54. Ibid., 92–93.

55. Ibid., xiv.

56. Kenneth Parker, "Being (God) the Father: What I Learned about Creating in the First Four Years of My Three Sons," unpublished manuscript, 2001.

57. Jürgen Moltmann, "The Motherly Father: Is Trinitarian Patripassianism Replacing Theological Patriarchalism?" in *God as Father?* ed. Johannes-Baptist Metz and Edward Schillebeeckx (New York: Seabury, 1981), 53.

58. Ibid., 54.

59. The date of the quotation is September 10, 1978. Noted in Hadewych Snijdewind, "Ways toward a Non-Patriarchal, Christian Solidarity," in *God as Father?* ed. Johannes-Baptist Metz and Edward Schillebeeckx (New York: Seabury, 1981), 88.

60. See Kyle Pruett, *The Nurturing Father: Journey toward the Complete Man* (New York: Warner, 1987).

61. Rob Palkovitz makes this argument in "The Recovery of Fatherhood?" in *Religion, Feminism, and the Family,* ed. Anne Carr and Mary Stewart Van Leeuwen (Louisville: Westminster, 1996), 320–25.

62. John W. Miller also sees in this passage an image of a merciful father (*Calling God "Father,"* 76–77).

63. Diane Tennis, *Is God the Only Reliable Father?* (Philadelphia: Westminster John Knox, 1985).

64. See John M. Hass, "The Christian Heart of Fatherhood: The Place of Marriage, Authority, and Service in the Recovery of Fatherhood," *Touchstones: A Journal of Mere Christianity* 14, no. 1 (January–February 2001), 51. See the special section "Return to the Father's House" for additional articles on the topic.

65. Henry B. Biller, "The Father Factor and the Two Parent Advantage: Reducing the Paternal Deficit," unpublished paper, 1994. Biller found a thirty-minute-a-day

average, with only 25 percent of young children spending an hour a day or more with their fathers. His figures were widely reported in the popular press.

66. A story in the *New York Times* describes an At-Home Dads Convention outside Chicago which was attended by eighty-five dads from twenty states. Many lead groups or have created web sites that focus on men's issues. The 1993 census figures suggest that there may be some 2 million stay-at-home-dads. See Rick Martin, "At Home Fathers Step Out to Find They Are Not Alone," *New York Times*, February 2, 2000. This is still a very small, but growing, minority.

8. Welcoming the Children

1. See also Marcia Bunge, ed., *The Child in Christian Thought* (Grand Rapids, Mich.: Eerdmans, 2001), and *The Vocation of Parenting* (forthcoming).

2. John Paul II, *On the Family* (Washington, D.C.: United States Catholic Conference, 1981), no. 14.

3. Adrian Thatcher, *Marriage after Modernity: Christian Marriage in Postmodern Times* (New York: New York University Press, 1999), 133–37. Thatcher notes that John Chrysostom spoke of a three-in-one-flesh unity in a mother, father, and baby. His claim that Augustine argued against divorce because of his concern for children is less convincing (139).

4. See, for instance, ibid., 142–52. Thatcher notes that Jon Davies also uses the phrase "a preferential option for children" sarcastically in order to mock liberation theology. Thatcher has no such intention. See Davies, "A Preferential Option for Children," in *The Family in Theological Perspective*, ed. Stephen C. Barton (Edinburgh: T. & T. Clark, 1996).

5. National Conference of Catholic Bishops, *Putting Children and Families First* (Washington, D.C.: United States Catholic Conference, 1991), 1–2. The abortion rate dropped to about 1.4 million by 2000. The bishops also lament the fact that more than half of mothers of children under age six work. Listing this as one of the facts exposing children's suffering seems to overlook the diversity in women's work situations as well as the positive aspects of those situations.

6. Ibid., 3.

7. Ted Peters, *For the Love of Children: Genetic Technology and the Future of the Family* (Louisville: Westminster John Knox, 1996), 21.

8. Diane Jacobs-Malina, *Beyond Patriarchy: The Images of Family in Jesus* (New York: Paulist, 1993), 169.

9. Christine Gudorf, "Dissecting Parenthood," *Conscience* (Autumn 1994): 17, 19.

10. Laura Schlessinger, *Parenting by Proxy: Don't Have Them If You Won't Raise Them* (New York: HarperCollins, 2000), 34.

11. Ibid., 47.

12. Rodney Clapp, *Families at the Crossroads: Beyond Traditional and Modern Options* (Downers Grove, Ill.: InterVarsity, 1993), 44–48.

13. James Francis, "Children and Childhood in the New Testament," in *The Family in Theological Perspective*, ed. Stephen C. Barton (Edinburgh: T. & T. Clark, 1996), 72–73.

14. Ibid., 68–71. Francis admits that the child's "intuitive spontaneity" was evidently seen as valuable in that it enabled them to see what wise adults sometimes missed, 71.

15. Ibid., 75.

16. Ibid., 79.

17. Herbert Anderson and Susan B. W. Johnson, *Regarding Children: A New Respect for Childhood and Families* (Louisville: Westminster John Knox, 1994), 17.

18. See for instance, Schlessinger, or the works of James Dobson, of Focus on the Family.

19. Maureen Junker-Kenny and Norbert Mette, eds., *Little Children Suffer* (Maryknoll, N.Y.: Orbis, 1996), viii–ix.

20. Janet Pais, *Suffer the Children: A Theology of Liberation by a Victim of Child Abuse* (Mahwah, N.J.: Paulist, 1991), 149.

21. Rita Nakashima Brock, "And a Little Child Will Lead Us: Christology and Child Abuse," in *Christianity, Patriarchy, and Abuse: A Feminist Critique*, ed. Joanne Carlson Brown and Carole R. Bohn (New York: Pilgrim, 1989), 54–55.

22. Ibid., 57.

23. Ibid., 59.

24. Ann Loades, "Dympna Revisited: Thinking about the Sexual Abuse of Children," in *The Family in Theological Perspective*, ed. Stephen C. Barton (Edinburgh: T. & T. Clark, 1996), 257. This is particularly important as a contrast to popular emphasis on strict obedience. Acknowledging the reality of abuse forces a different perspective.

25. Pais, *Suffer the Children*, 149.

26. Joseph Martos, *Doors to the Sacred: A Historical Introduction to the Sacraments in the Catholic Church* (Garden City, N.Y.: Doubleday, 1981), 168–201.

27. Jean Guarino. "What Good Are Godparents?" *U.S. Catholic* 56 (August 1991): 20–22.

28. Joseph Martos, "Godparents Are Obsolete," *U.S. Catholic* 57 (September 1992): 13–14.

29. Guarino, "What Good Are Godparents?" 23. See also Carlos Vidal, "Godparenting among Hispanic Americans," *Child Welfare* 67, no. 5 (September–October 1988).

30. Bonnie Miller-McLemore, a Methodist theologian, mentions godparents as one among many sources that would help religious communities become more involved in caregiving to children. See *Also a Mother* (Nashville: Abingdon, 1994), 192.

31. Martos, "Godparents Are Obsolete," 14–15.

32. However, he does appreciate his devoted godparents and refers to their children, who are not relatives, as his "godcousins."

33. *On the Family*, no. 36.

34. Miller-McLemore, *Also a Mother*, 171.

35. Ibid., 172.

36. One might also find support for this idea in John Boswell's account of Christian rescue and adoption of abandoned children. The church opposed the practice of abandonment because of the sexual sins that were behind illegitimate births and a general duty to state and family, but not out of "an inherent obligation of procreator to child." See Boswell, *The Kindness of Strangers: The Abandonment of Children in Western Europe from Late Antiquity to the Renaissance* (New York: Pantheon, 1988) 430.

37. Stanley Hauerwas, "The Family as a School for Character," in *Perspectives on Marriage: A Reader,* ed. Kieran Scott and Michael Warren (New York: Oxford University Press, 1993), 151.

38. Ibid., 152.

39. Ibid., 148. Theologian Jeff Astley criticizes Hauerwas's emphasis on the church, arguing the families do form character whereas many actual church communities are incapable of doing so. Both important influences are needed, but Hauerwas's emphasis is necessary in view of the fact that American Christians are far less receptive to the influence of churches than to the influence of parents. See Jeff Astley, "The Role of Family in the Formation and Criticism of Faith," in *The Family in Theological Perspective,* ed. Stephen C. Barton (Edinburgh: T. & T. Clark, 1996), 201–2.

40. Anton A. Bucher, "Children as Subjects," in *Little Children Suffer,* ed. Maureen Junker-Kenny and Norbert Mette (Maryknoll, N.Y.: Orbis, 1996), 44.

41. Ibid., 45–49. For instance I may intend to communicate love to my child by spanking him, but if my child does not accept my reasoning, he will not learn that physical discipline means love. I cannot simply force him to think the way I do. On the child as agent, see also Douglas Sturm, "On the Suffering and Rights of Children: Toward a Theology of Childhood Liberation," *Cross Currents* (Summer 1992): 149–73.

42. Ibid., 47.

43. Ibid., 45.

44. John Paul II, *On the Family,* no. 26.

45. Ibid., no. 14.

46. National Conference of Catholic Bishops, "Follow the Way of Love," *Origins* 23 (December 2, 1993): 439.

47. Miller-McLemore, *Also a Mother,* 143.

48. Ibid., 147.

49. Ibid., 156.

50. Ibid., 161.

51. Francis, "Children and Childhood in the New Testament," 72.

52. Don Browning et al., *From Culture Wars to Common Ground: Religion and the American Family Debate* (Louisville: Westminster John Knox, 1997), 297. Miller-McLemore defines mutuality this way: "The adult both gives *and* gets, and the child both gets *and* gives" (166). She notes that in the early years when children need more than they can ever give back, "the necessity to give, in response to the needs of the child, depends upon a broader context of give-and-take."

53. Although there has been some progress on this front, one has only to glance at recent studies on housework in dual-career households to understand that women play

this role in most families. See Arlie Hochschild, *The Second Shift* (New York: Avon, 1989).

54. Miller-McLemore, *Also a Mother*, 126.

55. For an example, see the McGinnis family's list of chores in Jim and Kathy McGinnis, "The Week That Was, That Is, and Will Be Forever," in James McGinnis, ed., *Helping Teens Care* (New York: Crossroad, 1991), 15.

9. Divorce and Remarriage in Christian Families

1. See Judith Wallerstein, Julia M. Lewis, and Sandra Blakeslee, *The Unexpected Legacy of Divorce: A Twenty-Five Year Landmark Study* (New York: Hyperion, 2000), 295.

2. For an analysis of recent divorce trends, see Michael Lawler, *Family: American and Christian* (Chicago: Loyola Press, 1998), 47–80.

3. Most Scripture scholars believe these are the actual words of Jesus. A dissenting view can be found in Mary Rose D'Angelo, "Remarriage and Divorce Sayings of Jesus," in *Divorce and Remarriage: Religions and Psychological Perspectives*, ed. William P. Roberts (Kansas City, Mo.: Sheed & Ward, 1990), 78–106.

4. See Gerald Coleman, *Divorce and Remarriage in the Catholic Church* (New York: Paulist, 1988), 68.

5. John Crossan calls the anti-divorce teaching "an especially well attested saying of Jesus" (Crossan, *The Historical Jesus: The Life of a Mediterranean Jewish Peasant* [San Francisco: HarperSanFrancisco, 1991], 301). Joseph Fitzmyer, in his influential article "Matthean Divorce Texts" (*Theological Studies* 37 [1976]: 197–226), claims that recent studies of the Qumran texts do nothing to challenge the idea that the most primitive anti-divorce texts are sayings of Jesus (224).

6. Duane Warden, "The Words of Jesus on Divorce," *Restoration Quarterly* 39, no. 3 (1997): 146.

7. E. P. Sanders and Margaret Davies, *Studying the Synoptic Gospels* (Philadelphia: Trinity Press International, 1989), argue that it is not possible to know whether the exception clause is authentic, but Sanders has an extremely skeptical view of knowing anything about the New Testament. Others are much less uncertain.

8. Fitzmyer, "Matthean Divorce Texts," 224.

9. Richard Hays, *The Moral Vision of the New Testament: A Contemporary Introduction to New Testament Ethics* (San Francisco: Harper, 1996), 353.

10. See John P. Meier, *The Vision of Matthew: Christ, Church, and Morality in the First Gospel* (New York: Crossroad, 1991), 254–56; Fitzmyer, "Matthean Divorce Texts," 221; Bruce Vawter, *The Four Gospels: An Introduction* (Garden City, N.Y.: Doubleday, 1967), 276.

11. Raymond Collins, *Divorce in the New Testament* (Collegeville, Minn.: Liturgical Press, 1992), 209.

12. See ibid. for a summary of this position.

13. William A. Heth, "The Meaning of Divorce in Matthew 19:3–9," *Churchman* 98, no. 2 (1984): 138.

14. Ibid., 142.

15. Hays, *The Moral Vision of the New Testament*, 355.

16. John Paul II, *On the Family* (Washington, D.C.: United States Catholic Conference, 1981), no. 20.

17. Ibid.

18. Ibid.

19. Bernard Cooke, "What God Has Joined Together...," in *Perspectives on Marriage: A Reader*, 2d ed., ed. Kieran Scott and Michael Warren (New York: Oxford University Press, 2001), 348–49.

20. Ibid., 351–53.

21. I do not mean to imply that this is always the case. Certainly, there are times (especially in cases of abuse) when no unity of purpose is possible. In these cases, the church would recommend permanent separation, and I would concur.

22. Margaret Farley, *Personal Commitments* (San Francisco: Harper & Row, 1986).

23. Margaret Farley in *Moral Theology: Challenges for the Future*, ed. Charles Curran (New York: Paulist, 1990), 227–29.

24. In agreeing with official church teaching, I am taking an unusual stand. Most moral theologians would allow for at least some exceptions to the no divorce rule. Many would argue that lifelong marriage is an ideal but, given the finiteness of persons, the church ought to allow for failure instead of condemning it.

25. Paul R. Amato and Bruce Keith, "Parental Divorce and the Well-Being of Children: A Meta-Analysis," *Psychological Bulletin* 110, no. 1 (1991): 26–46.

26. Ibid., 40.

27. Wallerstein, "Children after Divorce: Wounds That Don't Heal," in *Perspectives on Marriage: A Reader*, ed. Kieran Scott and Michael Warren (New York: Oxford University Press, 1993), 370–73.

28. Ibid., 369.

29. Wallerstein, Lewis, and Blakeslee, *The Unexpected Legacy of Divorce*, xxvi–xxx.

30. Ibid., xxv.

31. Ibid., 298–301.

32. Sara McLanahan and Gary Sandefur, *Growing Up with a Single Parent* (Cambridge: Harvard University Press, 1994), 1.

33. Ibid., 2.

34. Ibid., 19.

35. Ibid., 3–4, 27.

36. Ibid., 6–7.

37. Barbara Dafoe Whitehead, "Dan Quayle Was Right," *Atlantic Monthly* (April 1993): 71–72.

38. Barbara Dafoe Whitehead, "The Decline of Marriage as the Social Basis of Childrearing," in *Promises to Keep: Decline and Renewal of Marriage in America*, ed. David Popenoe, Jean Elshtain, and David Blankenhorn (Lanham, Md.: Rowman & Littlefield, 1990), 11–12.

39. See also P. Lindsay Chase-Lansdale, Andrew J. Cherlin, and Kathleen E. Kiernan, "The Long-Term Effects of Parental Divorce on the Mental Health of Young Adults: A Developmental Perspective" *Child Development* 66 (1995): 1614–34; Judith

Mishne, "The Grieving Child: Manifest and Hidden Losses in Childhood and Adolescence," *Child and Adolescent Social Work Journal* 9, no. 6 (1992): 471–90; Peter J. Riga, "Children as Victims of Divorce," *Linacre Quarterly* (February 1994): 32–43; D. R. Morrison and Andrew Cherlin, "The Divorce Process and Children's Well-Being — A Prospective Analysis," *Journal of Marriage and the Family* 57, no. 3 (August 1995): 800–12; Elizabeth Thompson et al., "Family Structure, Gender, and Parental Socialization," *Journal of Marriage and the Family* 54 (1995): 368–78; Marsha Kline et al., "The Long Shadow of Marital Conflict: A Model of Children's Postdivorce Adjustment," *Journal of Marriage and the Family* 53 (May 1991): 297–309.

40. David Gately and Andrew I. Schwebel, "Favorable Outcomes in Children after Parental Divorce," *Journal of Divorce and Remarriage* 18 (1992): 57–78.

41. LeeAnn Kot and Holly M. Shoemaker, "Children of Divorce: An Investigation of the Developmental Effects from Infancy through Adulthood," *Journal of Divorce and Remarriage* 31, no. 1/2 (1999): 161–78.

42. "Homily 20 on Ephesians," in *Marriage in the Early Church*, ed. David Hunter (Minneapolis: Fortress, 1992), 83.

43. Although children are my focus here, it is worth noting that though some research shows that parents are happier after divorce, other important research challenges this notion. Norval Glenn of the University of Chicago claims that if divorce puts an end to unhappy marriages, we should now have a lot more happy marriages. However, from 1973 until 1993, the percentage of people who said they were very happy in their marriages decreased, from 72 percent to 60 percent. In his view, the greater emphasis on marital happiness (versus marital permanence) leads adults to assume a state of "permanent availability" that works against satisfaction. See Glenn, "Values, Attitudes, and American Marriage," in *Promises to Keep: Decline and Renewal of Marriage in America*, ed. David Popenoe, Jean Elshtain, and David Blankenhorn (Lanham, Md.: Rowman & Littlefield Publishers, 1996), 17–31.

44. See Wallerstein, *Unexpected Legacy of Divorce*, who notes that in difficult marriages, children can thrive because of the stability and modeling the parents provide (307).

45. See James Young, "Remarried Catholics: Searching for Church Belonging," in *Perspectives on Marriage: A Reader*, 2d ed., ed. Kieran Scott and Michael Warren (New York: Oxford University Press, 2001), 392.

46. According to Wallerstein, most parents do not do this. Divorce often comes as a surprise to children and is sometimes announced after one spouse has left (*Unexpected Legacy of Divorce*, 46–50).

47. Ibid., 307–8.

48. However, perhaps more couples can make this choice. Linda Waite of the University of Chicago claims that "86 percent of unhappily married couples who stick it out find that, five years later, their marriages are happier." See Linda J. Waite and Maggie Gallagher, *The Case for Marriage: Why Married People Are Happier, Healthier, and Better Off Financially* (New York: Broadway Books, 2000), 148.

49. National Conference of Catholic Bishops, "Follow the Way of Love," *Origins* 23 (December 2, 1993), 437.

50. For an excellent analysis of domestic church, see Florence Caffrey Bourg, *"Where Two or Three Are Gathered": Family as Domestic Church* (South Bend, Ind.: University of Notre Dame Press, 2003).

51. Joanne Heaney-Hunter, "Domestic Church: Guiding Beliefs and Daily Practices," *Christian Marriage and Family*, ed. Michael Lawler and William P. Roberts (Collegeville, Minn.: Liturgical Press, 1996), 59.

52. National Conference of Catholic Bishops, "Follow the Way of Love," 436–37.

10. What Is Family For?

1. Christopher Lasch, *Haven in a Heartless World: The Family Besieged* (New York: Basic Books, 1977), 156.

2. Jean Bethke Elshtain, "The Family and Civic Life," in *Rebuilding the Nest: A New Commitment to the American Family*, ed. David Blankenhorn et al. (Milwaukee: Family Service America, 1990).

3. Robert Bellah et al., *Habits of the Heart: Individualism and Commitment in American Life* (New York: Harper & Row, 1985), 115.

4. Ibid., 116.

5. John Paul II, "Speech at Arrival," St. Louis, January 26, 1999, *www.vatican.va/holy_father/john_paul_ii/travels/*.

6. This tradition of writings from the popes and bishops on social issues like war and peace, work and workers, and race and poverty is usually traced to 1891, when Pope Leo XIII wrote on the labor question and asserted that workers have certain inalienable rights, including the right to unionize. Ever since then, most of church's popes and many of its national conferences of bishops have addressed the important social issues of their day.

7. John Paul II, *On Social Concern* (Washington, D.C.: United States Catholic Conference, 1987), 38.

8. See Donal Dorr, *Option for the Poor: A Hundred Years of Catholic Social Teaching*, rev. ed. (Maryknoll, N.Y.: Orbis, 1992), 2.

9. John Paul II, *On the Family* (Washington, D.C.: United States Catholic Conference, 1981), no. 47.

10. See Judith Stacey, *Brave New Families: Stories of Domestic Upheaval in Late Twentieth Century America* (New York: Basic Books, 1991), 3–19.

11. *On the Family*, no. 17.

12. Robert Bellah et al., *The Good Society* (New York: Vintage, 1991).

13. *On Human Labor* (Washington, D.C.: United States Catholic Conference, 1981), no. 6.

14. Amitai Etzioni, *The Spirit of Community: The Reinvention of American Society* (New York: Simon & Schuster, 1993), 82.

15. Mark Mellman et al., "Family Time, Family Values," in *Rebuilding the Nest*, 73–92.

16. Bellah et al., *The Good Society*, 23.

17. Ibid., 255.

18. James and Kathleen McGinnis, *Parenting for Peace and Justice: Ten Years Later* (Maryknoll, N.Y.: Orbis, 1990).

19. See Duane Elgin, *Voluntary Simplicity: Toward a Way of Life That Is Outwardly Simple, Inwardly Rich*, rev. ed. (New York: Quill, 1993).

20. Daniel Gaines, "Mapping Out Your Own Road," *Los Angeles Times*, October 1, 1995, D2.

21. *On Social Concern*, no. 47.

22. Ibid., no. 38.

23. Kavanaugh, *Following Christ in a Consumer Society*, rev. ed. (Maryknoll, N.Y.: Orbis, 1991).

24. Ibid., 60.

25. Women especially spend an inordinate amount of time shopping. Studies of housework show that despite the increased use of appliances, time spent doing housework has not decreased, largely because of shopping. See Heidi Hartmann, "The Family as Locus of Gender, Class, and Political Struggle: The Example of Housework," in *Feminism and Methodology: Social Science Issues*, ed. Sandra Harding (Bloomington: Indiana University Press, 1987), 125.

26. The voluntary simplicity movement provides helpful narratives of downsizing. Though not all those who downsize end up being more involved in their communities, many do. A 1995 Merck Family Fund study found that 28 percent of Americans polled said that they had made a lifestyle change in the past five years that had resulted in a decrease in their earnings, so this can be considered a significant trend; see Elaine St. James *Living the Simple Life: A Guide to Scaling Down and Enjoying More* (New York: Hyperion, 1996) or Joe Dominguez and Vicki Robin, *Your Money or Your Life: Transforming Your Relationship with Money and Achieving Financial Independence* (New York: Penguin, 1992). Amy Dacyczyn's *The Tightwad Gazette: Promoting Thrift as a Viable Alternative Lifestyle* (New York: Viking, 1998) is particularly helpful for families and includes a wealth of how-to information and success stories from middle-class families who are living well (and often sharing more) on $20,000–30,000 a year.

27. Bellah, *The Good Society*, 260.

28. David Hollenbach, "A Prophetic Church and the Catholic Sacramental Imagination," in *The Faith That Does Justice: Examining the Christian Sources for Social Change*, ed. John C. Haughey (New York: Paulist, 1977), 256.

29. See Marcus Borg, *Conflict, Holiness, and Politics in the Teaching of Jesus* (Harrisburg, Pa.: Trinity Press International, 1998), 93–109.

Bibliography

Aldous, Joan, Gail M. Mulligan, and Thoroddur Bjarnason. "Fathering over Time: What Makes the Difference?" *Journal of Marriage and Family* 60 (November 1998): 809–20.

Amato, Paul R., and Bruce Keith. "Parental Divorce and the Well-Being of Children: A Meta-Analysis," *Psychological Bulletin* 110, no. 1 (1991): 26–46.

Anderson, Herbert, and Susan B. W. Johnson. *Regarding Children: A New Respect for Childhood and Families.* Louisville: Westminster John Knox, 1994.

Astley, Jeff. "The Role of Family in the Formation and Criticism of Faith." In *The Family in Theological Perspective*, ed. Stephen C. Barton. Edinburgh: T. & T. Clark, 1996.

Bailey, William. "Fathers' Involvement and Responding to Infants: 'More' May Not Be 'Better.'" *Psychological Reports* 74 (1994): 92–94.

Barclay, John M. G. "The Family as the Bearer of Religion in Judaism and Early Christianity." In *Constructing Early Christian Families: Family as Social Reality and Metaphor*, ed. Halvor Moxnes. New York: Routledge, 1997.

Barton, Stephen C. "The Relativisation of Family Ties." In *Constructing Early Christian Families: Family as Social Reality and Metaphor*, ed. Halvor Moxnes. New York: Routledge, 1997.

Baum, Gregory. "Bulletin: The Apostolic Letter *Mulieris dignitatem*." In *Motherhood: Experience, Institution, Theology*, ed. Elisabeth Schüssler Fiorenza and Anne Carr. Edinburgh: T. & T. Clark, 1989.

Bellah, Robert, et al. *Habits of the Heart: Individualism and Commitment in American Life.* New York: Harper & Row, 1985.

———. *The Good Society.* New York: Vintage, 1991.

Bernard, Jesse. "The Good-Provider Role." In *Perspectives on Marriage*, ed. Kieran Scott and Michael Warren. New York: Oxford University Press, 1993.

Biller, Henry B. *Fathers and Families: Paternal Factors in Child Development.* Westport, Conn.: Auburn House, 1993.

———. "The Father Factor and the Two Parent Advantage: Reducing the Paternal Deficit." Unpublished paper, 1994.

Blankenhorn, David. *Fatherless America: Confronting Our Most Urgent Social Problem.* New York: Basic Books, 1995.

Boswell, John. *The Kindness of Strangers: The Abandonment of Children in Western Europe from Late Antiquity to the Renaissance.* New York: Pantheon, 1988.

225

Bourg, Florence Caffrey. *"Where Two or Three Are Gathered": Family as Domestic Church.* South Bend, Ind.: University of Notre Dame Press, 2003.

Brock, Rita Nakashima. "And a Little Child Will Lead Us: Christology and Child Abuse." In *Christianity, Patriarchy, and Abuse: A Feminist Critique,* ed. Joanne Carlson Brown and Carole R. Bohn. New York: Pilgrim, 1989.

Brown, Peter. *The Body and Society: Men, Women, and Sexual Renunciation in Early Christianity.* New York: Columbia University Press, 1988.

Browning, Don, et al. *From Culture Wars to Common Ground: Religion and the American Family Debate.* Louisville: Westminster John Knox, 1997.

Bucher, Anton A. "Children as Subjects." In *Little Children Suffer,* ed. Maureen Junker-Kenny and Norbert Mette. Maryknoll, N.Y.: Orbis, 1996.

Bunge, Marcia, ed. *The Child in Christian Thought.* Grand Rapids, Mich.: Eerdmans, 2001.

Cahill, Lisa Sowle. *Between the Sexes: Foundations for a Christian Ethics of Sexuality.* Philadelphia: Fortress, 1985.

———. "Can We Get Real about Sex?" *Commonweal* 117 (September 14, 1990): 497–503.

———. "Marriage: Institution, Relationship, Sacrament." In *One Hundred Years of Catholic Social Thought: Celebration and Challenge,* ed. John A. Coleman. Maryknoll, N.Y.: Orbis, 1991.

———. *Women and Sexuality.* New York: Paulist, 1992.

———. *Sex, Gender, and Christian Ethics.* Cambridge: Cambridge University Press, 1996.

———, and Dietmar Mieth, eds. *The Family.* New York: Orbis, 1995.

Carr, Anne, and Mary Stewart Van Leeuwen, eds. *Religion, Feminism, and the Family.* Louisville: Westminster John Knox, 1996.

Chase-Lansdale, P. Lindsay, Andrew J. Cherlin, and Kathleen E. Kiernan. "The Long-Term Effects of Parental Divorce on the Mental Health of Young Adults: A Developmental Perspective," *Child Development* 66 (1995): 1614–34.

Chmiel, Mark. "Seven Sacraments of Everyday Life." *Praying: Spirituality for Everyday Living* (September 1998).

———, and Mev Puleo. "The Holy Contour of Life." Unpublished manuscript.

Chrysostom, St. John. "An Address." In *Christianity and Pagan Culture in the Later Roman Empire,* trans. M. L. W. Laistner. Ithaca, N.Y.: Cornell University Press, 1951.

Clapp, Rodney. *Families at the Crossroads: Beyond Traditional and Modern Options.* Downers Grove, Ill.: InterVarsity Press, 1993.

Coleman, Gerald. *Divorce and Remarriage in the Catholic Church.* New York: Paulist, 1988.

Collier, Jane, Michelle Z. Rosaldo, and Sylvia Yanagisako. "Is There a Family? New Anthropological Views." In *Rethinking the Family: Some Feminist Questions,* ed. Barrie Thorne with Marilyn Yalom. Boston: Northeastern University Press, 1992.

Collins, Raymond. *Divorce in the New Testament.* Collegeville, Minn.: Liturgical Press, 1992.

Coltrane, Scott. "The Future of Fatherhood." In *Fatherhood: Contemporary Theory, Research, and Social Policy,* ed. William Marsiglio. Thousand Oaks, Calif.: Sage Publications, 1995.

———. *Family Man: Fatherhood, Housework, and Gender Equity.* New York: Oxford, 1996.

Cooke, Bernard. "Christian Marriage: Basic Sacrament." In *Perspectives on Marriage: A Reader,* 2d ed., ed. Kieran Scott and Michael Warren (New York: Oxford University Press, 2001).

———. "What God Has Joined Together...." In *Perspectives on Marriage: A Reader,* 2d ed., ed. Kieran Scott and Michael Warren. New York: Oxford University Press, 2001.

Covino, Paul, ed. *Celebrating Marriage: Preparing the Wedding Liturgy: A Workbook for Engaged Couples.* Washington, D.C.: Pastoral Press, 1994.

Cowan, Carolyn Pape, and Philip A. Cowan. *When Partners Become Parents: The Big Life Change for Couples.* New York: Basic Books, 1992.

Cross, Nancy. "A Traditionalist's Dilemma: What to Do When the Pope Goes Feminist," *Crisis* 8 (January 1990): 32.

Crossan, John Dominic. *The Historical Jesus: The Life of a Mediterranean Jewish Peasant.* San Francisco: HarperSanFrancisco, 1991.

Curran, Charles, ed. *Moral Theology: Challenges for the Future.* New York: Paulist, 1990.

Dacyczyn, Amy. *The Tightwad Gazette: Promoting Thrift as a Viable Alternative Lifestyle.* New York: Viking, 1998.

Daly, Mary. *Beyond God the Father: Toward a Philosophy of Women's Liberation.* Boston: Beacon, 1973.

D'Angelo, Mary Rose. "Remarriage and Divorce Sayings of Jesus." In *Divorce and Remarriage: Religions and Psychological Perspectives,* Ed. William P. Roberts. Kansas City, Mo.: Sheed & Ward, 1990.

———. "Abba and 'Father': Imperial Theology and the Jesus Traditions," *Journal of Biblical Literature* 111, no. 4 (1992): 611–30.

Davies, Jon. "A Preferential Option for Children." In *The Family in Theological Perspective,* ed. Stephen C. Barton. Edinburgh: T. & T. Clark, 1996.

Day, Dorothy. *The Long Loneliness: An Autobiography.* San Francisco: Harper & Row, 1952.

———. *Loaves and Fishes.* Maryknoll, N.Y.: Orbis, 1997.

De Luccie, Mary. "Predictors of Paternal Involvement and Satisfaction," *Psychological Reports* 79 (1996): 1351–59.

Dienhart, Anna. *Reshaping Fatherhood: The Social Construction of Shared Parenting.* Thousand Oaks, Calif.: Sage Publications, 1998.

Dimock, Giles. "Women, the Woman, and the Church," *Social Justice Review* 83 (July–August 1992): 113–15.

Dobson, James. *Dare to Discipline*. Wheaton, Ill.: Tyndale Publishing House, 1973.

Dominguez, Joe, and Vicki Robin. *Your Money or Your Life: Transforming Your Relationship with Money and Achieving Financial Independence*. New York: Penguin, 1992.

Dorr, Donal. *Option for the Poor: A Hundred Years of Catholic Social Teaching*. Rev. ed. Maryknoll, N.Y.: Orbis, 1992.

Ehrensaft, Diane. *Parenting Together: Men and Women Sharing the Care of Their Children*. Chicago: University of Illinois Press, 1987.

Elgin, Duane. *Voluntary Simplicity: Toward a Way of Life That Is Outwardly Simple, Inwardly Rich*. Rev. ed. New York: Quill, 1993.

Elshtain, Jean Bethke. "The Family and Civic Life." In *Rebuilding the Nest: A New Commitment to the American Family*, ed. David Blankenhorn et al. Milwaukee: Family Service America, 1990.

Etzioni, Amitai. *The Spirit of Community: The Reinvention of American Society*. New York: Simon & Schuster, 1993.

Farley, Margaret. *Personal Commitments: Beginning, Keeping, Changing*. San Francisco: Harper & Row, 1986.

Finley, Mitch. *Your Family in Focus*. Notre Dame, Ind.: Ave Maria Press, 1993.

Fiorenza, Francis Schüssler. "Marriage." In *Systematic Theology: Roman Catholic Perspectives*, vol. 2, ed. Francis Schüssler Fiorenza and John P. Galvin. Minneapolis: Fortress, 1991.

Fitzmyer, Joseph. "The Matthean Divorce Texts and Some New Palestinian Evidence," *Theological Studies* 37, no. 2 (June 1976): 197–226.

———. *Luke*. Anchor Bible. Garden City, N.Y.: Doubleday, 1986.

Flannery, Austin, ed. *Vatican Council II: The Conciliar and Post Conciliar Documents*. Rev. ed. Northport, N.Y.: Costello Publishing Co., 1988.

Fleming, Austin. *Prayerbook for Engaged Couples*. Chicago: Liturgy Training Publications, 1990.

Francis, James. "Children and Childhood in the New Testament." In *The Family in Theological Perspective*, ed. Stephen C. Barton. Edinburgh: T. & T. Clark, 1996.

Friedan, Betty. *The Feminine Mystique*. New York: Dell, 1963.

Galinsky, Ellen. *Ask the Children: What America's Children Really Think about Working Parents*. New York: William Morrow, 1999.

Gallagher, Chuck. *The Marriage Encounter: As I Have Loved You*. Garden City, N.Y.: Doubleday, 1975.

Gately, David, and Andrew I. Schwebel. "Favorable Outcomes in Children after Parental Divorce," *Journal of Divorce and Remarriage* 18 (1992): 57–78.

Glendon, Mary Ann. "What Happened at Beijing," *First Things* 89 (January 1996): 30–36.

Glenn, Norval. "Values, Attitudes, and American Marriage." In *Promises to Keep: Decline and Renewal of Marriage in America*, ed. David Popenoe, Jean Elshtain, and David Blankenhorn. Lanham, Md.: Rowman & Littlefield Publishers, 1996.

Golant, Mitch, and Susan Golant. *Finding Time for Fathering.* New York: Ballantine Books, 1993.

Gould, Ezra P. *Mark.* International Critical Commentary. New York: Charles Scribner's Sons, 1961.

Griswold, Robert. *Fatherhood in America: A History.* New York: Basic Books, 1993.

Gross, Rita. "Female God Language in a Jewish Context." In *Womanspirit Rising: A Feminist Reader in Religion,* ed. Judith Plaskow and Carol Christ. San Francisco: HarperSanFrancisco, 1992.

Guarino, Jean. "What Good Are Godparents?" *U.S. Catholic* 56 (August 1991): 20–22.

Gudorf, Christine. "Parenting, Mutual Love, and Sacrifice." In *Women's Consciousness, Women's Conscience: A Reader in Feminist Ethics,* ed. Barbara Hilkert Andolsen, Christine E. Gudorf, Mary D. Pellauer. Minneapolis: Winston Press, 1985.

————. *Body, Sex, and Pleasure: Reconstructing Christian Sexual Ethics.* Cleveland: Pilgrim, 1994.

————. "Dissecting Parenthood." *Conscience* 14 (Autumn 1994): 15–22.

Hammerton-Kelly, Robert. *God the Father: Theology and Patriarchy in the Teaching of Jesus.* Philadelphia: Fortress, 1979.

Harrison, Carol P. "The Silent Majority: The Family in Patristic Thought." In *The Family in Theological Perspective,* ed. Stephen C. Barton. Edinburgh: T. & T. Clark, 1996.

Hartmann, Heidi. "The Family as Locus of Gender, Class, and Political Struggle: The Example of Housework." In *Feminism and Methodology: Social Science Issues,* ed. Sandra Harding. Bloomington: Indiana University Press, 1987.

Hass, John M. "The Christian Heart of Fatherhood: The Place of Marriage, Authority, and Service in the Recovery of Fatherhood," *Touchstones: A Journal of Mere Christianity* 14, no. 1 (January–February 2001): 47–52.

Hauerwas, Stanley. "The Family as a School for Character." In *Perspectives on Marriage: A Reader,* ed. Kieran Scott and Michael Warren. New York: Oxford University Press, 1993.

Hays, Richard. *The Moral Vision of the New Testament: A Contemporary Introduction to New Testament Ethics.* San Francisco: HarperCollins, 1996.

Heaney-Hunter, Joanne. "Domestic Church: Guiding Beliefs and Daily Practices." In *Christian Marriage and Family,* ed. Michael Lawler and William P. Roberts. Collegeville, Minn.: Liturgical Press, 1996.

Hebblethwaite, Margaret. *Motherhood and God.* London: Geoffrey Chapman, 1984.

Heiman, Carrie J. *The Nine-Month Miracle.* Liguori, Missouri: Liguori Publications, 1986.

Heth, William A. "The Meaning of Divorce in Matthew 19:3–9," *Churchman* 98, no. 2 (1984): 136–52.

Hochschild, Arlie. *The Second Shift*. New York: Avon, 1989.

———. *The Time Bind: When Work Becomes Home and Home Becomes Work*. New York: Henry Holt, 1997.

Hollenbach, David. "A Prophetic Church and the Catholic Sacramental Imagination." In *The Faith That Does Justice: Examining the Christian Sources for Social Change*, ed. John C. Haughey. New York: Paulist, 1977.

Horsley, Richard. *Sociology of the Jesus Movement*. New York: Crossroad, 1989.

Hunter, David, ed. *Marriage in the Early Church*. Minneapolis: Fortress, 1992.

Jacobs, Andrew. "A Family Affair: Marriage, Class, and Ethics in the Apocryphal Acts of the Apostles." *Journal of Early Christian Studies* 7 (1999): 105–38.

Jacobs-Malina, Diane. *Beyond Patriarchy: The Images of Family in Jesus*. New York: Paulist, 1993.

Jerome, St. "Against Jovinian." In *Women and Religion: A Feminist Sourcebook of Christian Thought*. Trans. and ed. Elizabeth Clark and Herbert Richardson. San Francisco: HarperCollins, 1977.

John Paul II, Pope. *On Human Labor*. Washington, D.C.: United States Catholic Conference, 1981.

———. *On the Family*. Washington, D.C.: United States Catholic Conference, 1981.

———. *On the Original Unity of Man and Woman*. Boston: Daughters of St. Paul, 1981.

———. *On the Theology of Marriage and Celibacy*. Boston: Daughters of St. Paul, 1986.

———. *On Social Concern*. Washington, D.C.: United States Catholic Conference, 1987.

———. *On the Dignity and Vocation of Woman*. Washington, D.C.: United States Catholic Conference, 1988.

Johnson, Elizabeth. *She Who Is: The Mystery of God in Feminist Theological Discourse*. New York: Crossroad, 1992.

Johnson, W. Brad. "Father Uninvolvement: Impact, Etiology, and Potential Solutions," *Journal of Psychology and Christianity* 12, no. 4 (1993): 301–11.

Junker-Kenny, Maureen, and Norbert Mette, eds. *Little Children Suffer*. Maryknoll, N.Y.: Orbis, 1996.

Kavanaugh, John F. *Following Christ in a Consumer Society: The Spirituality of Cultural Resistance*. Rev. ed. Maryknoll, N.Y.: Orbis, 1991.

Kline, Marsha, et al. "The Long Shadow of Marital Conflict: A Model of Children's Postdivorce Adjustment," *Journal of Marriage and the Family* 53 (May 1991): 297–309.

Kohn-Roelin, Johanna. "Mother-Daughter-God." In *Motherhood: Experience, Institution, Theology*, ed. Anne Carr and Elisabeth Schüssler-Fiorenza. Edinburgh: T. & T. Clark, 1989.

Kot, LeeAnn, and Holly M. Shoemaker. "Children of Divorce: An Investigation of the Developmental Effects from Infancy through Adulthood," *Journal of Divorce and Remarriage* 31, no. 1/2 (1999): 161–78.

Laffey, Alice L. "Biblical Hermeneutics and Divorce." In *Religions of the Book*. Annual Publication of the College Theology Society, ed. Gerard S. Sloyan. New York: University Press of America, 1996.

Lamb, Michael. "Introduction: The Emergent American Father." In *The Father's Role: Cross Cultural Perspectives*, ed. Michael Lamb. Hillsdale, N.J.: LEA Publishers, 1987.

LaPorte, Jean. *The Role of Women in Early Christianity*. Lewiston, N.Y.: Edwin Mellen Press, 1982.

Lasch, Christopher. *Haven in a Heartless World: The Family Besieged*. New York: Basic Books, 1977.

Lassen, Eva Marie. "The Roman Family: Ideal and Metaphor." In *Constructing Early Christian Families: Family as Social Reality and Metaphor*, ed. Halvor Moxnes. New York: Routledge, 1997.

Lawler, Michael. *Marriage and Sacrament: A Theology of Christian Marriage*. Collegeville, Minn.: Liturgical Press, 1993.

———. *Family: American and Christian*. Chicago: Loyola Press, 1998.

Leo XIII. *On the Condition of the Working Classes*. Boston: Daughters of St. Paul, 1942.

Loades, Ann. "Dympna Revisited: Thinking about the Sexual Abuse of Children." In *The Family in Theological Perspective*, ed. Stephen C. Barton. Edinburgh: T. & T. Clark, 1996.

Luther, Martin. "Lectures on Genesis." In *Woman and Religion: A Feminist Sourcebook of Christian Thought*, ed. Elizabeth Clarke and Herbert Richardson. San Francisco: HarperCollins, 1977.

MacIntyre, Alasdair. *After Virtue: A Study in Moral Theory*. Notre Dame, Ind.: University of Notre Dame Press, 1981.

Mahoney, John. *The Making of Moral Theology: A Study of the Roman Catholic Tradition*. Oxford: Clarendon Press, 1987.

Mann, C. S. *Mark*. Anchor Bible. Garden City, N.Y.: Doubleday, 1986.

Marsiglio, William. "Fatherhood Scholarship: an Overview and Agenda for the Future." In *Fatherhood: Contemporary Theory, Research, and Social Policy*, ed. William Marsiglio. Thousand Oaks, Calif.: Sage, 1995.

Martos, Joseph. *Doors to the Sacred: A Historical Introduction to the Sacraments in the Catholic Church*. Garden City, N.Y.: Doubleday, 1981.

———. "Godparents Are Obsolete." *U.S. Catholic* 57 (September 1992): 13–14.

———. "Marriage in the Bible." In *Perspectives on Marriage: A Reader*, ed. Kieran Scott and Michael Warren. New York: Oxford University Press, 1993.

McFague, Sallie. *Models of God: Theology for an Ecological, Nuclear Age*. Philadelphia: Fortress, 1987.

————. "God as Mother." In *Motherhood: Experience, Institution, Theology*, ed. Anne Carr and Elisabeth Schüssler-Fiorenza. Edinburgh: T. & T. Clark, 1989.

McGinnis, James, and Kathleen McGinnis. *Parenting for Peace and Justice: Ten Years Later*. Maryknoll, N.Y.: Orbis, 1990.

————. "The Week That Was, That Is, and Will Be Forever." In *Helping Teens Care*, ed. James McGinnis. New York: Crossroad, 1991.

McGowan, Jo. "Marriage versus Living Together." In *Perspectives on Marriage: A Reader*, ed. Kieran Scott and Michael Warren. New York: Oxford University Press, 1993.

McLanahan, Sara, and Gary Sandefur. *Growing Up with a Single Parent: What Hurts, What Helps*. Cambridge: Harvard University Press, 1994.

Meier, John P. *The Vision of Matthew: Christ, Church, and Morality in the First Gospel*. New York: Crossroad, 1991.

Mellman, Mark, et al. "Family Time, Family Values." In *Rebuilding the Nest: A New Commitment to the American Family*, ed. David Blankenhorn, Steven Bayme, and Jean Elshtain. Milwaukee: Family Service America, 1990.

Mich, Marvin L. Krier. *Catholic Social Teaching and Movements*. Mystic, Conn.: Twenty-Third Publications, 1998.

Miller, John W. *Calling God "Father": Essays on the Bible, Fatherhood, and Culture*. New York: Paulist, 1999.

Miller-McLemore, Bonnie J. "Let the Children Come." *Second Opinion* 17 (July 1991): 10–25.

————. *Also a Mother: Work and Family as Theological Dilemma*. Nashville: Abingdon Press, 1994.

Mishne, Judith. "The Grieving Child: Manifest and Hidden Losses in Childhood and Adolescence," *Child and Adolescent Social Work Journal* 9, no. 6 (1992): 471–90.

Modras, Ronald. "Pope John Paul II's Theology of the Body." In *The Vatican and Homosexuality: Reactions to the "Letter to the Bishops of the Catholic Church on the Pastoral Care of Homosexual Persons,"* ed. Jeannine Gramick and Pat Furey. New York: Crossroad, 1988.

Moltmann, Jürgen. "The Motherly Father: Is Trinitarian Patripassianism Replacing Theological Patriarchalism?" In *God as Father?* ed. Johannes-Baptist Metz and Edward Schillebeeckx. New York: Seabury, 1981.

Morrison, D. R., and Andrew Cherlin. "The Divorce Process and Children's Well-Being — A Prospective Analysis," *Journal of Marriage and the Family* 57, no. 3 (August 1995): 800–12.

National Conference of Catholic Bishops. *Marriage in Christ*. Collegeville, Minn.: Liturgical Press, 1991.

————. "Follow the Way of Love." *Origins* 23 (December 2, 1993): 433–43.

————. *Putting Children and Families First*. Washington, D.C.: United States Catholic Conference, 1991.

Nelson, James. "Varied Meanings of Marriage and Fidelity." In *Perspectives on Marriage: A Reader*, ed. Kieran Scott and Michael Warren. New York: Oxford University Press, 1993.

Nelson-Pallmeyer, Jack. *Families Valued: Parenting and Politics for the Good of All Children*. New York: Friendship Press, 1996.

O'Connor, Flannery. "The Lame Shall Enter First," in *The Complete Stories*. New York: Noonday Press, 1946.

————. *The Habit of Being*. Ed. Sally Fitzgerald. New York: Noonday Press, 1979.

Orsi, Robert. *The Madonna of 115th Street: Faith and Community in Italian Harlem, 1880–1950*. New Haven: Yale University Press, 1985.

Osiek, Carolyn. "The New Testament and the Family." In *The Family*, ed. Lisa Sowle Cahill and Dietmar Mieth. Maryknoll, N.Y.: Orbis, 1995.

Pais, Janet. *Suffer the Children: A Theology of Liberation by a Victim of Child Abuse*. Mahwah, N.J.: Paulist, 1991.

Palkovitz, Rob. "The Recovery of Fatherhood?" In *Religion, Feminism, and the Family*, ed. Anne Carr and Mary Stewart Van Leeuwen. Louisville: Westminster John Knox, 1996.

Parker, Kenneth. "Being (God) the Father: What I Learned about Creating in the First Four Years of My Three Sons." Unpublished manuscript, 2001.

Peters, Ted. *For the Love of Children: Genetic Technology and the Future of the Family*. Louisville: Westminster John Knox, 1996.

Pius XI, Pope. *Christian Marriage* (1930). New York: Paulist, 1939.

Post, Stephen G. *A Theory of Agape: On the Meaning of Christian Love*. Lewisburg, Pa.: Bucknell University Press, 1990.

————. *Spheres of Love: Toward a New Ethics of the Family*. Dallas: Southern Methodist University Press, 1994.

————. "Adoption Theologically Considered," *Journal of Religious Ethics* 25, no. 1 (Spring 1997): 149–68.

————. *More Lasting Unions: Christianity, the Family, and Society*. Grand Rapids, Mich.: Eerdmans, 2000.

Pruett, Kyle. *The Nurturing Father: Journey toward the Complete Man*. New York: Warner, 1987.

Purvis, Sally. "Mothers, Neighbors and Strangers," *Journal of Feminist Studies in Religion* 7 (Spring 1991): 19–34.

Rahner, Karl. *Theological Investigations*. Vol. 10. New York: Herder and Herder, 1973.

Rich, Adrienne. *Of Woman Born: Motherhood as Experience and Institution*. New York: W. W. Norton, 1986.

Riga, Peter J. "Children as Victims of Divorce," *Linacre Quarterly* 61 (February 1994): 32–43.

Robinson, Geoffrey. *Marriage, Divorce, and Nullity: A Guide to the Annulment Process in the Catholic Church*. Collegeville, Minn.: Liturgical Press, 1984.

Ruddick, Sarah. "Maternal Thinking." In Rethinking the Family, rev. ed., ed. Barrie Thorne, with Marilyn Yalom. Boston: Northeastern University Press, 1992.

Ruether, Rosemary Radford. "Motherearth and the Megamachine." In Womanspirit Rising: A Feminist Reader in Religion, ed. Carol P. Christ and Judith Plaskow. San Francisco: HarperSanFrancisco, 1992.

St. James, Elaine. Living the Simple Life: A Guide to Scaling Down and Enjoying More. New York: Hyperion, 1996.

Sanders, E. P. Jesus and Judaism. Philadelphia: Fortress, 1985.

————, and Margaret Davies. Studying the Synoptic Gospels. Philadelphia: Trinity Press International, 1989.

Schlessinger, Laura. Parenting by Proxy: Don't Have Them If You Won't Raise Them. New York: HarperCollins, 2000.

Schüssler Fiorenza, Elisabeth. In Memory of Her: A Feminist Theological Reconstruction of Christian Origins. New York: Crossroad, 1989.

————. "Women in the Early Christian Movement," In Womanspirit Rising: A Feminist Reader in Religion, ed. Judith Plaskow and Carol Christ. San Francisco: HarperSanFrancisco, 1992.

————. Discipleship of Equals: A Critical Feminist Ecclesiology of Liberation. New York: Crossroad, 1993.

Spohn, William. Go and Do Likewise: Jesus and Ethics. New York: Continuum, 1999.

Stacey, Judith. Brave New Families: Stories of Domestic Upheaval in Late Twentieth Century America. New York: Basic Books, 1991.

————. "Backward toward the Postmodern Family: Reflections on Gender, Kinship, and Class in the Silicon Valley." In Rethinking the Family: Some Feminist Questions, ed. Barrie Thorne. Boston: Northeastern University Press, 1992.

Stackhouse, Max L. Covenant and Commitments: Faith, Family, and Economic Life. Louisville: Westminster John Knox, 1997.

Sturm, Douglas. "On the Suffering and Rights of Children: Toward a Theology of Childhood Liberation." Cross Currents (Summer 1992): 149–73.

Tennis, Diane. Is God the Only Reliable Father? Philadelphia: Westminster John Knox, 1985.

Thatcher, Adrian. Marriage after Modernity: Christian Marriage in Postmodern Times. New York: New York University Press, 1999.

Theissen, Gerd. Sociology of the Early Palestinian Christianity. Philadelphia: Fortress, 1989.

Thompson, Elizabeth, et al. "Family Structure, Gender, and Parental Socialization," Journal of Marriage and the Family 54 (1995): 368–78.

Thorne, Barrie, with Marilyn Yalom, eds. Rethinking the Family: Some Feminist Questions. Boston: Northeastern University Press, 1992.

Vawter, Bruce. The Four Gospels: An Introduction. Garden City, N.Y.: Doubleday, 1967.

Vidal, Carlos. "Godparenting among Hispanic Americans," *Child Welfare* 67, no. 5 (September–October 1988): 453–59.

Waite, Linda. "Does Marriage Matter?" *Demography* 32 (November 1995): 483–507.

———, and Maggie Gallagher. *The Case for Marriage: Why Married People Are Happier, Healthier, and Better Off Financially.* New York: Broadway Books, 2000.

Wallerstein, Judith. "Children of Divorce: Wounds That Don't Heal." In *Perspectives on Marriage: A Reader,* 2d. ed., ed. Kiernan Scott and Michael Warner. New York: Oxford University Press, 2001.

Wallerstein, Judith, Julia M. Lewis, and Sandra Blakeslee. *The Unexpected Legacy of Divorce: A Twenty-Five-Year Landmark Study.* New York: Hyperion, 2000.

Warden, Duane. "The Words of Jesus on Divorce." *Restoration Quarterly* 39, no. 3 (1997): 141–53.

Whitehead, Barbara Dafoe. "Dan Quayle Was Right," *Atlantic Monthly* 271 (April 1993): 71–72.

———. "The Decline of Marriage as the Social Basis of Childrearing." In *Promises to Keep: Decline and Renewal of Marriage in America,* ed. David Popenoe, Jean Elshtain, and David Blankenhorn. Lanham, Md.: Rowman & Littlefield, 1996.

Witte, John. *From Sacrament to Contract: Marriage, Religion, and Law in the Western Tradition.* Louisville: Westminster John Knox, 1997.

Woodhead, Linda. "Faith, Feminism, and the Family," in *The Family,* Concilium, ed. Lisa Sowle Cahill and Dietmar Mieth. Maryknoll, N.Y.: Orbis, 1995.

Yoder, John Howard. *The Politics of Jesus: Vicit Agnus Noster.* Grand Rapids, Mich.: Eerdmans, 1972.

Index

237